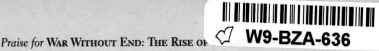

Praise for WAR WITHOUT END: THE RISE OF ~~~~ GLOBAL RESPONSE

"Dilip Hiro's *War Without End* puts the bin Laden story and all Islam-based terrorism into the broadest possible context . . . It is valuable in explaining and weaving together the various schools of thought, organizations and historical events that together recount the history of 'fundamentalist' violence."　　　　　—Thomas W. Lippman, *The Washington Post*

"Comprehensive and relevant . . . it consists of a meticulous assembling of the facts to support inevitable conclusions which, thereby, gain even greater force . . . This is an immensely useful compendium of the background to the new world that we face . . . It should become compulsory reading."　　　　　—George Joffe, *Middle East International*

"The strength of Hiro's book lies in his providing a clear context of events, thus illustrating the extent of the crisis that now exists between Islamists, led, inspired and influenced by bin Laden, and the Western nations now at war with him."　　　　　—Mark Huband, *Financial Times* (London)

Praise for THE LONGEST WAR: THE IRAN-IRAQ MILITARY CONFLICT

"The best book on the subject so far."
　　　　　—Patrick Seale, *The Observer* (London)

"Written with exemplary objectivity by journalist Dilip Hiro,"
　　　　　—James Adams, *Sunday Times* (London)

"Takes us well beyond images of Khomeini dart boards and Saddam voodoo dolls to reveal calculating interest groups whom the West might have manipulated more skillfully."　　　　　—*Los Angeles Times*

Praise for DESERT SHIELD TO DESERT STORM: THE SECOND GULF WAR

"*Desert Shield to Desert Storm* . . . is an excellent guide to the political economy of oil and indebtedness."
　　　　　—Christopher Hitchens, *Independent on Sunday* (London)

ALSO BY DILIP HIRO

Nonfiction

War Without End:
The Rise of Islamist Terrorism and Global Response (2002)
India: The Rough Guide Chronicle (2002)
Neighbors, Not Friends: Iraq and Iran After the Gulf Wars (2001)
Sharing the Promised Land: A Tale of Israelis and Palestinians (1999)
Dictionary of the Middle East (1996)
The Middle East (1996)
Between Marx and Muhammad:
The Changing Face of Central Asia (1995)
Lebanon, Fire and Embers:
A History of the Lebanese Civil War (1993)
Desert Shield to Desert Storm: The Second Gulf War (1992)
Black British, White British:
A History of Race Relations in Britain (1991)
The Longest War: The Iran-Iraq Military Conflict (1991)
Holy Wars: The Rise of Islamic Fundamentalism (1989)
Iran: The Revolution Within (1988)
Iran Under the Ayatollahs (1985)
Inside the Middle East (1982)
Inside India Today (1977)
The Untouchables of India (1975)
Black British, White British (1973)
The Indian Family in Britain (1969)

Fiction

Three Plays (1985)
Interior, Exchange, Exterior (Poems, 1980)
Apply, Apply, No Reply & A Clean Break
(Two Plays, 1978)
To Anchor a Cloud (Play, 1972)
A Triangular View (Novel, 1969)

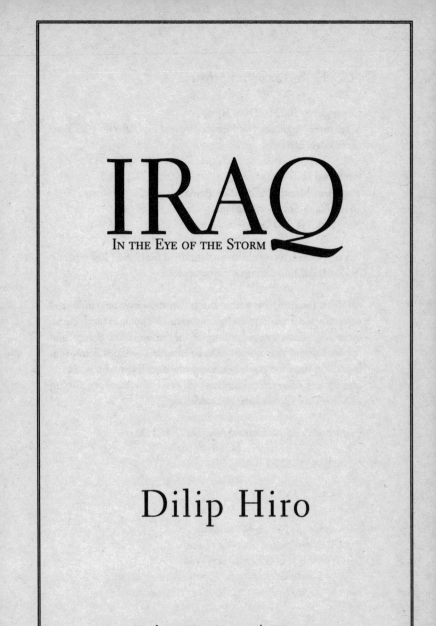

IRAQ

IN THE EYE OF THE STORM

Dilip Hiro

THUNDER'S MOUTH PRESS / NATION BOOKS

NEW YORK

IRAQ: IN THE EYE OF THE STORM

Published by
Thunder's Mouth Press/Nation Books
161 William Street, 16th Floor
New York, NY 10038

Nation Books is a co-publishing venture of the Nation Institute and
Avalon Publishing Group Incorporated.

Library of Congress Control Number: 2002113816

ISBN 1-56025-477-7

9 8 7 6 5 4 3 2 1

Book design by Simon M. Sullivan
Printed in the United States of America
Distributed by Publishers Group West

CONTENTS

Iraq: no-fly zones

TURKEY

Habour

36° parallel
(June 1991–)

SYRIA

Sinjar   Mosul
                Shaqlawa   Hajj Umran
                Salahuddin   H'rian
                Irbil   Ranya   Hiro
                Koy Sanjak   Qala Diza
                Suleimaniya
        Kirkuk
                        Halabja

IRAN

Jabal
Maqbul   Alam   Kifri
Tharthar   Tikrit   Qasr-e Shirin
Lake   Dur   Kalar
        Samarra   Khanaqin
Muthanna
        Dujayal

ANBAR
PROVINCE
        Habbaniya   Taji   Baghdad
        Ramadi   Rashidiya
33° parallel   Falluja
(Sept 1996–)
Trebil   Hakam   Musayib
        Rafah   Atheer   Kut
        Karbala   Hilleh
32° parallel   Kufa
(Aug 1992–
Sept 1996)   Najaf   Amara

IRAQ

Euphrates

        Ur   Qurna
        Nasiriyeh   Arvand
SAUDI   Rud
                Khorramshahr   Abadan
ARABIA   Rumeila oilfield
                Umm al Qasr   Shatt
                Zubair   al arab

KUWAIT

        Kuwait City

        The
        Gulf

——·—— International boundary

------- Iraqi front line

Area controlled by Kurdish
regional administration

Security zone
('Safe Haven' 1991)

N

0   200 miles
0   300 kilometres

vii

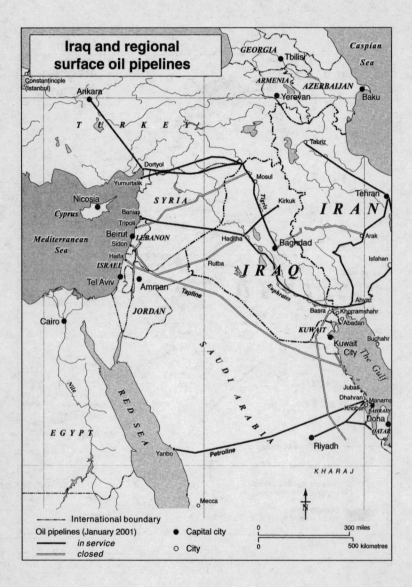

Iraq and regional surface oil pipelines

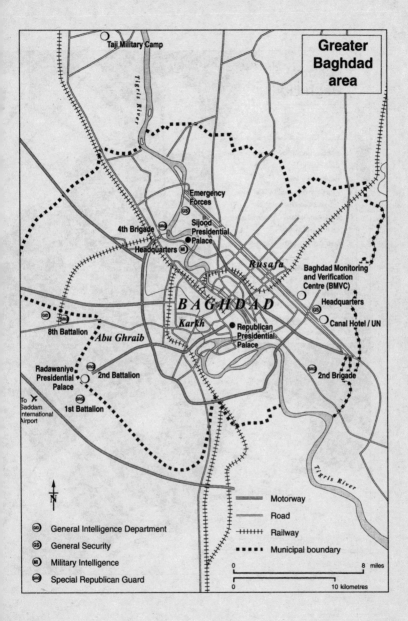

Greater
Baghdad
area

Taji Military Camp

Tigris River

Emergency
Forces

4th Brigade

Sijood
Presidential
Palace

Headquarters

Rusafa

Baghdad Monitoring
and Verification
Centre (BMVC)

Headquarters

BAGHDAD

Canal Hotel / UN

Karkh

Republican
Presidential
Palace

8th Battalion

Abu Ghraib

Radawaniye
Presidential
Palace

2nd Battalion

2nd Brigade

To
Saddam
International
Airport

1st Battalion

Tigris River

N

	Motorway
	Road
++++++	Railway
■■■■	Municipal boundary

GID General Intelligence Department

GS General Security

MI Military Intelligence

SRG Special Republican Guard

0 ————————— 8 miles

0 ————————— 10 kilometres

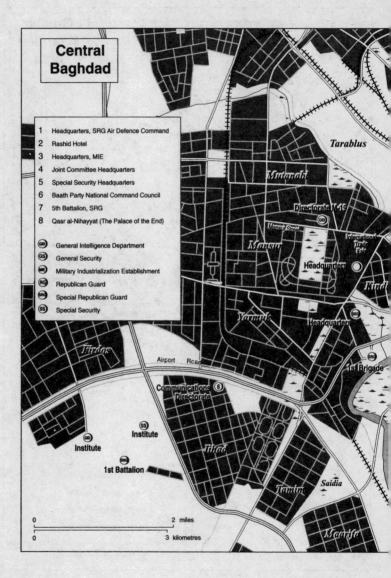

Central Baghdad

1 Headquarters, SRG Air Defence Command
2 Rashid Hotel
3 Headquarters, MIE
4 Joint Committee Headquarters
5 Special Security Headquarters
6 Baath Party National Command Council
7 5th Battalion, SRG
8 Qasr al-Nihayyat (The Palace of the End)

(GID) General Intelligence Department
(GS) General Security
(MIE) Military Industrialization Establishment
(RG) Republican Guard
(SRG) Special Republican Guard
(SS) Special Security

Tarablus

Mutanabi

Directorate M-19

Mansur Shopt

International Trade Fair

Mansur

Headquarters

Kindi

Yarmuk

Headquarters

Firdos

Airport Road

1st Brigade

Communications (6) Directorate

(SS) Institute

(GID) Institute

Jihad

(SRG) 1st Battalion

Tamim

Saidia

Maarifa

0   2 miles
0   3 kilometres

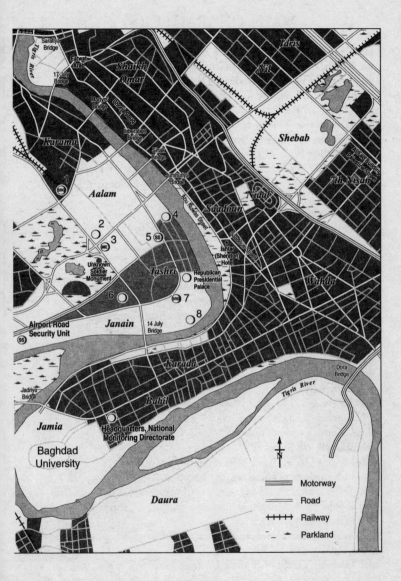

MAIN CHARACTERS

Madeleine Karbol Albright, *US Secretary of State, 1997–2001*

Kofi Annan, *Ghanian Secretary-General of United Nations, 1997–*

Tariq Aziz (aka Yahunna, Mikhail), *Deputy Prime Minister of Iraq, 1991–*

Masud Barzani, *Leader of Kurdistan Democratic Party, 1987–*

Samuel (Sandy) Berger, *US National Security Adviser, 1997–2001*

Tony Blair, *Prime Minister of Britain, 1997–*

George Bush, *US President, 1989–1993*

George Walker Bush, *US President, 2001–*

Richard Butler, *Australian Executive Chairman of Unscom, 1997–2000*

Ahmad Chalabi, *Leader of opposition Iraqi National Congress, 1992–*

Bill Clinton, *US President, 1993–2001*

Dick Cheney, *US Vice-President, 2001–*

Charles Duelfer, *American Deputy Executive Chairman of Unscom, 1993–2000*

Rolf Ekeus, *Swedish Executive Chairman of Unscom, 1991–97*

Faisal I, *King of Iraq, 1921–33*

Rashid Gailani, *Prime Minister of Iraq, 1933, 1936–38, 1940–41*

Saddam Hussein, *President of Iraq, 1979–*

Muhammad Baqir al Hakim, *Leader of opposition Supreme Assembly of Islamic Revolution in Iraq, 1982–*

Gen. Hussein Kamil Hassan, *Elder son-in-law of Saddam, Minister of Industry and Military Industrialization, 1991–95; defected in 1995*

Qusay Saddam Hussein, *Younger son of Saddam, Head of National Security Bureau of Iraq, 1992–*

Gen. Ali Hassan al Majid, *Cousin of Saddam, Commander of Northern Command of Iraq, 1991–*

Adnan Nouri, *Leader of opposition Iraqi National Accord, 1990–*

Colin Powell, *US Secretary of State, 2001–*

Abdul Karim Qasim, *Prime Minister of Iraq, 1958–63*

Donald Rumsfeld, *US Secretary of Defense, 2001–*

Scott Ritter, *American Chief Inspector of Unscom, 1991–98*

Nuri al Said, *Prime Minister of Iraq, 1930–32, 1939–40, 1941–44, 1946–47, 1949, 1950–52, 1954–57, 1958*

Gen. Wafiq Jassim al Samarrai, *Head of Military Intelligence of Iraq, 1991–92; defected in 1994*

Jalal Talabani, *Leader of Patriotic Union of Kurdistan, 1976–*

Hans von Sponeck, *German Head of the UN Office of Humanitarian Coordinator in Iraq, 1998–2000*

PREFACE

Before vacating the White House on 20 January 2001, the one thank-you note that President Bill omitted to write should have been addressed to Iraqi president Saddam Hussein: "My dear Saddam: But for you I would not have occupied the White House for eight years."

A sick joke? A spoof? No, a fact based in history and logic. After his victory in the Gulf War between the United States–led coalition and Iraq in March 1991, President George Bush Sr.'s popularity soared to 91 percent. His reelection seemed so certain that leading Democratic politicians did not enter the race for the party's nomination. Into this vacuum stepped the comparatively unknown governor of the obscure southern state of Arkansas, Bill Clinton.

Iraq thus joined Iran in impinging directly on the US presidential election, a remarkable achievement for a Third World country. One of the main reasons why President Jimmy Carter lost his campaign for reelection in 1980 was his failure to free the American hostages held by Iran ruled by Ayatollah Ruhollah Khomeini.

While Khomeini is gone, Saddam is very much with us. Since he is the only one who matters in Iraq, there is no open interplay between different concepts and politicians on how to administer the state. On top of that, twelve years of a United Nations–imposed economic siege of the country has sharply reduced contacts between Iraqis and non-Iraqis.

No wonder, it is hard for the people of the region—much less those living in the West—to comprehend how ordinary Iraqis manage to survive. To fill that lacuna, I unveil my book with a narrative of daily life in the benighted country by synthesizing material from personal and assorted published sources.

What follows next is a brief chronicle of Iraq, spiced periodically with an anecdote or telling quote. Into this foil I relate the history of the governing Baath Party and the rise and rise of Saddam Hussein. Inevitably there is opposition to a reign as rigid as that of Saddam, and that is the subject of chapter 5.

Since the end of the Gulf War, however, a second center of power has emerged in Baghdad: the United Nations, with a panoply of organizations charged with everything from disarming Iraq to feeding tens of thousands of its indigent families. The saga of the UN inspectors and Iraq takes up the bulk of chapter 6, with the United States overtly confronting Iraq at several points, and covertly plotting coups to overthrow Saddam. During this period Baghdad's relations with its neighbors underwent change, a phenomenon I cover in the following chapter. My theme-centered text ends with chapter 8, which deals with petroleum. In it I show how oil has shaped the policies not only of the government of Iraq but also those of the major Western powers, starting with Britain.

The final chapter traces the above themes chronologically after 11 September 2001, not because Iraq had anything to do with the atrocities of that day on the American soil, but because it has become a memorable date in world history.

Since its invasion of Kuwait in 1990, Iraq has been a recurring item on the agenda of the United Nations Security Council, especially after it resolved to disarm Iraq of its weapons of mass destruction. This has proved a long, tortuous process, interspersed with periodic air strikes on Iraq by the United States, assisted by Britain. The withdrawal of UN inspectors by their executive chairman in December 1998 so that the Pentagon could unleash its hundred-hour blitzkrieg against Iraq broke the continuity of the UN efforts to disarm the Iraqi regime. The issue of the return of the inspectors to Iraq remained in limbo even after the passage of a new, comprehensive Security Council resolution in December 1999—until the 9/11 attacks, followed by the inclusion of Iraq as part of the three-member "axis of evil" by US president George W. Bush in early 2002. Since then, due largely to the hawks in the present administration gaining an upper hand in formulating and implementing US policy in the Middle East, the issue of a "regime change" in Baghdad has been pushed to the top of the international agenda—as well as the domestic one during the run-up to the mid-term congressional elections. So once again Iraq is in the eye of the storm—and is set to remain there for several months at the very least.

* * *

For the names of regional places and people, I have used the spellings adopted by the print media. In certain cases, I have changed the names of my interviewees.

A word about Iraqi male names. In 1972 the government decreed that instead of using the family name, indicative of the clan, tribe, or the area of origin, men should use a maximum of three personal names—self, father, and grandfather. This order was issued primarily to mask the fact that al Tikritis—originating in the native area of President Ahmad Hassan Bakr and his relative, Saddam Hussein—held far too many top positions. Though this law has not been formally revoked, the use of the family names has crept back. At the first mention of an important Iraqi male in the text, I provide his family name in parentheses if appropriate.

To encourage debate on Iraq, I have listed both "Frequent Comments and Questions" and "Infrequent and Infrequent Comments and Questions" and offered short answers. They are equal in length.

Appendix III contains the questions Iraq submitted to the United Nations secretary-general in March 2002. The reader will find it more rewarding to go through the list after finishing the book rather than before.

The postscript is not indexed.

Dilip Hiro

London, October 2002

CHAPTER 1
LIFE IN IRAQ

Iraqis are caught between internal pressure and external. But external pressure is much worse. It impinges on every aspect of our life daily— from electricity to drinking water to car repairs to textbooks to medicine. We see no end as yet.

—Abdul Razak, a US-educated retired professor in Baghdad

One hundred and twenty-two degrees Fahrenheit in the shade. Late-July Baghdad (lit., Gift of God), the heart of Mesopotamia, the land between the Euphrates and the Tigris, rich and fertile in the midst of an arid zone. The famed Tigris, however, is so depleted that I can cross it without wetting my underpants if I so wish. But I don't. A sturdy baseball cap protects me from the blazing sun. Athir al Anbari, my plump translator-guide with bushy eyebrows and a mole on his left nostril, eyes me with envy. Having forgotten his baseball cap in a hasty exit from his home after siesta, he has to make do with a flimsy local newspaper to fend off the Mesopotamian sun's hot temper.

We are in the Fathwat al Arab (The Arab Quarters) neighborhood in central Baghdad, within hearing distance of a muezzin calling from the minaret of the elegant al Gailani Mosque. Athir knocks at a door at random. It turns out to be the house of Yassin Abdul Hamid, a sixty-eight-year-old patriarch in a long white shirt and matching rubber sandals with a faraway look in his myopic eyes. He is the head of a joint family of fourteen lodged in a modest two-story building. Of his four grown-up sons, two are car mechanics, another is a waiter at a private club, and the fourth, Afif, runs a small shop selling food grains—something Yassin Hamid did himself until the government bought up his store in the course of nationalization of food distribution in 1980, transforming him into a civil servant, a job he kept for six years before retiring. "No matter what happens, there is always business in foodstuffs," he remarks.

Athir and I are now seated on a carved, cushioned bench in a rectangular reception lobby, delineated on one side by a whitewashed wall decorated with a thick carpet—incongruously embroidered with a central European royalty scene with voluptuous milky white princesses—and the Holy Kaaba (Black Stone) in Mecca, the site of the Muslim pilgrimage; and on another by a wall covered partially by a sturdy refrigerator. "Before the sanctions this refrigerator was full of everything," Yassin Hamid says with palpable nostalgia. "Now it has only water and bread. No more fish or meat or chicken. Before the sanctions we ate fish almost daily." Most conversations in Iraq, I soon discover, are peppered with the phrases "before the sanctions (*hisar*, in Arabic)" and "after the sanctions," meaning the economic sanctions administered by the United Nations 661 Sanctions Committee of the Security Council.[1]

The post-sanctions period is subdivided between before and after the UN oil-for-food scheme, which went into operation in December 1996, with the post-scheme food rations being 50 percent higher than those before the scheme. During the earlier period, so acute was the food deprivation of the populace that eggs and chicken became currency. "Said rented out a room in their house for two trays of eggs [60 eggs] a month," notes Nuha al Radi, an Iraqi sculptress and potter, in her diary on November 6, 1994. "Quite clever of him. Now the tenant is losing money as the price of eggs rises ever upwards. Mu'taza's mum said she asked the people renting her house for one chicken a year. They refused."[2]

Both Said and Mu'taza are typical of urban dwellers, who form 70 percent of Iraq's population. A study by the UN's Food and Agriculture Organization showed that in 1995 only those 10 percent of city and town residents who were engaged in trade and other lucrative commercial activities were doing well. The rest were doing badly. So badly indeed that many of them had drifted back to their native villages, where agricultural produce was on the rise due to the official drive to make the country self-sufficient in food. This was an ambitious enterprise for a country that imported 70 percent of foodstuffs before 1990, and which now faced a UN ban on imports of seeds, pesticide, fertilizer, and spare parts for farm machinery. No wonder that the proportion of those engaged in agriculture doubled in less than a decade to 40 percent—a unique phenomenon in the Third World.[3]

The drive for self-sufficiency in food gave a financial and political boost to the fortunes of landlords with large holdings, thus reversing the traditional policy of the Arab Socialist Baath Party (ABSP)—Baath, for short—of favoring small landholders and farm workers at the expense of rich landlords. Furthermore, the government raised the social and official status of large landholders by restoring the administrative and financial powers they enjoyed before the 1968 coup by the Baath Party. The state-run Iraqi television took to showing affluent tribal leaders singing and dancing the national *dabka* dance, and heaping praise on President Saddam Hussein—a scene Yassin Hamid mentions in passing.

His family's chief source of sustenance since the start of the Gulf War in January 1991 has been the rations provided by the Ministry of Trade. The patriarch shows me the rationing document for supplies of wheat flour, rice, sugar, tea, vegetable oil, milk, salt, lentils, white beans, detergent, and toilet soap. It is a long, sturdy sheet with twelve vertical rows of stamps—each signifying an item—one row for each month, with a wide column to the right carrying the address and other details of the household topped by a message from President Saddam. It reads,

> To the Iraqi Woman: 1. The economic life of Iraq is organized according to the program that Iraq will win

the war and hope that the battle will be resolved and benefit Iraq and the [Arab] nation. 2. The rationing is the socialist solution in this difficult period. 3. Rationing is the backbone on which to build the solidarity of our social life in this troublesome period.

Meat and fish do not figure on the document, nor do vegetables or fruit. The ministry supplies bare necessities, the monthly rations per person being: flour 20 lb.; rice 7 lb.; cooking oil 2 ¾ lb.; lentils 1 lb.; beans ½ lb.; powdered milk 1 lb.; sugar 4 ½ lb.; tea ⅓ lb.; soap ½ lb.; and detergent ¾ lb.

Buying these supplies for some 20 million Iraqis costs the government $1.2 billion a year, paid for from the sum of its income from petroleum exports shipped under the strict UN regime whereby Iraq's oil revenue is deposited into an escrow account of the UN at BNP Paribas Bank SA in New York. During the first three years of the scheme, the six-monthly amount that Baghdad is allowed to earn from oil exports was raised from $2.1 billion to $5.6 billion, and then the ceiling was removed altogether. But by the time the UN has deducted 30 percent of the Iraqi income for the Compensation Fund for those who suffered due to Iraq's invasion of Kuwait, 13 percent for the Kurdistan region outside the central government's jurisdiction, and another 7 percent for the UN's administrative costs, the Baghdad regime receives about half of the total.

For its part, instead of recovering the $5 per capita cost of the monthly rations from its citizens, the Iraqi authorities charge only US 12 cents (Iraqi dinar, IQD 250)—the price of three eggs in the open market—just to cover the distribution cost. That means a typical five-member Iraqi family receives free rations worth $25 a month, four times the remuneration of a middle-level government employee.[4]

The net outcome is the strengthening of Saddam's regime, the exact opposite of what the US administrations under George Bush

Sr., Bill Clinton, and George W. Bush Jr. have been attempting to achieve. "The risk of having rations withdrawn is too high a price for dissent [as most people cannot afford to buy food in the open market]," says Abdullah Mutawi, a lawyer associated with the New York–based Center for Economic and Social Rights (CESR), and a member of two American fact-finding missions to Iraq in the 1990s.[5]

Though larger than before, the rationed quantities the Iraqi government supplies monthly are still not enough. So most families have to supplement them by purchasing their basic necessities on the open market. There the prices are astronomical. I discover this during my visit to the Shorja Market, located between the Martyrs' and Liberation bridges—a panoply of white canvas coverings crammed between gray cement concrete buildings, relieved here and there by multicolor parasols. One lb. of rice costs 160 Iraqi dinars; 1 lb. of sugar 300 dinars; and 1 lb. of beans 350 dinars. Two bananas, one for Athir and one for me, sets me back 600 dinars.

I am tempted to buy a couple of 100-leaf notebooks for 1,000 dinars each and a few China-made ballpoint pens selling at 50 dinars each—for Salih, the fourteen-year old son of Yassin Hamid. But I am not sure Athir al Anbari will take the trouble to deliver them. So I put out of my mind the mournful words of Yassin Hamid, "The pity is that Salih cannot imagine how things were before the sanctions, when he was only four."

I would have liked to visit Salih's school, but it is closed for summer vacation. Luckily, one of the guests at my modest Al Fanar (lit., Tower) Hotel, along the bank of the Tigris, is Francesca Noe, a wiry, middle-aged Italian social worker, overworked yet enthusiastic, who has studied the Iraqi educational system thoroughly. "Before the Gulf War," she tells me, "there were free school meals for children, which were stopped after the conflict, when they were needed most. Also after the war the authorities ended the free bus transport for pupils they had before, which was especially helpful in rural areas. Before the war, only 6 percent of the children were not enrolled in primary school. Five years later the figure shot up to 16 percent. School-age children are being put to work for family business or sent out by their parents to vend in the streets or beg." The trend accelerated: During the 1997–98 academic year, the dropout rate at the primary level soared to 53 percent.[6] While the world at large registered a substantial rise in literacy during the 1990s, the figure in Iraq fell from 90 to 66 percent.

Referring to a 1994 study by Unicef's Emergency Fund, Noe tells me that about two-thirds of children went to school on an empty stomach. Another Unicef study in 1997 shows that about a third of Iraqi children are chronically malnourished, a figure higher than that in Ghana or Mali. That is about a million Iraqi children, Noe calculates. "There is a direct correlation between lack of nourishment and learning ability."

The facilities at the educational institutions have deteriorated sharply, she continues. The local authorities have failed to maintain the buildings properly because the budgets for maintenance and cleaning were cut by 90 percent. "So you see broken windows, no lights, and toilets in bad repair, and desks and chairs in a poor state."

Then there is the psychological damage done by the American bombardments, which occurred in 1991, 1993 (twice), 1996, and 1998. A Unicef study revealed that four out of five primary school children had fear of losing family or friends due to bombing. Thus we have a new generation growing up in Iraq with hatred for the United States that stems from their personal experiences.

When Fransesca tells me that low salaries have driven many teachers to take up better-paid manual or semi-skilled jobs, I think of Thaier Younis, the driver for my out-of-Baghdad trips. He is a tall, muscular man in his midthirties, courteous and dignified, more at ease with English than my official trcnslator-guide. It turns out that before the sanctions he was a geography teacher at a secondary school.

"As a schoolteacher now I would earn 3,000 dinars (US $4) a month, just enough to buy a kilogram [2.2 lb.] of meat, a tray of 30 eggs, or one flashlight cell," Thaier tells me. "Schools are in a bad way," he continues, shaking his head. "I have two school-going children. They use old, tattered textbooks." Because of the US dollar tips he gets from foreign visitors like me, Thaier is comparatively well off. Unlike him, most parents find notebooks, pencils, and pens too expensive to purchase.

Before the Gulf War the education ministry paid for the textbooks and stationery. Now it covers only half the cost, and many parents cannot afford the rest. "The UN has withheld permission for producing paper in Iraq, so teachers have resorted to teaching orally with the aid of audio- and videocassettes," he tells me.

The situation is equally dire at the university level, with the dropout rate soaring to 30 percent due to the economic pressure on the students' families struggling to survive. "Loma [a friend] was telling me about her university classes; she teaches computer studies," notes Nuha al Radi in her diary. "She has 60 students. They have no paper and no pencils. They write on the back of receipts, pharmacy bills, account books, anything that has a blank side to it. The university does not supply her with paper to photocopy the exams, so she has to write the exam on the blackboard; those at the back cannot see it, so when the ones in front have copied the questions, those at the back move to the front. There are only 10 working computers, so they take turns on the machines."[7]

Little wonder that the quality of teaching at the higher levels has deteriorated. The only way university teachers can keep the system functioning is by photocopying textbooks, in violation of the international copyrights convention. But the problem is that many photocopiers are broken down due to lack of spare parts, which are not allowed to be imported.

Among those who have been irked by the heartless decisions of the UN 661 Sanctions Committee in Iraq is Hans von Sponeck, the German head of the Baghdad-based UN Office of Humanitarian Coordinator in Iraq (UNOHCI) from 1998 to 2000. "It is not only about food and medicine," he says. "But it is also about intellectual genocide—with professional journals, international newspapers, books, writing materials, computers, all considered nonessential by the Sanctions Committee, and vetoed."[8]

The barring of the international mail over twelve ounces to Iraq by the UN 661 Sanctions Committee, at the behest of the United States and Britain, has resulted in a virtual embargo on all business mail. "We see no professional literature and we cannot keep abreast of developments in our fields," complains a physician in Baghdad. This is just one manifestation of the educational, professional, and cultural embargo that has severely damaged the country's university system and intellectual life. "Iraqi university teachers and students are unable to import textbooks, journals, or even newspapers as sources of the latest research," says Noe. "Nor do they have access to international computer data banks or even Internet. All they have is outdated research data. They are unable to attend foreign seminars or conferences even if they are invited because it is extremely expensive for them to go abroad."

The deleterious impact of international isolation on Iraq's recent university graduates and young politicians will manifest itself in the coming decades. Unlike the present generation of Iraqis, many of them educated at foreign universities and fluent in several European languages, the rising generation, limited to further education only at ill-equipped Iraqi universities, is growing up in an intellectual and professional vacuum.

What is true of education in Iraq is also true of other public services: agricultural irrigation, drinking water, public sanitation and health services, and electric supplies. With these services receiving only 10 percent of the needed resources from the impoverished government, they are in poor condition.

Even though Baghdad, with nearly a fifth of the national population, has top priority in public services, it looks shabby. The main roads are bearable, but turn into a side street and you see an unpaved, pot-holed passage, crisscrossed by dark veins of sewage and littered with uncollected garbage.

Driving into the middle-class neighborhood of Mustansiriya—famed for its university of the same name, established in 1235—around sunset, I expect to breathe the dry, refreshing air of the surrounding desert blowing through the jammed half-open windows of my ramshackle taxi. Instead I inhale air permeated with the fetid smell of sewage. Even the Tashri neighborhood, the privileged heart of the Saddam Hussein regime, is not free of this nauseating odor. Biochemical reactions, it seems, are immune to pressure from the politically powerful.

The problem stems from broken-down pumps—and is nation-wide. They cannot be repaired without imported parts. The import of pumps and pump parts is banned: They are regarded by the United States to have "dual"—meaning civilian and military—purpose. In general, since machinery spare parts are neither food nor medicine, their purchase is repeatedly blocked by the US and British represen-tatives on the Sanctions Committee. The ban on pumps and pump parts adversely affects irrigation, water supply, and sewage.

Due to the broken-down pumps, the sewage spills over into rivers, the source of drinking water. And that leads to such illnesses as typhoid and dysentery, which reached epidemic proportions in 1997, the year when Hikmat, the six-month-old grandson of Yassin Hamid, died due to dehydration caused by dysentery for which medicine was unavail-able. That year Hikmat became one of the 70,000 children under five to die due to lack of medicine—a threefold increase in the mortality rate of 9 percent in 1991.[9]

Whereas the sharp rise in the infant mortality rate in Iraq gets periodically mentioned in the Western media, what goes unreported is the increase in the death rate of adults above fifty. Two of my inter-viewees in their late sixties—Yassin Hamid from Fathwat al Arab and Muhammad Muftin Bagga from Saddam City, a down-at-the-heels sector of the capital—carry medical cards entitling them to almost-free drugs for their chronic illnesses. They complain that the drugs they need are often unavailable.

"For my high blood pressure I get Terrenin 100 mg tablets which are almost free," Bagga tells me. "But they are seldom available. In the open market one pill costs 10 dinars. That is 150 times the amount I pay when it's officially available." Thus a package of 20 such pills would consume the monthly income of his barber son Imad, who earns 25,000 to 30,000 dinars a month, the salary of a judge. At $12 a year, the per capita medical expenditure in Iraq is a tiny fraction of the $1,500 spent on drugs per person in Britain.[10]

For any item to arrive in Iraq from abroad, it has had to go through fourteen steps, most of these at the UN 661 Sanctions Committee in New York, which authorizes a member of the fifteen-strong committee to veto any contract without offering an explanation. Washington has been the most active in blocking contracts, followed, well behind, by London. Both have been accused, rightly, of politically motivated obstructionism.

Among other things, this has resulted in:

A ban on the import of vaccines into Iraq simply because they contain a minuscule quantity of a derivative of mustard, a substance that can be used for making a chemical warfare agent.

The barring of vaccines for foot and mouth disease for Iraqi livestock on the grounds that the vaccines could be used for producing biological warfare agents; this had led to the death of almost half of Iraq's livestock by 1999.[11]

The disallowing of new printing presses requested by Iraq, which wants to improve the quality of its bank notes and issue bank notes of 1,000 dinars, four times its highest currency denomination of 250 dinars, worth US 12.5 cents.

The 661 Committee agreeing, after repeated Iraqi requests, to allow Iraq to rehabilitate its analog telecommunications system, installed in the early-to-mid-1980s. Iraq finds that the companies that had installed its telecommunications equipment no longer make parts or equipment for the old analog system.

The banning of chemicals including chlorine and aluminum sulfate. In a water-purifying process, aluminum sulfate attracts dirt and other impurities, and sinks to the bottom of a water tank; chlorine acts as a disinfecting agent. Iraq produces chlorine domestically at a plant in Basra, but not enough, and it is of poor quality. "Before the sanctions we used to get chlorine from Turkey and Jordan," says Qasim al Muhandas at the Watbah Water Treatment Plant in northern Baghdad, built by a British company in 1935. "No more. We should use chlorine twice to turn raw water from the Tigris into drinking water. But we are managing by using chlorine only once. For aluminum sulfate we are using a local substitute, which is not as good. But we make do."

Make-do—mending, repairing, improving—during the 1990s becomes a way of life in Iraq. Improvising is the name of the game. At a small workshop in the Fathwat al Arab neighborhood, I see a diesel engine attached to a lathe. As soon as electric power goes off at the preannounced time of 2 P.M., the owner turns on the diesel engine and continues to work. In such establishments as hotels and government offices generators are always on stand-by. (At any event, lack of air-conditioning in temperatures of 122°F in the shade would be unbearable for office employees or hotel guests.) Even small commercial establishments like ice cream parlors have installed diesel-powered generators.

For me, the sight of a young, balding man repairing a hurricane lantern during my stroll in the Shorja Market encapsulates the depressing reality in Iraq today.

As people resort to mending equipment and machines, including motor vehicles, on an unprecedented scale, the demand for mechanics and repairers rises. Civil servants quit office jobs to run repair shops for cars, air conditioners, refrigerators, transistor radios, and television sets, and draft their sons into the trade. This is also the case with many teachers, engineers, doctors, accountants, academics, and lawyers. As a consequence, Iraq's class composition is transformed. Its salaried middle class shrinks by half.

Consider the case of Narmeen al Mufti, a slight woman, plain, short-haired, articulate, and well traveled, dressed always in jeans and a blouse. A divorcee, she looks after a son in his midteens. Before the Gulf War, as a Ministry of Culture and Information employee, she earned 100 dinars/$310 a month, and her expenses were 80 dinars, with half the sum spent on rent. She owned a car and employed a maid. After the war, she has had to take up three jobs—as a reporter at the daily *Baghdad Observer*, a feature writer at a weekly Arabic magazine, and a television news producer—a common pattern among middle-class professionals, with engineers deploying their cars as taxis after work, teachers giving private tuition to their pupils after school hours, and public-hospital doctors seeing patients at home.

Yet all these jobs together fetch Narmeen 35,000 dinars a month—only about a third of her expenses, much reduced due to the sale of her car and the sacking of her maid. To cover the monthly deficit of 65,000 dinars/$33, she tries hard to get occasional translation jobs from visiting foreign journalists who pay cash in US dollars (simply because they cannot use traveler's checks or credit cards due to the international ban on financial transactions with Iraq). But translation tasks are iffy.

Ideally, she would like to work for the Foreign Press Center or the Director of the International Media Section run by her old Ministry of Culture and Information. Just what Athir al Anbari is currently doing. He started out as a journalist with the Iraqi News Agency, run by the Ministry of Information, and worked for fifteen years. By the early 1990s hyperinflation had shrunk his salary to four dollars a month. Unable to cope, he took a test for a translator's job at the International Media Section and succeeded in getting hired. That put him in contact with foreign journalists who at the end of a working day often gave him a tip of ten dollars, or 20,000 dinars, a princely sum. But such jobs are few and far between.

So, consequently, professionals like Narmeen have had to tap a source available more widely. And that for her—as well as hundreds of thousands of other professionals—is money received from relatives living abroad.

Assuming an average individual remittance of one hundred dollars a month by the estimated one million Iraqi expatriates, the annual sum comes to $1.2 billion, the amount the government spends on providing free rations to all its citizens. But these Iraqi expatriates cannot transfer money to the banks in Iraq. So they use the *hawala* (lit., trust)—an informal money-transfer system that has been in use since travelers on the Silk Road employed it to avoid being robbed en route. London alone has more than a dozen such *hawala* dealers.

The sender gives cash to a *hawala* dealer in one of the countries where Iraqi expatriates are based for 1 percent commission. The dealer gives him a code of one letter and four numbers. The sender then conveys the code to the recipient in Iraq who calls on the local agent of the *hawala* dealer based in the originating country, says the code, and gets the money. Both sides then tear up the records. It beats Western Union: The commission is low and there is no hassle of identification. The system works smoothly partly because by now there is a constant injection of US dollars, legitimate and otherwise, into the Iraqi economy.

There is now a recognized dollar economy in Iraq. This sector involves the United Nations with its multitude of activities, ranging from Unicef to the World Food Program to UNOHCI; foreign embassies; and Western nongovernmental organizations (NGOs), all of whom pay their local employees in dollars. Then there are hotels, which require foreign guests to pay in dollars, and the bus and taxi services between Amman and Baghdad, where cash payment is strictly in US dollars. Also, 3,000 Iranian pilgrims to Shia holy shrines a week provide $350 each in cash. Then there are UN-sanctioned Iraqi oil exports to Jordan. Finally, there are the contraband petroleum sales to the buyers in Iraqi Kurdistan as well as Syria, Iran, and the United Arab Emirates. All of which adds up to a substantial amount of US dollars.

In the early and mid-1990s the number of Iraqis working abroad shot up dramatically. The reasons were economic: raging hyperinflation, caused by UN economic sanctions and the destruction of half of the cereal and seed stocks as well as 95 percent of the breeding stocks of poultry and livestock[12] that reduced the value of one Iraqi dollar from US$3.2 to US $1/3000 to 1/10,000th of its prewar value. A diary entry by Nuha al Radi encapsulates the disastrous impact on living standards: "Dinner at the Hatra Hotel; nouvelle cuisine—five bits of very charcoaled meat, three slices of tomato and three small triangles of bread for 4,000 dinars. My Toyota Corona cost that much in 1981."[13]

Soon banks started counting money by weighing it in bundles as customers arrived clutching gunny sacks and people gossiped about "photocopy money." The professionals suffered grievously. "My dentist told me that in the old days he would charge 20 dinars for a filling, his actual costs came to four dinars and he would pocket 16 dinars," al Radi wrote in her diary in January 1995. "With that he could buy five chickens. Now a filling costs 1,250 dinars and his profit is 400 dinars, which would just buy him a chicken leg."[14]

Many Iraqi professionals started emigrating. They obtained tourist visas for travel to Jordan, Lebanon, the Gulf states, Europe, and North America, and never returned. To stop the intellectual-professional hemorrhage, in 1995 the authorities required doctors and engineers to pay a 1,000,000 dinars/$1,000 guarantee to ensure their return. Undeterred, many mortgaged their houses to pay the guarantee and departed—forever.

Besides the self-employed doctors and engineers, all those with fixed salaries suffered badly. That meant about a third of the country's workforce which was on the government payrolls. The authorities refused to raise salaries to keep pace with inflation, fearing that such a step would make matters worse.

"Unemployment soared in 1992 when the government de-mobbed 600,000 soldiers to reduce its soaring budget deficit," says Athir. "But there were no jobs for them—the only exception being reconstruction projects, which required mostly unskilled workers." The misery that visited the vast majority of citizens was so acute that the authorities banned the consumption of alcohol in public so as not to fuel the popular ire at those who openly indulged in this practice—or at the regime that allowed it. They also shut down the state-owned breweries producing beer and *arak*, a locally distilled spirit.

The regime tried to portray President Saddam as a man of piety as he launched "the campaign of the faith," with the education ministry augmenting Islamic input into school and college curricula.

While suffering Iraqis turned increasingly to religion for solace, petty crime soared, with cars disappearing from parking lots only to be cannibalized for parts. Burglaries, previously a rare occurrence in Iraq, became commonplace. Thieving became so rampant that Western-educated Iraqis joked that the fable of "The Thief of Baghdad," with which Iraq is often associated in the popular Western psyche, was not a fable after all. Pilfering of foreign guests' possessions spread even to the prestigious Al Rashid Hotel, the haunt of diplomats and foreign journalists.

Driven to desperation, more and more Iraqis resorted to underhand means to cope with their dire economic condition. "Many of these methods are illegal, and illegal businesses are on the rise," said Hans von Sponeck. "Relying on them is creating in Iraq a generation of fixers, manipulators of the system rather than thinkers or strategists."[15]

Apparently, what von Sponeck had in mind was the emerging class of smugglers and licensed importers. Together they became the new influential class and got co-opted into the political system. Most smugglers were petty bourgeoisie with blood ties to influential village clans in central and southern Iraq. They were active along the borders with Iran, Turkey, and Syria, where controls were lax— exporting Iraqi oil and oil products and importing food and essential consumer goods. There was also a new category of middlemen, those who were licensed by the government to purchase wholesale UN-approved flour, rice, tea, cooking oil, baby food, and other foodstuffs in Jordan, and then sell these to the rationing authorities with high markups. They and the smugglers became enthusiastic backers of the Baathist regime.

Hans von Sponeck also had in mind the rise of prostitution, increased domestic violence, and decline in women's employment. "In Baghdad you see prostitutes in the street in the middle of the night, something unheard-of in Arab countries," he said. "Shame-faced Iraqis would tell you, 'They are Sudanese.' You see young girls as prostitutes. Behind the Vatican embassy is a hotel where prostitution goes on day and night."[16] The arrival of open prostitution in Baghdad and other cities was symptomatic of both the economic degradation of the populace brought about by stringent sanctions, and the resulting loss of self-dignity that affected not only women, but also men, a lamentable tragedy.

In the economic field, sanctions and sanctions-busting have become a way of life, with a small section of society having acquired a vested interest in perpetuating them. Overall the UN embargo enables Saddam to shift the blame for Iraq's severe socioeconomic problems from himself to the United States.

The early estimations of Washington have failed to materialize.

The conventional wisdom in the Bush Sr. administration—shared by its successor—was that as the Iraqi people began to suffer the devastating effect of the UN sanctions they would increasingly blame Saddam for their woes. That would create an environment in which an irate but courageous member of his immediate family or bodyguard would assassinate him: the Silver Bullet Solution. Alternatively his overthrow would come about through a coup at the top by a few disaffected generals of the elite Republican Guard.

By the early twenty-first century neither had happened. "There are various reasons why most Iraqis have not made the connection between the cause—Iraq's aggression against Kuwait—and the effect, the UN sanctions and international isolation," explained "Dhia," a London-based Iraqi lawyer who visits Baghdad periodically. "Iraqis don't take individual responsibility for the invasion of Kuwait. The sanctions, emanating from that event have created a popular feeling of 'us' and 'them,' against the West. When it comes to apportioning blame, most Iraqis say that Saddam put them in harm's way but did not cause harm. That was caused by the West, led by America. 'Saddam did not drop bombs on us, or cut off our electricity and phones and water supplies; others did that,' they say." Sanctions provided Saddam with a perfect alibi for all the ills in Iraq. "If roads are pot-holed, if phones don't work, if there aren't enough medicines in hospitals, Saddam blames the sanctions. On the other hand, he takes credit for any improvement, however slight—like, say, flower beds appearing in Saadoun Street in Baghdad, a thoroughfare." Furthermore, explained Dhia, "due to the communications and educational embargo, middle-class Iraqis have lost touch with reality. They do not read foreign papers or watch foreign television. All they are exposed to are the Iraqi state television and radio, which offer a very distorted view of the outside world. Most people in Iraq don't know what a fax is, or a mobile phone. E-mail is a rarity even in Baghdad, and very expensive."

Sanctions loom large in the daily life of Iraqis. Whether middle-class professionals or small shopkeepers or manual workers, Iraqis talk about the sanctions as the British do about the weather and Americans about baseball. Will the economic siege of Iraq end? they wonder. If yes, then how and when? I received a variety of answers to these questions.

But on one point all my respondents were of one mind: The sanctions are there solely because of the United States. "If America pulls its hand out of the Security Council, then the embargo will end," says the portly wife of Muhammad Bagga, Umm Jassim, wrapped up in a black cloak.

That Americans are coldhearted when it comes to dealing with Iraq and Iraqis is a view shared unanimously by my respondents irrespective of their age, class, or sex. I doubt though if they know of the interview of US secretary of state Madeleine Albright with Lesley Stahl on CBS's 60 *Minutes* program on May 12, 1996. "More than 500,000 Iraqi children are already dead as a direct result of the UN sanctions," said Stahl. "Do you think the price is worth paying?" Albright replied: "It is a difficult question. But, yes, we think the price is worth it."[17]

Later the American strategy on the sanctions was articulated succinctly by Samuel Berger, President Clinton's national security adviser, in an article in the *Washington Post*, where he established a direct link between UN sanctions and the oil-for-food program. "Our proposal to increase the flow of humanitarian aid to Iraq . . . is in direct opposition to the proposals to lift sanctions," he explained in January 1999. "If sanctions were lifted, the international community no longer could determine how Iraq's oil revenues are spent. . . . Billions of dollars now reserved for the basic needs of the Iraqi people would become available to Saddam Hussein to use as he pleased. Under the current program we . . . force Saddam Hussein to spend the nation's valuable treasure on the people of Iraq. That makes the oil-for-food program part of the sanctions regime."[18]

What of the views of ordinary Iraqis on the subject? "Only God will decide the lifting of sanctions," said Samira at Yassin Hamid's household. "May be two months, may be many years. Sometimes we think they will drag on and on." By contrast, Abdul Razak was unwavering. "I don't think sanctions will ever be lifted fully and formally. What will happen, though—over the next ten years or so—is that they will be eroded."

His views were echoed by Muhammad Bagga, a slim sixty-eight-year-old war veteran with a lean, craggy face. "The sanctions will never be lifted because of America and Britain, and their clients in the Arab world. Though the Americans are responsible for the sanctions, Britain is our first enemy. It is the British who created Israel. They were in the Gulf before the Americans. The big Western powers got angry because Saddam Hussein wanted to benefit all Arabs as well as Iraqis from Iraq's oil."

In his small, crowded drawing room, Bagga proudly pointed to the picture on the wall showing Saddam Hussein pinning a bravery badge on his long white shirt in 1988 during the Iran-Iraq War after his son, Najib, a thirty-five-year-old lieutenant, had been killed on the battlefield. Najib was his second son to die in the war, the first, named Jassim, having perished two years earlier at the age of thirty-two. Images of the neatly dressed young men in uniform hung from the same wall that displayed the photograph of their father being decorated by the country's president and commander-in-chief. The fact that the young Baggas were both Shia Muslim, and had died fighting the Shia-majority Islamic Republic of Iran, made their deaths all the more poignant.

I wondered if Muhammad Bagga saw any link between that war and the one that followed in 1991. But by the time this thought struck me I was miles away from his home, in my hotel facing the Tigris.

CHAPTER 2

BABYLON TO BAATHIST ERA

The blazing August afternoon sun of the Mesopotamian plain failed to dampen the enthusiasm of my translator-guide, Ilham Mubarak, to give me a convoluted history lesson during a walking tour of Babylon, fifty-five miles south of Baghdad. I trudged wearily behind him more concerned about suffering a sunstroke than absorbing the chronicle of Babylon since the Akkadian era. But when pacing around the restored palace of Nebuchadnezzar (r. 605–562 B.C.) he insisted on showing me the rooms used for storing ice (brought down from the mountains to the north), I refused point-blank, anxious as I was to seek refuge under a tree in the nearby, semi-parched park. The irony of explaining the secrets of keeping cool in ancient Mesopotamia to a visitor on a day when the temperature rose to a ferocious 125°F was lost on Ilham Mubarak, a rotund, middle-aged man with a perpetual half smile on his face.

I was more interested in examining the bas-reliefs of the mythical animals that decorated the wall of the sturdy Gate of Ishtar, a leading goddess of Babylon—chiefly because the wall provided an island of shade. "War decorations," said Ilham.

His words transported me to an enormous wall mural, three hundred by one hundred feet, I had seen in his company in Baghdad a few days earlier. Executed in an abstract style, it shows an Iraqi prisoner of war being tortured during the 1980–88 Iran-Iraq War, with his arms being torn apart by two Iranian jeeps, pulling him in opposite directions.

As the longest conventional armed conflict of the twentieth century, the Iran-Iraq War occupies an important place in the world's military history. It had a profound impact on Iraq, which emerged as a military behemoth with 1.2 million soldiers. Such power intoxicated President Saddam Hussein, and paved the way, inadvertently, for his invasion of Kuwait in 1990, resulting in the 1991 Gulf War between Iraq and the US-led coalition of twenty-eight countries, including thirteen Muslim states, the last major conventional war of the twentieth century.

At the turn of that century the Mesopotamian provinces of Basra and Baghdad had been part of the Ottoman Empire since 1638 when Sultan Murad IV, a Sunni Muslim, signed a peace treaty with the Iranian Safavids, followers of Shia Islam, and demarcated the frontiers between their empires. Reversing the trend of the past, when the Safavids persecuted the Sunni minority in Mesopotamia, the Ottomans favored Sunnis at the expense of the majority Shias.[1]

Following the dissolution of the Ottoman Empire in November 1918 in the wake of its defeat in World War I, the League of Nations gave Britain the mandate over Mesopotamia in April 1920, thus making the British targets of the Mesopotamian hostility that had so far been directed against the Ottoman Turks. As it was, by then the local nationalist military officers had declared the territory independent under the constitutional monarchy of Abdullah ibn Hussein al Hashem. He in turn offered his throne to his elder brother Faisal I. Rallying around the military leaders, the general public resisted the British mandate.

Faced with a popular rebellion, the British brought in military reinforcements from their Indian empire and crushed it. They then formalized their relations with Faisal I—formally enthroned in August 1921—by signing a treaty with him that placed military and economic control of the country in their hands.

The 1922 Anglo-Iraqi Treaty was grudgingly ratified by an elected Constituent Assembly two years later. Faisal I legitimized his regime by ratifying the constitution drafted by the assembly and holding parliamentary elections.

Nineteen twenty-five saw the resolution of the issue of the sovereignty of Mosul. The League of Nations' arbitration committee separated the province, inhabited by ethnic Kurds, from Turkey and awarded it to King Faisal I. So now his Kingdom of Iraq consisted of the historic Baghdad and Basra provinces, inhabited by ethnic Arabs, and the Kurdish-majority province of Mosul—with ethnic Kurds forming about one-sixth of the kingdom's population.

Descendants of Indo-European tribes, Kurds appear in the history of the early empires of Mesopotomia, where they are described as Kardouchoi. They trace their distinct history as mountain people to the seventh century B.C. when they were part of the Scythian empire (c. ninth to third century B.C.). In the seventh century A.D. they embraced Islam but retained their language. During the Ottoman and Persian empires they mounted periodic uprisings against the central power. Kurdish nationalism manifested itself in the late nineteenth century *inter alia* in the publication of the first periodical in Kurdish in 1897. With the breakup of the Ottoman Empire, Kurds found themselves living in Turkey, Iraq, and Syria.

Though the expectations of the Turkish Petroleum Company (TPC), owned largely by the British Anglo-Persian Oil Company (APOC), to strike oil in commercial quantities in the Kurdish region in Iraq did not materialize, it succeeded in finding the mineral in the nearby Kirkuk area in 1927. With this, northern Iraq acquired strategic importance.

Three years later London signed a twenty-five-year treaty with Iraq that required the Iraqi ruler to formulate a common foreign policy with Britain and allow the posting of British troops in his country in exchange for a British guarantee to protect his country against foreign attack. This was the price London extracted from Baghdad before ending its mandate in October 1932, enabling Iraq to become a member of the League of Nations. Most Iraqis, however, considered their independence incomplete so long as British troops were stationed on their soil.

Faisal I died in 1933; his only son, Ghazi, I succeeded him. During his rule factions emerged among military officers. In 1936 he encouraged commander-in-chief Bakr Sidqi to overthrow the unpopular civilian government of Yassin al Hasehmi. His nationalist views made him a popular figure. Fond of sports cars, he died in 1939 as a result of a car "accident," for which most Iraqis held Britain responsible.

His four-year-old son, Faisal II, became the formal ruler under the regency of his uncle Abdul Ilah ibn Ali. The prevalent anti-British sentiment in the military hierarchy prevented the pro-British prime minister Nuri al Said from declaring hostilities against Germany when World War II broke out in September 1939. In April 1941 Rashid Ali Gailani, a nationalist prime minister, led a successful coup against the British. Faisal II and his mother fled, along with Abdul Ilah and other members of the royal family.

This anti-imperialist victory is much lauded in the history books of Iraq today. A bronze statue of Rashid Gailani, a bespectacled man of medium height and build, standing erect on a marble pedestal, his right hand gently tugging a lapel of his double-breasted suit, adorns a platform that honors Iraq's recent heroes at Baghdad's Andalus Square. Among the military officers who joined Gailani in his mission was Khairallah Talfa (al Masallat), who would later become the guardian and political mentor of Saddam Hussein.

Gailani's rule, however, proved transient as he failed to repel the British counteroffensive against him in May. Among other things, Khairallah Talfa lost his military post, and returned to his native village of Auja near Tikrit, one hundred miles north of the capital, where, nursing his strong anti-imperialist feelings, he would instill Iraqi nationalism into his ambitious, strong-willed ward, Saddam Hussein.[2]

Britain reinstalled Nuri al Said as prime minister. The royal family returned to Baghdad. Yet anti-British sentiment was so strong among civilians and soldiers that it was only in 1943 that Nuri al Said declared war against Germany. As a result Iraq became one of the founding members of the United Nations after the end of World War II in 1945.

In the wake of the Arab defeat in the Palestine War (1948–49) — also called the First Arab-Israeli War — the sentiment in Iraq turned strongly anti-Western and anti-Zionist. Yet Nuri al Said led Iraq into the Western-led Baghdad Pact, and refused to condemn the 1956 Anglo-French-Israeli aggression against Egypt, called the Suez War.

The upshot was a military coup on July 14, 1958 by Free Officers led by forty-four-year-old Brigadier Abdul Karim Qasim, instantaly recognized by an ascetic face, a toothbrush mustache, and big ears. King Faisal II and his family members were assassinated as was Nuri al Said. To most Iraqis, the overthrow and elimination of the royal family marked the end of the indirect British rule they had endured since their nominal independence in 1932. Therefore July 14, 1958, captured visually in the Liberation Monument in Baghdad's Liberation Square — showing an Iraqi man freeing himself by bending the bars of British subjugation — remains an important date in Iraqi history. Later the Baathist regime would name the bridge connecting the Tashri neighborhood, housing the Republican Presidential Palace, with the U-bend in the Tigris "14 July" while another bridge upstream carried the name "Liberation." Republican Iraq withdrew from the Baghdad Pact, thus opting out of the Cold War between NATO and the Soviet bloc, and adopting a nonaligned policy in international affairs.

REPUBLICAN IRAQ

Qasim promulgated a provisional republican constitution with supreme executive and legislative authority invested in the three-member Sovereignty Council assisted by a cabinet. Qasim's non-aligned stance went down badly in Washington — as did his convening a meeting of the representatives of the oil-rich Iran, Kuwait, Saudi Arabia, and Venezuela in Baghdad in September 1960 to form the Organization of the Petroleum Exporting Countries (OPEC). With OPEC coordinating the hydrocarbon policies of its constituent members, it would become a vital element in the world of oil on which the economies of Western nations and Japan would come to rely heavily.

Qasim was overthrown in 1963 by a group of military officers belonging to the Baath Party, working in conjunction with the US Central Intelligence Agency. Once in power, the Baathists fell out among themselves on the questions of the relationship with Egypt led by pan-Arabist president Gamal Abdul Nasser and the degree of socialism to be achieved. This enabled the prestigious but non-Baathist president Abdul Salam Arif to usurp total power. Following his death in an air accident in 1966, his brother Abdul Rahman Arif assumed the presidency.

On the eve of the June 1967 Arab-Israeli War, Arif prevaricated and dispatched an Iraqi division to Jordan to participate in the conflict only after Baathists and others had staged demonstrations in Baghdad. By the time the Iraqi troops arrived in Jordan, the war was over. Arif, however, joined the Arab oil boycott of the West, which lasted only until the end of August. But when he resumed oil shipments to the West, five ministers resigned in protest. As popular disenchantment with his rule escalated in demonstrations for an elected parliament, he resorted to repression and withdrew his promise to hold a general election by May.

Against this background, former Baathist military officers, led by fifty-six-year-old Ahmad Hassan Bakr, a balding, chubby-faced, avuncular former major-general, conspired with Arif's leading security and presidential guard commanders to topple the president. They did so on July 17, 1968.[3] This was neither the first nor the last time the Arab-Israeli conflict impacted the course of modern Iraqi history.

IRAQ UNDER THE BAATHISTS

Better organized than in 1963, the Baathists consolidated their hold on power, with the self-appointed five-member Revolutionary

Command Council (RCC) assuming supreme authority. They immediately imposed ceilings on agricultural land holdings, confiscated the excess without compensating the owner, and distributed it to landless peasants. They encouraged agricultural cooperatives and introduced state-owned collective farming. By so doing, they built a popular base in rural Iraq.

They also pacified the Kurdish insurgency, which revived in 1969, by signing a fifteen-point agreement with the nationalist Kurdistan Democratic Party (KDP) in March 1970 to be implemented over the next four years. The accord promised a fair degree of autonomy to the Kurdish-majority region and the appointment of a Kurd as a vice president of the republic. But in 1974, when the RCC rejected the KDP's nominee for vice president, the accord broke down.

The KDP, armed by the Shah of Iran and Israel, resumed its insurgency. The hostilities claimed 60,000 civilian and military casualties before coming to an end in March 1975, when—with the cessation of aid from the Shah (and Israel, which channeled its arms through him) as a result of the Iraqi-Iranian Accord signed in Algiers—the Kurdish rebellion collapsed. The resulting treaty demarcated the fluvial frontier of Iraq and Iran along the median line of the main navigable channel of the Shatt al Arab. This signified Baghdad abandoning its claim to both banks of the Shatt and conceding to Tehran's demand to share the waterway.

The end of the Kurdish rebellion coupled with a fivefold increase in Iraq's revenue from the export of petroleum—whose price rocketed due to the Arab oil embargo against the West for siding with Israel in the October 1973 Arab-Israeli War—boosted the popularity of the Baathist regime.

Yet the largest single group in Iraq, Shias—forming 56–61 percent of the population—nursed a grievance: They were grossly underrepresented in the upper echelons of the military, police, and intelligence, as well as the Baathist and governmental hierarchy. None of the RCC members, now numbering seventeen, was Shia. And the secular

Baathist government also tried to weaken the authority of the Shia religious establishment based in Najaf, the prime center of Shia learning. It was here that Ayatollah Ruhollah Khomeini, an archenemy of the Shah of Iran, had found refuge after his expulsion from Iran in 1964. He would be expelled from Najaf fourteen years later.

The rise of an Islamic republic in the Shia-majority Iran under Khomeini in early 1979 provoked militancy among Iraqi Shias, to the extent that the increasingly powerful first vice president of the republic, young Saddam Hussein, a Sunni, acted severely against them, much to the unease of the older President Bakr. While Khomeini took to appealing to Iraqis to overthrow the "non-Muslim" Baathist regime, Baghdad encouraged the ethnic Arabs in the oil-rich Iranian province of Khuzestan to demand autonomy and sabotage oil installations. The differences between Bakr and Saddam on how to tackle the Shia problem became irreconcilable. So on July 17, 1979, the eleventh anniversary of the Baathist seizure of power, Saddam Hussein became chairman of the Revolutionary Command Council and president of Iraq after forcing Bakr to step down.

To counter Tehran's claim that the Iraqi regime was dictatorial, the RCC held elections to the 250-member Parliament in June 1980, thus reviving an institution that had been dead since the 1958 coup. On the fifth anniversary of the 1975 Iran-Iraq treaty of International Boundaries and Neighborliness, Saddam declared in the newly convened Parliament that he was abrogating the treaty forthwith.

This was the prelude to the Iraqi invasion of Iran.

THE IRAN-IRAQ WAR

On September 22, 1980 Iraq invaded Iran, a country three-and-a-half times as large and four times more populous than itself. Its army crossed the border at several points while its air force bombed Iranian military installations and economic targets. Angered by the

Iranians' hostage-taking at the US embassy in Tehran in November 1979, the Carter administration had encouraged Iraq, through diplomatic back channels, to attack Iran. Now, however, Washington declared itself neutral in the war. Saddam expected the conflict to last a month and lead to the overthrow of the Khomeini regime. Instead, it dragged on for ninety-five months.

The war, fought over land, sea, and air, went through several phases.

Contrary to Saddam's expectations that ethnic Arabs in Iranian Khuzestan would welcome his troops as liberators, and that there would be large-scale defections from Iran's military, the Arab Iranians sided firmly with the Tehran government, whose armed forces remained intact. Indeed, many Iranians who did not like the Islamic regime, volunteered to fight for their country as patriots. As a result, the Iraqi gains did not exceed 10,000 square miles of Iranian territory in the southern and central sectors. The wet winter helped bring about a military standoff.

The stalemate continued until the next spring. Then Iran regained almost all of its lost territory. In early June 1982 Baghdad declared itself ready for a truce. But Tehran refused to cease fire until Saddam had been removed from office.

In July 1982, in a role reversal, the Iranians marched into Iraq and tried to conquer Basra. With nine divisions locked in the largest infantry combat since World War II, fierce battles raged for a fortnight. Finally Iran managed to hold on to a mere 32 square miles of Iraq. In April 1983 Iran's offensive in the southern sector to reach the strategic Basra-Baghdad highway failed partly because Iraq used chemical weapons. Tehran's second attempt in early 1984 to sever the strategic highway also ended in failure. But the next February Iran captured Iraq's oil-rich Majnoon Islands in the southern marshes.

Iraq escalated its attacks on Iranian oil tankers, using French-made Exocet air-to-ship (surface-skimmer) missiles, and intensified its air raids on the Kharg oil terminal in the Upper Gulf, which handled most of Iran's petroleum exports. Tehran retaliated by hitting the oil tankers of Kuwait and Saudi Arabia—aiding Iraq financially, logistically, and intelligence wise—as they made their way north through the Straits of Hormuz. In 1985 Iraq hit thirty-three ships in the Gulf and Iran fourteen.

The war of attrition escalated during 1986, with Iraq striking eighty-six ships and Iran forty-one. Having concluded that Iran would not lose the war, Washington began intervening overtly on the Iraqi side to save it from defeat. The Iranian assault in February 1986 in the south, which resulted in the capture of 310 square miles in the Fao Peninsula, broke the stalemate. In March, following a report by UN experts confirming Iraq's use of poison gas, the UN Security Council combined its condemnation of Iraq for deploying chemical weapons with its disapproval of Iran for prolonging the conflict. The next month, Kuwait's and Saudi Arabia's flooding of the oil market caused the petroleum price to fall below ten dollars a barrel, down from twenty-seven dollars in December. This sharply reduced Iran and Iraq's oil income, but Iraq was cushioned by the huge sums it received from its Gulf allies, the West, and the Soviet Union.

From July 1986, assisted by Pentagon expertise (which secretly seconded its Air Force officers to work with the Iraqis), Iraq began using its air force more aggressively than before, hitting Iran's economic and infrastructure targets and extending its air strikes to the Iranian oil terminals in the Lower Gulf. In January 1987 Iran's offensives brought its forces within seven miles of Basra, but failed to capture it.

On July 20, the UN Security Council unanimously passed Resolution 598, calling for a cease-fire and the withdrawal of warring forces. The ten-article text included a clause for an impartial commission to determine war responsibility, one of Iran's major demands. But this was not enough to satisfy Tehran. Iraq said it would accept the resolution if Iran did the same.

Four days later a Kuwaiti supertanker on the first Gulf convoy escorted by US warships hit a mine, believed to have been planted by the Iranians. The subsequent naval buildup by the United States, Britain, and France brought sixty Western warships into the region, which was tantamount to opening a second front against Iran.

On the seventh anniversary of the war, September 22, 1987, Iraq had nearly 400 combat aircraft, six times the figure for Iran. Baghdad possessed 4,500 tanks, 3,200 armored fighting vehicles, and 2,800 artillery pieces versus Tehran's respective totals of 1,570, 1,800, and 1,750. Iraq had 955,000 regular troops versus Iran's 655,000; Iraq's Popular Army, at 650,000, was slightly larger than Iran's Revolutionary Guards Corps (IRGC), at 625,000.

In October, claiming that Iran had fired on a US patrol helicopter, the US navy sank three Iranian patrol boats. Then US warships destroyed two Iranian offshore oil platforms in the Lower Gulf in retaliation for an Iranian missile attack on a US-flagged supertanker docked in Kuwaiti waters. Tehran's war effort was severely hobbled due to the shortage of manpower and money and the damage done to its bridges, factories, and power plants by ceaseless US-assisted Iraqi bombing.

During the first half of 1988, Iraq went on the offensive in a big way, including firing long-range surface-to-surface missiles at Tehran, which demoralized the population. In April Iraq recaptured the Fao Peninsula, using chemical weapons extensively—a fact witnessed and confirmed at the time by the Pentagon's Defense Intelligence Agency officers—while US warships blew up two Iranian oil rigs, destroyed one Iranian frigate and immobilized another, and sank an Iranian missile boat. The next month, using chemical arms, Iraq staged offensives in the northern and central sectors, and then in the south, and made gains. It capped its victories with the recapture of the Majnoon Islands in the south. Iraq would use 110,000 chemical munitions against Iran before the war's end.

On July 3, 1988 a US cruiser shot down an Iran Air airbus carrying 290 people over the Lower Gulf, mistaking it for a combat aircraft. Perceiving this as a prelude to more aggressive intervention by the Pentagon, a fortnight later Tehran unconditionally accepted UN Security Council Resolution 598. Khomeini stated that acceptance of a truce was "in the interest of the revolution and the system at this juncture," thereby implying that if Iran continued to fight, its army would disintegrate. Though the cease-fire did not go into effect until August 20 under UN supervision—after the failure of both sides to make last-minute territorial gains—Saddam declared the war over on August 8 with Iraq as the winner. "I remember the day well, as do all other Iraqis," Abdul Razak told me, his eyes shining. "There were celebrations for three days, with much dancing in the streets. And the day is memorable, 8888, four eights in a row. It is a much-celebrated public holiday now."

Overall, the war was a draw. Neither country lost much territory, nor was there a change of regime in either nation. The conflict enabled Khomeini to consolidate the Islamic revolution. And Iraq emerged as the most powerful military force in the region, outstripping Turkey and Egypt.

Baghdad never released the war casualty figures. But it was estimated that between 160,000 and 240,000 Iraqis died. Iran put the number of its dead at about 200,000—the figure including the missing in action and 11,000 civilians—and the injured at 500,000.

According to estimates from the Stockholm International Peace Research Institute (SIPRI), the war cost Iran something in the range of $74–91 billion, with military imports costing some $11 billion, while Iraq spent between $94–$112 billion, and imported $42 billion worth of military hardware. The latter proved to be an underestimate, as Iraqi deputy premier Tariq Aziz later cited the figure of $102 billion. Whereas Tehran raised no foreign loans, Baghdad borrowed a staggering $83–98 billion—$8 billion from the Soviet Union, $25–35 billion from the West and Japan, and $50–55 billion from the Gulf monarchies, chiefly Saudi Arabia and Kuwait.

Iraq kept its economy running by employing 1.5 to 2 million foreign workers. That is how it managed to achieve a staggering force ratio—regular military personnel/1,000 inhabitants—of 63.3, nearly five times the figure for Iran. At this level, the Pentagon would have 19 million military troops. By prosecuting the war on borrowed money and manpower, Saddam was able to continue building ambitious public works—such as four of the present twelve bridges over the Tigris in Baghdad, and the $7 billion Saddam International Airport—during the conflict.

Yet Iraq could not escape altogether the adverse consequences of a war that halved its per capita income and resulted in an estimated $200 billion worth of damage to its infrastructure. By contrast, the Gulf War cost the US-led coalition $82 billion, with Washington's share being $18 billion, just $5 billion more than Japan's, and a fraction of the $51 billion borne by Saudi Arabia and Kuwait.

IRAQ BETWEEN THE WARS

When Iraq demobilized the first batch of 200,000 troops in 1989, there were no jobs for them. This resulted in clashes between the returning Iraqi soldiers and Egyptian expatriates, the largest group of foreign workers, in which several hundred Egyptians were killed.

Iraq's reconstruction plans were hamstrung by the demands of foreign debt servicing and high defense expenditure that consumed seven-eighths of the oil-export revenue. Its income was limited by the OPEC quota of 2.64 million oil barrels per day (bpd). With Kuwait exceeding its OPEC quota, petroleum prices began falling. Aware of Baghdad's economic vulnerability, Kuwait chose oil as the lever to pressure Baghdad into settling their border dispute while demanding that Iraq repay the $12–14 billion it had borrowed from Kuwait during the war.[4]

The flouting of the OPEC quota by Kuwait and the United Arab Emirates in the spring of 1990 depressed oil prices well below OPEC's reference level of $18 a barrel. During a closed session of the extraordinary Arab summit in Baghdad on May 30, Saddam revealed that every US dollar drop in the price of an oil barrel deprived Iraq of $1 billion annually. "War is fought with soldiers, and harm is done by explosions, killing and coup attempts, but it is also done by economic means sometimes. . . . I say to those who do not mean to wage war on Iraq that this is in fact a kind of war against Iraq."[5]

Saddam's plea fell on deaf ears. Overproduction continued, with Kuwait exceeding its OPEC quota by 40 percent, and the UAE by 30 percent. Petroleum prices fell to $11 a barrel, a level at which Iraq's oil income was just enough to meet current expenses, leaving nothing to service foreign debts or fund urgently needed reconstruction.

Meanwhile the United States was diplomatically active. On July 25, its ambassador to Iraq, April Glaspie, had a meeting with Saddam, which was meticulously recorded, and which would figure prominently in subsequent chronicles, with the authors almost invariably stating that Saddam interpreted Glaspie's stance as a green light. "We have no opinion on the Arab-Arab conflicts, like your border disagreement with Kuwait," she told Saddam. "I was in the American embassy in Kuwait in the late 1960s. The instruction we had during this period was that we should express no opinion on this issue [of borders], and the issue is not associated with America. [US Secretary of State] James Baker has directed our official spokesmen to emphasize this instruction."[6] She conveyed the State Department's hope that Saddam would be able to solve the border problem through the good offices of "your Arab brothers." But the talks between Iraqi vice president Izzat Ibrahim, a lean, sprightly man with a walrus mustache, and Kuwaiti crown prince Shaikh Saad al Sabah, a dark, burly potentate, in Jiddah on July 31, went badly. Shaikh Saad warned Ibrahim, "Don't threaten us. Kuwait has very powerful friends. You will be forced to pay back all the money you owe us."[7]

Among these "powerful friends," the United States was preeminent. "We remain strongly committed to supporting the individual and collective self-defense of our friends in the Gulf," stated the US Defense Department on July 31. Expecting the worst, it put its naval force in the Gulf on high alert.

The behavior of the Pentagon and Shaikh Saad convinced Saddam that further negotiations with Kuwait were futile.

CHAPTER 3

IRAQ AND THE INVASION OF KUWAIT

At 2 A.M., the coolest hour in the southern Iraqi desert, on Thursday, August 2, 1990, six divisions of the elite Republican Guard advanced the seventy-five miles from the Iraqi-Kuwaiti frontier to the capital, Kuwait City, within four hours. They were assisted by the Special Forces that were brought into the emirate by ship and helicopter a few hours after the border crossing. Helicopter-borne troops seized the offshore islands of Warba and Bubiyan.

During the second stage of the offensive, Iraq's fighter aircraft struck key installations in and around Kuwait City while its commandos and airborne units attacked the ruler's Dasman Palace along the coast, the radio and television station, and the Central Bank. The Iraqis' main target was the palace. While Iraqi units in armored personnel carriers, brought in by landing craft, surrounded it, helicopter-borne troops landed on its roof, and in its spacious gardens dawn broke. By then, most of the residents of the palace had fled south into Saudi Arabia in a convoy of Mercedes-Benz limousines. The ruler, Shaikh Jaber III al Ahmad al Sabah, was tipped off an hour before the invasion. Around 4:30 A.M. he and his immediate entourage rushed to the US embassy to board an American military helicopter brought in earlier from one of the US warships in the Gulf, and flew to Bahrain, and then to the Saudi kingdom. By 10 A.M. Iraq completed its occupation of the Emirate of Kuwait.

The UN Security Council's Resolution 660 condemned Iraq and urged a cease-fire and an unconditional withdrawal of its troops from Kuwait. On August 6, it passed Resolution 661, imposing mandatory

35

sanctions and embargo on Iraq and occupied Kuwait. That day King Fahd of Saudi Arabia invited US forces to his realm to bolster its defenses. President George Walker Herbert Bush dispatched 40,000 American troops to the Saudi kingdom.

In mid-August Saddam offered a peace proposal that involved the withdrawal of Israel from the Occupied Arab Territories in "Palestine, Syria and Lebanon," and the formulation of arrangements for the "situation in Kuwait" in line with the UN resolutions. It was rejected summarily by the US and Kuwait. In early October, Amnesty International, the London-based human rights organization, published a report portraying widespread arrests, torture, and summary executions in Kuwait by the occupying Iraqi forces.

On November 29 the UN Security Council adopted Resolution 678 by 12 votes to two (Cuba and Yemen), with one abstention (China), under Chapter VII, authorizing "all necessary means" to implement the earlier resolutions in order "to restore international peace and security in the area," unless Iraq fully implemented these resolutions before January 15, 1991.

Opinion in the US Congress was almost evenly divided between those who wanted the UN economic sanctions to bring about the Iraqi evacuation of Kuwait and those who advocated using military force. It was only by 53 votes to 47 that the Senate authorized Bush Sr. to use the military pursuant to Security Council Resolution 678—followed by the House of Representatives doing so by 250 votes to 183. Among the opposing senators was Sam Nunn, the crusty chairman of the Senate Armed Services Committee. Iraq's Parliament unanimously decided to go to war rather than withdraw from Kuwait, and empowered Saddam Hussein to conduct it.

THE 1991 GULF WAR

Both sides deployed massive military forces and hardware. Iraq's more than half a million men were equipped with 4,200 tanks and

700 combat-ready warplanes and helicopters. They faced 700,000 Western troops, including 550,000 Americans, whose war machine consisted of 4,000 tanks, 2,900 combat aircraft and helicopters, and 107 warships, stationed in the Gulf, the Arabian Sea and the Gulf of Oman, the Red Sea, and the eastern Mediterranean. The US navy was armed with 700-plus nuclear weapons on warships and submarines. In addition were the 220,000 Arab and Muslim troops, equipped with 1,200 tanks and 500 warplanes and combat helicopters.

The coalition's air campaign, code-named Operation Desert Storm, started with aerial bombing and the firing of cruise missiles from US warships on January 16. Two days later Iraq fired 12 Scud ground-to-ground missiles at Tel Aviv and Haifa; and on 22 January three more Iraqi Scuds landed in Tel Aviv but missed the targeted Israeli defense ministry headquarters. Saddam's action stemmed from his resolve to show that the Israeli heartland was no longer immune from attacks by the Arab world; to hurt Israel for its continued occupation of the Palestinian Territories and in the process provoke it to insist on joining the US-led coalition and thereby cause the exit of its Arab and Muslim members; and to avenge belatedly Israel's destruction of the two French-built Osirak light water civilian nuclear reactors at Tuweitha, fifteen miles south of Baghdad, in a lightning, clandestine air attack in June 1981. Coalition air sorties in the first week totaled 12,000, and in the second and third weeks 20,000, with the US accounting for seven-eighths of the total. During the fourth week (February 7–13) the coalition concentrated on destroying Iraq's transport infrastructure of bridges and roads.

On February 15, Baghdad agreed to deal with UN Security Council Resolution 660, if the coalition forces left the region, if Israel withdrew from the Occupied Arab Territories, and if "the nationalist and Islamic forces" of Kuwait were allowed to settle the country's future. Kuwait, Saudi Arabia, and Egypt rejected the proposal. President Bush called on the Iraqi people and military to remove Saddam from office, and then comply with all UN resolutions.

At 1200 Greenwich mean times (GMT) on February 23, Iraq said that, following its acceptance of the eight-point Soviet peace plan, it had decided to withdraw from Kuwait immediately and unconditionally. At 1630 GMT the UN Security Council began a closed-door session, with the Western powers declaring that they were not interested in bridging the gap between the Soviet plan and the United States' twelve conditions. At 1800 GMT Bush ordered the coalition's commander, Gen. Norman Schwarzkopf, to expel the Iraqis from Kuwait. By then retreating Iraqis had begun to set Kuwaiti oil wells ablaze, 640 in all.

At 0100 GMT on February 24, the coalition launched its ground offensive from Saudi Arabia, code-named Operation Desert Saber, with ground troops advancing on two axes. It would last one hundred hours. The next day at 2130 GMT Moscow presented a new peace plan, and an hour later Iraq accepted it. Baghdad ordered a withdrawal from Kuwait. By noon on February 26 the Iraqi troops had withdrawn from Kuwait City and its suburbs, and a long convoy of Iraqi tanks, armored personnel carriers, trucks, buses, and hijacked vans and cars was on its way to Basra along the six-lane Highway 80.

As it approached Mitla ridge, north of Jahra, twenty miles west of Kuwait City, its head and tail were hit by US ground-attack aircraft. This immobilized the convoy. The slaughtering of the retreating Iraqis by the Pentagon continued for the next forty hours until the truce at 0800 local time on February 28. In the words of Colin Smith, the chief roving correspondent of the London *Observer*, the aerial assault was "one of the most terrible harassments of a retreating army from the air in the history of warfare." When the weather turned unsuitable for aerial bombing in the afternoon, the task of "taking out" the retreating Iraqis fell to the US army and marines. "We got there [Highway 80] just before dusk, and essentially shot up the front of this column," reported Tony Clifton of *Newsweek*. "The group of vehicles we hit included petrol tankers and tanks, so the tanks exploded in these great fountains of white flame from the ammunition. . . . You could see the little figures of soldiers coming out with their hands up. It really looked like a medieval hell—the hell you see in [the paintings of Hieronymus] Bosch, because of the great red flames and then these weird little contorted figures. . . . It was all conducted at a distance of say, half a mile, and in darkness."[1]

On February 27 at 0200 GMT Bush ordered a truce if Iraq would put down its arms. At 0440 GMT Iraq complied and a temporary cease-fire went into effect at 0500 GMT—with the coalition's Western armies occupying over 2,000 square miles of southern Iraq between Samawa and the Kuwait border—thus ending 167 days of prewar crisis and 42 days of warfare.

With an estimated 25,000–30,000 fatalities caused by the coalition's attacks on the 12 retreating Iraqi divisions, added to an estimate of 32,600 deaths resulting from the coalition's air campaign, the Iraqi total came to 57,600–62,600. By contrast, of the 376 coalition deaths, the United States sustained 266 (including 125 due to accidents during the prewar seven-month field training), and Britain 29. An estimated 2,000–5,000 Kuwaitis, mostly civilians, died. In its 110,000 air sorties the coalition dropped on the Iraqi targets a total of 99,000–140,000 tons of explosives—equivalent to five to seven of the nuclear bombs dropped on the Japanese city of Hiroshima during World War II.[2] Such intense bombing, preceded by the most comprehensive economic sanctions imposed by the UN, plunged Iraq into a preindustrial state, reducing its oil output by two-thirds.

Since then, many politicians and commentators in the West and the Middle East have repeatedly asked why the coalition forces did not overthrow Saddam. This question was addressed in 1992 by Gen. Sir Peter de La Billiere, who commanded the troops of Britain, which contributed the second largest Western force to the Coalition. "We did not have a [UN] mandate to invade Iraq or take the country over, and if we had tried to do that, our Arab allies would certainly not have taken a favorable view," he explained in his book, *Storm Command.* "Even our limited incursion into Iraqi territory had made some of them uneasy. The Arabs themselves had no intention of invading another Arab country. The Islamic forces [i.e., forces of the 13 Muslim members of the coalition] were happy to enter Kuwait for the purpose of restoring the legal government, but that was the limit of their ambition. No Arab troops entered Iraqi territory." Sir Peter had no doubt that the Western troops would have reached Baghdad in another day and a half. "But in pressing on to the Iraqi capital we would have moved outside the remit of the United Nations authority, within which we had worked so far. We would have split the coalition physically, since the Islamic forces would not have come with us, and risked splitting it morally and psychologically as well, thus undoing all the goodwill which we had taken so much trouble to achieve. The American, British and French would have been presented as the foreign invaders of Iraq and we would have undermined the prestige which we had earned around the world for helping the Arabs resolve a major threat to the Middle East. The whole Desert Storm would have been seen purely as an operation to further Western interests in the Middle East." Finally, what would have been achieved by such a move? "Saddam Hussein . . . would have slipped away into the desert and organized a guerrilla movement, or flown to some friendly state such as Libya and set up a government-in-exile. We would then have found ourselves with the task of trying to run a country shattered by war, which at the best of times is deeply split into factions. . . . Either we would have to set up a puppet government or withdraw ignominiously without a proper regime in power, leaving the way open for Saddam to return. In other words, to have gone on to Baghdad would have achieved nothing except to create even wider problems."[3]

The Shia Uprising

The ink had hardly dried on the cease-fire terms on March 3, when Saddam's regime faced a rebellion by Shia insurgents in the South.

It began in Nasiriyeh, the headquarters of the army's southwestern command, when a group of armed men arrived from the nearby Suq al Shuyukh, a town occupied by the American forces, and organized hundreds of Iraqi army deserters. (Among their leaders was Maj.-Gen. Tawfiq Yasseri, who would go into exile after the failure of the uprising and set up the opposition Iraqi National Coalition.) Together they stormed the garrison and seized it. The uprising spread rapidly to other Shia-majority towns and cities, including Basra, Karbala, and Najaf. The insurgents attacked army premises and seized weapons.

Popular protest, often triggered by the tearing up of Saddam's posters by army deserters and excited by slogans like "There is no god but God, and Saddam is His enemy" (*La illah il Allah, Saddam adou Allah*), escalated into an orgy of looting and destruction of public property and summary executions of local Baath Party rulers as well as intelligence and military officers.

Saddam was alarmed. His government immediately demobilized all soldiers aged thirty-five to thirty-eight to contain the mutiny. It awarded bonuses to conscripts and elite Republican Guard troops. It increased food rations, instituted in January 1991, by a quarter.

However, what really undermined the popular backing for the uprising, and helped Saddam, was the intervention, overt and covert, by Iran. Its president, Ali Akbar Hashemi Rafsanjani, declared: "You [Saddam] know well that you are undesirable in your country as well as in the region. So, don't further stain your bloodied hands by killing more innocent Iraqis. Yield to the people's will, and step down."[4] Having fought Iran for eight years, most Iraqi soldiers and civilians, irrespective of their religious affiliation, resented interference by Tehran in their domestic affairs.

This coincided with reports that thousands of armed men had crossed into Iraq from Iran. They reportedly included not only ranks of Iran's Islamic Revolutionary Guards Corps but also the forces of the Tehran-based Supreme Assembly of Islamic Revolution in Iraq

(SAIRI), led by Ayatollah Muhammad Baqir al Hakim, a lean-faced, thinly bearded, sad-eyed Shia cleric opposed to the Iraqi regime, who now stressed the Islamic nature of the uprising.

"[T]he initial uprisings were an explosion of pent-up rage and revenge, characterized by an orgy of looting and destruction without any sustaining organization or ideological vision," noted Anthony H. Cordesman and Ahmed S. Hashim, American specialists on the Gulf. "[W]hen the uprisings began to take on more organized form, they were led by Shia religious leaders and infiltrators from Iran. Many rebel leaders raised the green banner of Islam, [and] portraits of Khomeini and Muhammad Baqir al Hakim. . . . The atrocities committed against government officials were seen as the portent of the bloodshed to come if the rebels prevailed."[5]

Iran's intervention and SAIRI's dominance of the Shia uprising alarmed the Bush Sr. administration, which had second thoughts about a popular overthrow of the Iraqi regime. Brent Scowcroft, Bush's national security adviser, would later tell ABC News, "I frankly wished [the uprising] hadn't happened. I envisioned a post-war government being a military government. . . . It's the colonel with the brigade patrolling his palace that's going to get him [Saddam] if someone gets him."[6] This tied in neatly with the statement of Richard Haas, then director for Near East affairs on the US National Security Council, "Our policy is to get rid of Saddam, not his regime."[7]

The prospect of a fragmented Iraq, with the Shia South, adjoining Kuwait and Saudi Arabia's eastern region where its Shias are concentrated, siding with Iran, worried the Saudi and Kuwaiti rulers—not to mention the US administration. Inimical though they were to Saddam, Riyadh, Kuwait, and Washington did not wish to see his regime replaced by one modeled on Iran, thus enabling Tehran to emerge as the uncontested leader of the Gulf.

It was against this backdrop that Saddam reassembled his forces in the South, particularly the Republican Guard, which was almost wholly Sunni, and its military hardware, including seven hundred tanks and fourteen hundred armored personnel carriers it had managed to withdraw from the Kuwaiti theater of operations before the cease-fire. On March 9, it launched a counterattack against the Shia rebels. Unsurprisingly, the US forces did not intervene.

By March 16, Saddam's forces had quashed the rebellion after meeting stiff resistance in Basra, Najaf, and Karbala. The total death toll during the fortnight-long rebellion was put at 30,000.[8] Most of the deaths resulted from the artillery bombardment of residential areas by government troops. They also forced 70,000 Shias, including many clerics and most of the 8,000 theological students of Najaf, to flee into Iran. "All along Al Abbas Street, which leads to the Shia shrine of Imam Abbas [in Najaf], buildings were burnt out or smashed by gunfire," reported Patrick Cockburn of the London *Independent*. "At the end of the street a tank stands in front of the porch of the shrine whose top has been hit." This shrine as well as Imam Hussein's suffered damage, including bullet marks and gaping holes caused by artillery shells.

In a radio and television address on March 16, Saddam accused Tehran of supporting the saboteurs of the South, and "the stooges and agents of foreign enemies" in the [Kurdish] North. He celebrated the end of the rebellion in the South by visiting Najaf and praying at the shrine of Imam Ali. He allocated forty-four pounds of gold, 110 pounds of silver, and cash to rebuild the damaged shrine, and appealed to all Iraqis to donate money to the holy places of Iraq.[9]

The Kurdish Rebellion

While Saddam tackled the South, the Kurdish nationalists struck. On the morning of March 14, most of the ranks of Fursan (lit., horse-riders), the 100,000-strong Iraqi army auxiliary force consisting of Kurds, changed sides. The regular Iraqi forces found themselves facing ultimatums from the Fursan. Some fought, others surrendered. By the evening, in twelve major towns in a hundred-mile-long arc, authority passed to the Kurdish insurgents, known as *peshmargas* (i.e., those who face death). Since Saddam's invasion of Kuwait, Kurdish nationalist leaders had been cultivating the auxiliaries, most of them young recruits who had joined the Fursan either at the behest of their tribal chiefs, who received money and favors from Baghdad, or because they had lost their land and jobs in the forced resettlement of Kurds into protected villages in the government's drive to quell earlier Kurdish nationalist insurgencies. Within a week the insurgents controlled not only the three provinces of Suleimaniya, Irbil, and Dohak—forming the official Kurdistan Autonomous Region (KAR)—but also large parts of the Tamim province, with its capital in the oil city of Kirkuk.

Bush Sr. faced a dilemma. Should the United States intervene militarily in an incipient civil war in Iraq by severing Baghdad's supply lines to the Republican Guard, compelling Saddam to keep his aircraft grounded, and arming the insurgents with antitank and antiaircraft missiles? An intense debate ensued in Washington, with input from Riyadh and Ankara.

The scenario of an independent Kurdistan worried Turkey, with a large Kurdish population concentrated in its southeastern sector. During his meeting with Bush at Camp David on March 24, Turkish president Turgut Ozal explained how an independent Iraqi Kurdistan would become the nucleus for a Greater Kurdistan for the Kurdish populations of Turkey, Iran, and Syria, thus destabilizing the whole region. Two days later, in his meeting with Scowcroft, who visited Saudi Arabia secretly, King Fahd too urged a hands-off policy.

Following the US National Security Council meeting on March 27, the White House spokesman announced that President Bush had no intention of placing his administration in the midst of a civil war in Iraq, pointing out that "it had made no promises to the [Iraqi] Shias or Kurds." Reflecting the public mood, he added, "The American people have no stomach for a military operation to dictate the outcome of a political struggle in Iraq."[10]

Using heavy artillery, multiple rocket launchers, and helicopter gunships, the Iraqi armored and infantry divisions, commanded by Gen. Ali al Majid, mounted an all-out assault on Kirkuk, and drove out the lightly armed rebels by nightfall. This led to a massive Kurdish exodus to the mountainous Iranian and Turkish borders. As the Iraqi army recaptured town after town, the size of the Kurdish exodus increased, finally involving 1.5 million people, about half of the region's population. The Kurds feared brutal and extensive reprisals by Baghdad, a repeat of its behavior in the mid-1970s and late 1980s.

Their leaders' appeal to the United States, Britain, and France to act through the United Nations to save Kurds from "genocide and torture" went unheeded. This happened primarily because the events did not fit the scenario that the Western powers had hastily conceived for postwar Iraq: a military coup against Saddam that would put pro-Western Iraqi generals in charge of a united Iraq. In early March Washington was informed by Minaf Hassan al Tikriti, a senior Iraqi diplomat in Moscow who had defected to the Saudi embassy there, that his brother, Gen. Hakim Hassan al Tikriti, commander of the helicopter forces in the army, was planning a coup.[11] What US officials failed to realize was that following his brother's defection Gen. Hakim al Tikriti would have been put under intense government surveillance, thus ensuring the failure of his plan.

During the first week of April, Baghdad's forces retook Irbil, Dohak, Zakho, and Suleimaniya, enabling the government to act magnanimously and offer a general amnesty to rebellious Kurds. On April 6, the RCC declared, "Iraq has totally crushed all acts of sedition and sabotage in all cities of Iraq." It emerged later that "sedition and sabotage" had spread to all but four of the eighteen Iraqi provinces, the exceptions being Baghdad, Anbar (capital Ramadi), Salahuddin (capital Tikrit), and Nineva (capital Mosul).

The RCC's statement came a day after the UN Security Council had passed Resolution 688 by ten votes to three (Cuba, Yemen and Zimbabwe), with two abstentions (China and India). Unlike all previous resolutions on Iraq, this one was not passed under the UN Charter's Chapter VII (Action with Respect to Threats to the Peace, Breaches of the Peace, and Acts of Aggression), which authorizes military action by member-states. The Western powers agreed to this to forestall a veto by China. The resolution condemned the repression of Iraqi civilians, including most recently in the Kurdish-populated area, and demanded that the Iraqi government end this repression, and allow access to international humanitarian organizations to help those in need of assistance.

As it was, all Iraqis were in acute need of foreign economic help. The report by Martti Ahtissari, a senior UN diplomat, published on March 22, said that comprehensive sanctions on Iraq in August "seriously affected" its ability to feed its people. This was noted by the drafters of the Security Council's Resolution 687, a document of thirty-four paragraphs, passed under Chapter VII. Adopted on April 3, 1991 by twelve votes to one (Cuba), with two abstentions (Ecuador and Yemen), it removed the embargo on food, eased restrictions on essential civilian needs, and unfroze Iraq's foreign assets. However, the lifting of the remaining (still extensive) restrictions was tied to the elimination of Iraq's nonconventional weapons, and compensation to those who had suffered from Iraq's actions.

Resolution 687 could be summarized as follows. One, a formal cease-fire would come into effect only after Iraq officially accepted the document. Two, following the deployment of UN military observers in the demilitarized zone along the Iraqi-Kuwaiti border, the coalition troops would vacate southern Iraq. Three, Baghdad must agree unconditionally to destroy or remove under international supervision all chemical and biological weapons, and all ballistic missiles with ranges greater than ninety-four miles, and related production facilities. A similar procedure would be instituted to remove all nuclear weapons–usable material. Iraq must provide lists of locations, amounts and types of these arms and materials, as well as chemical and biological weapons, by April 17. The UN secretary-general would set up a commission charged with making on-site inspections by May 17. These actions represented steps toward *achieving the goal of establishing in the Middle East a zone free from weapons of mass destruction*. Four, Iraq was liable for damages arising from its invasion of Kuwait. A fund would be created to meet the claims, and a commission established by May 2 to administer it. Five, Iraq must pledge not to support international terrorism.

After protesting that Resolution 687 impinged on Iraq's sovereignty, Baghdad accepted it on April 6. But it rejected Resolution 688, and stuck to this position. These two resolutions would come to dominate society and state within Iraq as well as Baghdad's external relations over the next decade and beyond.

Meanwhile, the feelings of ordinary Iraqis on the great tragedy that had visited them was summed up succinctly by Nuha al Radi in her diary. "After the War ended, the Allies spent all day and all night flying over our heads and breaking the sound barrier," reads her entry on April 15, 1991. "Our torture went on for months—20 or 30 times, day and night, jets broke the sound barrier over our heads, horrific deafening noise, swooping down, rubbing our noses in the dirt. . . . Bush says he has nothing against the Iraqi people. . . . [But] It's us, and only us, who've been without electricity and water—a life of hardship."[12]

Whereas US warplanes' flights over Baghdad ended as summer approached, this could not be said of the Kurdish region in the North. In late August talks on Kurdish autonomy between the Iraqi Kurdistan Front, a coalition of eight Kurdish groups, and Baghdad finally broke down when Saddam insisted on the Front surrendering all its heavy weapons, closing down its radio station, and cutting all foreign links. The Iraqi forces and Kurdish irregulars clashed briefly. Having withdrawn from northern Iraq, the United States, Britain, and France stationed their combat aircraft at Turkey's Incirlik military base to maintain air surveillance of Iraq above the 36th parallel to protect the largely Kurdish population. Ankara allowed this arrangement for six months subject to parliamentary approval, starting October 1991, when Saddam withdrew his forces from the three Kurdish provinces.

His authority was curtailed further in August 1992 when the Western allies declared the predominantly Shia sector of Iraq below the 32nd parallel to be a "no fly" zone for his regime. However, that did not affect the Baghdad government's administrative powers. While accusing the Western powers of trying to dismember Iraq, Saddam refrained from ordering his military to down the patrolling aircraft. The reason was expressed by his deputy premier, Tariq Aziz, later: Active Iraqi resistance to the air exclusion zone in the South would have given President Bush Sr. an opportunity to flex his military muscle and boost his chances of reelection.

In the event, Bush Sr. lost to Democrat Bill Clinton in the November 1992 presidential election. This pleased Saddam, who reckoned that there was now a chance of a fresh start with the new occupant of the White House, since Clinton had no personal animus against him. At the same time he saw a chance to roll back the southern no fly zone, for which he saw no basis, during the transitional period in the American presidency, from early November 1992 to January 21, 1993.

In late December, when Iraq began challenging the southern air exclusion zone, a US F-16 shot down an Iraqi MiG fighter in the area. In response, the Iraqi air force deployed twenty antiaircraft missile launchers inside the zone, and transported missiles to arm the launchers on January 4–5, 1993. The United States, Britain, and France demanded the removal of the missiles within forty-eight hours. While voicing defiance in public, Saddam complied.

On January 10, though, Iraq refused to allow inspectors of the UN Special Commission (Unscom) on disarming Iraq, flying in from Bahrain, to use the Iraqi airspace below the 32nd parallel. When the UN protested, Baghdad banned UN flights. So on January

13, 114 US, British, and French warplanes hit sites near five Iraqi air bases below the 32nd parallel, targeting ground-to-air missile sites, radar sites, and telecommunications systems. Iraq rescinded its ban on UN flights, but insisted that the UN planes circumvent the southern no fly zone.

Rejecting the Iraqi condition, on January 17, the US navy fired forty-five Tomahawk cruise missiles at the Zafaraniya factory on the outskirts of Baghdad. One missile hit Al Rashid Hotel, much favored by visiting foreign journalists, and killed three civilians. Washington justified its actions on the grounds that Iraq had violated Resolutions 687 and 715 (concerning long-term monitoring of Iraq's military industry). The final Western attack on Iraq occurred the next day when seventy-five aircraft struck targets below the 32nd parallel and left twenty-one people dead. On the eve of the inauguration of President Clinton on January 21, Baghdad announced a unilateral cease-fire "to enable the new [US] administration to study the no fly zones." But the Clinton White House displayed no such sign, and the clashes in the southern air exclusion zone continued for four more days.

Militarily and diplomatically, the latest confrontation between Iraq and the Western powers altered nothing. But Saddam gained politically at home. The Western bombing in the southern no fly zone and outside (in and around Baghdad) distracted Iraqis from their daily hardships. Instead of blaming Saddam, they rallied around him in the face of renewed US-led bombardment, and started blaming the Western powers' intransigence rather than their government's conduct for their economic plight.

CHAPTER 4

THE BAATH AND SADDAM

At a major road intersection in Baghdad's middle-class neighborhood of Mustansiriya, I was struck by a hand-painted portrait of Saddam on an electric pole shining in the late-afternoon sun. I asked my official translator-guide, Ilham Mubarak, if I could take a snapshot. "Yes," he replied. I got out of the taxi. I clicked the shutter. Then, noticing the "Al Fadhil Street" sign in English and Arabic just to the right-hand side of the portrait, I turned my camera slightly to recompose the shot. Click! Then one more—to be on the safe side.

Suddenly a few young men in trousers and colorful bush shirts appeared. They waved at me, gesturing that I follow them. I froze. They talked to Ilham, standing a few yards behind me. Ilham's perpetual half smile disappeared, but he remained cool. As he followed the young men, he said to me in English, "Take your pictures." But I did not.

Unknown to me and Ilham, across the street was the Mustansiriya branch of the governing Arab Baath Socialist Party—Baath Party, in common parlance—recognizable not by any sign, large or small, but by a bunch of young men in shirtsleeves with submachine guns lounging at the entrance to a compound leading to the party office. My misdemeanor, I reckoned, was that I had tried to photograph a Baath Party office, a "sensitive site."

Ilham returned shortly. "It's all right," he said. "But there is a former employee of the foreign ministry who wants to practice his English with you." So we crossed the street together.

Outside the sentry post, I found Hamad, a man in his early forties, with a wide girth, sitting in a chair with a walking stick by his side. I inquired about the injury to his leg. "The damn American missiles," he replied, and bared the skin underneath his rib cage to show more scars. "I was in hospital for forty-four days—in 1993," he added. "The missiles that killed Laila Attar [a famous Iraqi painter]," I said. My statement surprised and pleased him as he nodded affirmatively.

Meanwhile, a young Baath zealot with a luxuriant black mustache and a missing right molar, called Hajir, kept pestering Ilham to appear before the Party Boss in the office. Hajir's insistent manner implied that he belonged to *Amn al Hizb* (lit., Party Security), charged with keeping tabs on members' loyalty and maintaining security cells within the organization. After resisting for a while, Ilham gave in. It was another 20 minutes or so before he emerged after an apparently taxing session with the Party Boss, looking grave but otherwise unscathed. So he should have. After all, he was part of the security network of the regime: He was required to submit reports on the foreign journalists he accompanied to the General Security (*Amn al Aam*) directorate.

The moral of the episode was unambiguous: "In Iraq, Baath Party Rules Okay."

As an entity that started clandestinely as the Arab Baath Party in 1950 with a few dozen members, the organization had come a very long way. Even in 1954 when—as a result of the amalgamation of the Arab Baath Party and Arab Socialist Party in Syria—the Arab Baath Socialist Party, a pan-Arab organization, came into being in Damascus, its Iraqi branch with the same name had only about two hundred members.

The party's basic principles were unity and freedom of the Arab nation within its homeland, and a belief in its special mission to end colonialism and promote "humanitarianism." To achieve this the party had to be nationalist, populist, socialist, and revolutionary. While rejecting the Marxist concept of class conflict, it favored land reform; public ownership of natural resources, transport, large-scale industry, and financial institutions; trade unions of workers and peasants; cooption of workers into management; and accepting nonexploitative private ownership and inheritance. It stood for a representative and constitutional form of government, and freedom of speech and association within the bounds of Arab nationalism.

According to the Baath, Arabs form a single nation that is currently divided into various regions (countries). Therefore the party is headed by a National Command that covers the whole Arab world and serves as the central executive authority. Under it are Regional Commands in those Arab states where the party is strong enough to justify establishing one. Below the Regional Commands are branches. These are composed of sections made up of divisions, each of which consists of a few three-member cells. Until 1966 the National Command was based in Damascus. A split led to a breakaway group establishing itself first in Beirut and then, following the Baathist coup in Iraq in 1968, in Baghdad.

The Baath Party in Iraq held its first (clandestine) regional congress in late 1955, when it decided to cooperate with other nationalist groups. It played only a marginal role in the antiroyalist military coup in 1958. Despite suppression by the new ruler, Abdul Karim Qasim, the party grew. By the time the Baathists, joined by non-Baathist allies, overthrew Qasim in early 1963, the party had 850–1,000 active members and 15,000 sympathizers. Once in power the Baathists fell out among themselves, allowing the non-Baathist president Abdul Salam Arif, followed by his brother Abdul Rahman, to usurp total authority.

Abdul Rahman's reluctance to join the June 1967 Arab-Israeli War immediately was used by the Baathists to build up popular support. In mid-July 1968 an alliance of Baathist leaders and non-Baathist military officers overthrew Arif, and a fortnight later the Baathists elbowed out the non-Baathist conspirators and monopolized power. By then the party had five thousand active members.

The governing five-member Revolutionary Command Council, headed by President Ahmad Hassan Bakr, institutionalized the entwining of the party with state machinery—especially the armed forces—as well as society at large. Later the party would establish a military bureau, headed by Saddam Hussein, with a mandate to impart political education to the officer corps, and monitor its political-ideological allegiance. The interim constitution of July 1970 formalized party supremacy by stating that the Revolutionary Command Council, the highest state body chaired by the republic's president, had the right to select its new members from the Baath's regional (i.e., national) leadership. The party followed a twin-track policy of widening its popular base by redistributing wealth and promoting social welfare, and simultaneously tightening its grip over the armed forces, police, and intelligence.

Once Saddam Hussein, who had earlier built up the party's militia, had acquired a seat on the enlarged RCC in November 1969, he busied himself with restructuring and strengthening the party as well as the state intelligence apparatus. His control of the security and intelligence agencies would play a vital role in his rise to the supreme authority, which he would achieve when his intelligence contacts informed him in June 1979 that President Bakr had sent a secret message to Syrian president Hafiz Assad, then visiting Baghdad, to expedite negotiations on unity between Syria and Iraq. Using that embarrassing information, Saddam would compel Bakr to resign.

In July 1973, on the fifth anniversary of the 1968 Baathist coup, the RCC sponsored the formation of the Baathist-led National Progressive and Patriotic Front (NPPF), consisting *inter alia* of Communists, Arab nationalists, and a Kurdish group, with the Iraqi Communist Party (ICP) being the single most important non-Baathist organization in the NPPF.

Established in 1934, the Communist Party was the oldest party in Iraq—and the strongest in the region. It was in touch with the Free Officers Organization that ended the pro-Western monarchy in 1958. Under Qasim, the party, made up of 8,000 active members, formed Peasant Leagues to help implement the land reform decreed by the new regime. Its strength was the envy of the Baathists who conspired with the CIA to carry out a witch-hunt against its activists after seizing power in 1963. As a consequence, 3,000–5,000 Communists were killed, the worst fate suffered by any political party in the Arab world before or since.

A decade later, along with other groups, the Communists signed the National Action Charter as a prerequisite to joining the NPPF. The non-Baathist signatories declared their loyalty to the Baathist revolution and promised to refrain from propagating their ideology among students and soldiers. In return NPPF constituents got seats in the thirty-strong cabinet, the Communists receiving a maximum of two. This arrangement lasted five years. Due to frequent policy differences with the Baathist leadership, the Communists quit the NPPF in 1978. Relations soured further when they endorsed the Soviet military intervention in Afghanistan in 1979, which Saddam criticized strongly. He barred the party from contesting the parliamentary poll held in 1980. Communist leaders condemned Saddam's invasion of Iran, which, to them, was an anti-imperialist state. Saddam repressed the party severely and denounced its members as unpatriotic—a charge that became hard to dismiss when Iran invaded and occupied Iraqi territory in mid-1982.

Iraq's war with Iran (1980–88) brought about a marked change in the Baath. In the name of increasing production, Saddam minimized the importance of Baathist socialism, and encouraged the private sector at the expense of the public sector. He also made the concept of pan-Arabism subservient to the idea of Iraqi nationalism, which the regime's propaganda machine deployed as the prime ideology to motivate citizens to join the war effort. In the tightly controlled general elections of 1980 and 1984, the Baath won 183 and 188 seats respectively out of 250, with the rest going largely to independents. In the 1989 vote, the Baath's share fell to 138.

The vagaries of the Baath's parliamentary strength made no difference to the total control that Saddam Hussein had been exercising over Iraq since 1979—which he acquired by trying sixty-eight Baathist civilian and military leaders on charges of participating in a major "anti-state conspiracy" and executing twenty-one of them, and then purging trade unions, the party militia, student unions, and local and provincial governments of the elements he considered half-hearted in their support of him.

SADDAM HUSSEIN

Born into the Begat clan of the al Bu Nasir tribe in Auja village near Tikrit, the son of Hussein Abd al Majid, a landless peasant, and Subha Talfa (al Massallat), Saddam (lit., fighter) was raised by his maternal uncle, Khairallah Talfa, due to the death of his father before his birth. He imbibed Khairallah's anti-imperialist views. Soon after his arrival in Baghdad, at the age of eighteen, for further education, he joined the Baath Party. Following the 1958 coup he engaged in fights between the Baathists and the followers of Prime Minister Qasim. As a member of the team that tried, unsuccessfully, to assassinate Qasim in October 1959, he was injured in the leg. He escaped to Syria and then to Egypt, where he studied law at Cairo University.

Following the Baathist coup in 1963, Saddam returned to Iraq and married Sajida, a daughter of Khairallah Talfa. After Abdul Salam Arif's usurpation of power from the Baathists, Saddam got involved in an abortive attempt to overthrow Arif. He was imprisoned but managed to escape in July 1966. Elected assistant general secretary of the Baath Party, he spent the next two years restructuring the organization. He was thirty-one when the Baath recaptured power in 1968.

Though not yet a member of the ruling Revolutionary Command Council, Saddam was quite influential thanks to his blood ties with its chairman, Ahmad Bakr, an avuncular cousin of Khairallah Talfa. Once he secured a place on the expanded RCC, he and Bakr came to dominate the party, mainly because of their duplicitous decimation of their RCC colleagues. He focused on strengthening the party as well as resolving the long-running Kurdish problem.

In 1970, Saddam set up the National Security Bureau (*Maktab Amn al Qawami*) under Nazim Kazar to coordinate and supervise the three existing intelligence agencies: General Security (GS, *Amn al Aam*), dating back to the British mandate in Iraq and functioning as part of the Interior Ministry, with its focus on the general public and governmental property; General Intelligence Department (GID, *Dairat al Mukhabarat al Ammaa*), concentrating on political opposition at home and abroad; and Military Intelligence (MI, *Istikhabarat al Askariya*). After Kazar's failed coup attempt in June 1973, Saadoun Shakir (al Tikriti), a cousin and a longtime confidant of Saddam, became head of the National Security Bureau and held the job for nearly two decades.

By the mid-1970s, Saddam had outshone Bakr in leadership, guile, ruthlessness, and organizational ability. It was Saddam who, during his visit to Moscow in early 1972 as the RCC's deputy chairman, stressed the ideological concurrence between Iraq and the Soviet Union—opposition to Western imperialism, Zionism, and American-sponsored peace moves—that led to the signing of the Iraqi-Soviet Friendship Treaty in April. It was Saddam again who signed the Algiers Accord with the pro-American Shah of Iran in 1975, which required the two governments to stop all infiltrations of a subversive nature.

At home, soon after replacing Bakr as the head of the RCC and president of Iraq, Saddam appointed his cousin, Ali Hassan al Majid, director of the General Security and instructed him to infuse Baathist ideology into its personnel. The transformation of the General Security into a political police force, carried out against the backdrop of the Iran-Iraq War, earned the service the disrepute of deploying torture, kidnapping, murder, and rape to intimidate dissenters and malcontents. Its agents became ever vigilant to discover the faintest sign of disaffection. In 1987, following Gen. al Majid's transfer to Kurdistan as its military commander, Gen. Abdul Rahman al Duri became the GS's new boss.

By far the largest intelligence agency was the General Intelligence Department, operating from its vast headquarters in Baghdad's affluent Mansur neighborhood. It functioned internally and externally. Domestically, it was divided into provincial bureaus; abroad, its agents were attached to the Iraqi embassies. Its mandate included keeping tabs on the Baath and other political parties; suppressing Shia and Kurdish opposition; monitoring subversive activities and conducting counterespionage; maintaining surveillance of all embassies and other foreign missions inside Iraq and monitoring Iraqi embassies abroad; collecting intelligence abroad; conducting sabotage and subversion against hostile states and aiding the groups and individuals opposed to their regimes; and establishing contacts with the antiregime groups in the countries hostile to Baghdad. In the Arab world, GID agents were most active in Amman, the Jordanian capital, a focal point for the activities of the intelligence agencies not only of the Arab countries but also Israel and the United States. They sniffed the city for any signs of anti-Saddam activity. Inside Iraq, the GID maintained clandestine contacts with its counterpart of the Kurdistan Democratic Party—a fact that surfaced when, following Saddam's military assistance to the KDP to wrest control of the regional capital of Irbil from its rival Patriotic Union of Kurdistan (PUK), in August-September 1996, its operatives worked fast to kill the CIA agents.[1] It maintained an extensive network of informers, often members of such popular organizations as the Union of Iraqi Students at home and abroad, and the Iraqi Women's Federation. Besides resorting to well-known methods of torture—administering electrical shocks to genitals, caning the soles of feet, hanging suspects upside down, burning sensitive parts of the body with cigarettes, immersing the head into water for oppressively long periods, depriving the suspect of sleep for days on end—the GID specialized in administering slow-acting poison to the suspects and holding hostage the families of the dissidents who proved elusive, often raping their young female relatives.

At the time of Nazim Kazar's fall in 1973, the GID was headed by Saddam's half-brother Barzan Ibrahim al Tikriti, an office he held for another decade. So he was well qualified to publish in May 1983 a highly publicized book, *Assassination Attempts on the Life of President Saddam Hussein*, including descriptions of nine such attempts but excluding the latest at Dujayal in the previous year.[2] In October, however, yielding to pressure from Washington to distance his regime from international terrorism to pave the way for the resumption of US-Iraq diplomatic ties, Saddam removed Barzan from this post because of his close association with the late Abu Nidal (real name, Sabri al Banna), a Palestinian leader involved in terrorist actions. He appointed Barzan as Iraq's ambassador to the UN in Geneva.

The GID's military counterpart was the Military Intelligence, with a history going back to the Iraqi independence in 1932. It assessed chief military threats to the country, oversaw security and counterintelligence in the military, ensured officers' loyalty to the regime, maintained a network of informers in the countries of the region, and cooperated with foreign intelligence agencies. Its standing received a big blow when Israeli warplanes surreptitiously destroyed a nuclear facility constructed by the French near Baghdad in June 1981. It was then instructed by Saddam to channel substantial resources into safeguarding Iraq's emerging military-industrial complex.

On hiding and camouflaging Iraq's strategic military-industrial projects, military and general intelligence received professional training and guidance from the Soviet Union. The KGB taught the Iraqi operatives how to locate their industrial facilities in a way that reduced their vulnerability to air raids, and how to hide their identifiable features—as recorded by aircraft or satellites—through ruse and practical means, like masking heat sources. It also stressed the vital importance of an early-warning system and rapid evacuation of a facility likely to be raided. The KGB recommended *inter alia* that Iraq should so design and construct new industrial-military facilities so that they might absorb the explosive impact of bombs, and install blow-away walls that—following bombing—leave intact the skeleton, which can be reconstructed swiftly. By following these instructions, the Iraqis succeeded in deceiving IAEA inspectors about their nuclear-arms program during their six-monthly inspections before the Gulf War.[3]

During the forty-three-day nonstop bombing by the anti-Iraq coalition during the Gulf War, the MI, then headed by Gen. Sabir al Duri, managed to save most of the Iraqi warplanes by having them stored in underground bunkers that withstood the impact of the Pentagon's deadly, high-tech bombs. After the war al Duri was replaced by Gen. Wafiq al Jassim Samarrai, a gaunt-faced career soldier with a luxurious mustache. In early 1992, following his transfer to a less important post at the Presidential Office, the post of the MI chief went to Gen. Muhammad Nimah al Tikriti.

In April 1992 the MI played a prominent role in aborting a conspiracy to stage a coup, masterminded by an affluent London-based Shia Iraqi, Saad Jabr, which led to the arrest of up to three hundred army officers and civilians, many of whom were executed.

Later that year, sensing disaffection in the officer corps, Saddam ordered the formation of the Military Security (MS, *Amn al Askariya*), and appointed Gen. Muhammad al Tikriti as its commander, with the instruction to report directly to the Presidential Office. The MS's job was to maintain internal security within the armed forces. It did so by having at least one unquestionably loyal officer in every military unit.[4] Both the MS and the MI had their headquarters in the Kadhamiya neighborhood in northern Baghdad.

Following a well-planned assassination attempt on him by a group of Shia soldiers belonging to al Daawa al Islamiya on July 11 1982 in Dujayal, forty miles north of Baghdad, in which ten of his bodyguards died,[5] Saddam established a special section within the General Security and called it Special Security. Two years later he upgraded it to a separate directorate, Special Security

Directorate (SSD, *Muderiye al Amn al Khas*) under Gen. Fanar Hassan al Tikriti, who was later succeeded by Gen. Hussein Kamil Hassan, a charming, attractive but none-too-bright son-in-law of Saddam.

Its primary task was the security of Saddam as well as his presidential palaces and guest houses. Its main executive instrument was the Emergency Forces (*Qawat al Himaya*), consisting of two hundred bodyguards. They formed the second circle around Saddam—the first circle around him being the forty-strong *Murafaqin* (lit., Companions), all of whom share the al Bu Nasir tribal affiliation with him. They were split into three groups. The Special Location Group focused on Saddam's security in the palaces he used; the Mobile Group (called Salih) secured the president and his immediate cordon of bodyguards; and the *Kulyab*, which consisted of Saddam's cook, butcher and food-taster, and his swimming and fishing companions.

The Special Security Directorate's other duties were to keep an eagle eye on all other intelligence and security agencies, and maintain a close watch on top military officers. It did so in close cooperation with the Special Republican Guard (SRG), formed in 1992, whose three brigades guarded the southern, northern, and western arteries of the capital. Additionally, there was a division of the Republican Guard stationed in Baghdad.

During the Iran-Iraq War, Saddam enlarged his military fivefold from the initial 250,000, vastly expanded the military-industrial complex and made progress in developing or producing chemical, biological, and nuclear weapons. He started applying his enlarged intelligence and military machines—including chemical arms—to root out insurgent nationalist Kurds in the North, who had allied with the enemy during the war with Iran.

Saddam's intelligence and security agencies proved their efficiency before and during the Gulf War by frustrating several attempts by the leading Western powers, Israel, and Saudi Arabia to assassinate him and/or overthrow his regime through a coup.

Aware of the intensified American plans against him, Saddam acted to thwart them. He divided evenly the top positions in the military, intelligence, and security agencies between Tikritis (those from Tikrit, his home base) and non-Tikritis. So a successful coup against him depended on a most unlikely alliance between Tikritis and non-Tikritis or the neutralization of one by the other. He placed the defense ministry and the Republican Guard in the respective hands of non-Tikriti generals, Saadi Tuma al Abbas and Mukhalif Iyad al Rawi. He balanced them with Tikritis: Gen. Hussein Wendawi as the military chief of staff, Gen. Medhahim Saib as the air force commander, and Hussein Kamil Hassan as minister of industry and military industrialization. The two wings of the civilian intelligence apparatus remained as before under his half-brothers—Sabawi Ibrahim al Tikriti and Barzan Ibrahim al Tikriti—with Military Intelligence assigned to Gen. Wafiq al Samarrai, a non-Tikriti. The appointment of a cousin, Gen. Ali Hassan al Majid, as interior minister in early March 1991 completed Saddam's grip over the formidable intelligence and security machine.[6]

After the post–Gulf War uprisings, when General Security agents became the insurgents' prime target, Saddam strengthened the intelligence agencies. He furnished the GS with its own paramilitary arm, the Emergency Forces (*Qawat al Tawaria*), and placed it under his half-brother, Sabawi Ibrahim al Tikriti, who stayed in the job for five years. (He was then replaced by Gen. Taha Abbas Ahbabi.) The agency expanded its already large network of informers. For example, the translator-guides provided by the Ministry of Culture and Information to visiting journalists (who are barred from using others) routinely submit reports on their charges to the GS. The drivers of the taxis based at hotels such as the two-hundred-room Al Rashid in Baghdad reported the movements of foreigners to the agency.[7]

Also, having quashed the post–Gulf War insurrections with the active backing of Sunni tribal leaders, Saddam set up the Tribal

Chiefs' Bureau (*Maktab al Shuyukh*) to formalize the relationship between them and the government. In return for cash subsidies and arms, loyal tribal chieftains agreed to crush dissidents within their tribes. He put his younger son-in-law, Col. Saddam Kamil Hassan (al Majid), a lookalike of the president who played him in a six-hour television docudrama of the life and times of Saddam Hussein, in charge of this bureau.[8]

By 1992, the aggregate size of the security and intelligence agencies of the state and the ruling party was probably about the same as the estimate of 60,000–80,000 at the height of the Iran-Iraq War in 1984.[9] There were probably about as many informers.

In May 1993 the Clinton administration, while unveiling its policy of containing not only Iraq but also Iran—the Dual Containment doctrine—adopted a tougher stance on Iraq, which included a public commitment to effect the downfall of Saddam's regime.

A denouement came in late June 1993, when the US navy hit the Iraqi GID complex in Baghdad with missiles on the assumption that Saddam had planned Bush Sr.'s assassination during the latter's trip to Kuwait in April as a guest of Emir Shaikh Jaber III al Sabah. Immediately after the former US president's visit, Kuwait arrested eleven Iraqis and five Kuwaitis—described as agents of Baghdad—for plotting the assassination. Their trial was set for June 5. The US State Department refrained from making any statement since the case was sub judice. But, on June 25, when the court case was still in progress, the White House announced that it had received a report from the Federal Bureau of Investigation (FBI) agents, sent earlier to Kuwait, saying that the assassination plot against Bush had been "serious" and that Iraq was the instigator. Baghdad denied the charge.

Of the twenty-three Tomahawk missiles that the US navy fired at the GID complex in Baghdad, three went astray, resulting in the destruction of neighboring houses and the deaths of eight people, including Leila Attar, a leading Iraqi painter. At the Security Council, Madeleine Albright, the US ambassador to the UN and a former professor of international affairs, argued that her country's "retaliation" was in line with Article 51 in Chapter VII of the UN Charter. That article reads, "Nothing in the present Charter shall impair the inherent right of individual or collective self-defense if an armed attack occurs against a Member of the United Nations, until the Security Council has taken measures necessary to maintain international peace and security."

In the absence of "an armed attack" by Iraq against the United States, this provision of the UN Charter did not apply. But that did not trouble the Clinton administration—nor did the doctoring of the evidence to show how a car bomb had been smuggled from Iraq into Kuwait across a fortified border that was presented to the Kuwaiti court, or the execution of four of the accused. By the time Pulitzer Prize–winner journalist-author Seymour Hersh had debunked the Kuwaiti charges in a *New Yorker* article in late October, it was too late. He revealed that far from "having a unique signature linking the [car bomb detonator to be used to kill Bush] to Iraq," the pictures that Albright displayed at the Security Council in June showed "mass-produced items, commonly used for walkie-talkies and model airplanes . . . most likely made in Taiwan or Japan or South Korea."[10]

By September 1994, Saddam had concluded that he had complied with all the conditions of UN Security Council Resolutions 687 and 715, and so it was time for the United Nations to lift, or ease, its economic sanctions. But the Unscom chief, Rolf Ekeus, in his six-monthly report, failed to give Baghdad a clean bill of health. Saddam therefore decided to highlight his demand for the easing of sanctions by creating a crisis. On October 7–8 he coupled his dispatch of two Republican Guard divisions to southern Iraq with a call on the Security Council to fix the date for lifting the embargo at its October 10 meeting. Washington portrayed Saddam's move as a plan to reinvade Kuwait, and augmented its forces to the region. Russia intervened. Saddam withdrew his troops to their pre-crisis positions in return for Moscow calling for the lifting of sanctions by the next spring.

During this crisis, a volunteer force of young men, called Firqat Fedayeen Saddam (Saddam's Self-Sacrificers Division), was set up by the president's elder son, Uday, a tall, clean-shaven man with large expressive eyes and a close-cropped head, who would receive severe injuries during a failed assassination attempt in December 1996. The new armed force would soon become 30,000 strong. Mandated to assist the regime in suppressing subversion, it functioned in close collaboration with the Special Republican Guard and the General Security.

The prospect of an end to the sanctions disappeared after the defection of Gen. Hussein Kamil Hassan, a former minister of military industrialization. He reportedly told Ekeus and others that Iraq had withheld much information on its WMD program, an account later disputed by Scott Ritter, Unscom's chief inspector.

On hearing of the defections on the morning of August 8, a national holiday to celebrate the victory over Iran, Saddam ordered the severing of telephone links with the outside world, and put on high alert the Republican Guard and the Special Republican Guard. Some RG units were deployed in the streets of Baghdad, where they resorted to searching people. The Firqat Fedayeen Saddam were posted along the 340 mile Iraqi-Jordanian highway ostensibly to prevent further defections.

In a nationwide broadcast on August 11 Saddam Hussein compared his senior son-in-law, Hussien Kamil, to Cain (who murdered his brother Abel), Judas (who betrayed Jesus Christ), and Abu Lahab (who opposed Prophet Muhammad, his nephew). He accused Hussein Kamil of defrauding the state treasury of many millions of dollars through front companies, and of spying for the CIA.[11]

Saddam realized that the root cause of the disaffection in his regime's innermost circle was the insatiable ambition and unpredictable violence of Uday. His unrestrained arrogance and ambition had led him to interfere, through the columns of his newspaper *Babil* (Babylon), in several ministries, thus acting as if he were a member of the RCC. This had begun to seriously undermine the role and influence of Saddam's long-serving aides as well as the Iraqi constitution, which describes the RCC as the country's supreme authority.

The Iraqi leader stripped Uday of all official positions he had garnered for himself, including his command of the Firqat Fedayeen Saddam, sparing him only the chairmanship of the Iraq Football Association. (Later members of the national team were to be flogged and humiliated at Uday's orders following poor performances.) Saddam also orchestrated criticism of Uday in the Iraqi media, and spread word that he had himself set afire Uday's collection of sports cars. Later he expropriated Uday when he thought that his son's wealth might be channeled to finance a coup against him.

To emphasize that it was the Baath Party and the RCC that really mattered, Saddam went on to offer himself as the party's sole candidate for president in a referendum which the RCC ordered in October. The exercise enabled Saddam to make full use of the party cadres whose loyalty and tenacity he had won by singling them out for economic perks and preferential treatment in medical care and university education. On the election day, these activists—like Hajir in Baghdad's Mustansiriya neighborhood—brought voters to the polling stations in droves.

Though the official figure of 99.96 percent of electors backing Saddam was blatantly exaggerated, the actual turnout of voters was large enough to impress the hundreds of foreign journalists who were invited to witness the exercise.

None of this, however, impacted favorably on the economy, which was in a dire state. This was reflected in the exchange rate, with as many as 3,000 dinars required to buy one US dollar, a figure higher than that prevailing in May 1994. In that month Saddam had dismissed Prime Minister Ahmad Hussein Khodayir due to his failure to stabilize the Iraqi dinar, and took over his job. This was on top of Saddam's presidency of the republic, command of the military, chairmanship of the RCC, and headship of the Baath Party.

Saddam's enhanced position had coincided with the unveiling of the rebuilt television tower in the Mansur neighborhood of Baghdad, which had been demolished by the Pentagon's missiles during the Gulf War. Renamed Saddam International (Challenge) Tower, the newer version, at 112 meters, was 12 meters higher than the original. It was topped by a two-level, rotating restaurant, called Babil. The compound of the tower was dominated by a full-length statue of Saddam Hussein in military uniform, carrying a revolver, his right arm outstretched. Around the bottom of the pedestal were scattered various parts of US missiles, like so many limbs of a carcass. The English text on the pedestal read: "This high standing monument of President Saddam Hussein was made exclusively from the remains of the aggressive American missiles which aimed this situation on January 17, 1991 during the grand immortal Battle of Umm al Marik [Mother of All Battles] as the Iraqi challenge against American imperialism."[12]

An aerial view of the capital gleaned from the glass walls of Babil Restaurant especially at night brought home Saddam's penchant for the cult of personality and for monumental public buildings. To the east along the winding Tigris you could see the twelve bridges, including the newest one constructed after the Gulf War, the impressive Double Decker Bridge, which—built with deficit financing—played its part in fueling hyperinflation. To the southeast, at the bottom of the U-bend in the Tigris, stood the eighteen-story Baghdad University building. In the near distance to the east were the Festival and Parade Ground, where massive parades were held on Army Day (January 5) and other state occasions, and the modernistic Monument of the Unknown Soldier, lit up in green, white and red, the colors of the national flag. Beyond these public buildings was the very private Republican Presidential Palace in Tashri along the left bank of the Tigris. To the north was the Baghdad Clock Tower, sprouting out of the Museum of the Leader (al Qaid), displaying every detail of Saddam's life.

On the ground, it was impossible to miss the signs of the personality cult. To see five images of Saddam—statues and stenciled and hand-painted portraits—within the first five minutes of a local taxi ride in Baghdad on arrival from Amman, as I did, was an experience likely to linger. On the eighth floor of the Ministry of Culture and Information, where officials deal with foreign journalists, I counted seven larger-than-life color prints of the Leader-President—often dressed in traditional Arab dress, engrossed in a book against the background of a shelf of weighty tomes—decorating the corridor walls.

During the journey from Baghdad to Karbala, Najaf, and Babylon, no square in even the humblest village was complete without a portrait of Saddam Hussein, dressed variously. At each of the three holy sites in Karbala and Najaf—the tombs of Imams Ali, Hussein, and Abbas—the image of Saddam at prayer had been built into the outside wall of the inner sanctum of the shrine reconstructed after the post–Gulf War uprisings.[13]

What added to Saddam's enormous ego was the generally favorable turn of events after his election as president in October 1995 for a seven-year term.

SADDAM AS "ELECTED" PRESIDENT

In February 1996, after the negotiated return of Hussein Kamil Hassan and his family to Baghdad, the erstwhile defector and his close male relatives were killed in a gun battle with a group led by his uncle Gen. Ali Hassan al Majid, intent on redeeming the clan's honor soiled by Hussein Kamil Hassan's defection and betrayal of state secrets.

Four months later Saddam aborted the most ambitious and meticulously planned coup attempt by the CIA, the British MI6, and the Saudi, Kuwaiti, and Jordanian intelligence agencies. He capped that with an intervention in the intra-Kurdish violence, at the invitation of one of the two warring Kurdish parties, that resulted in the expulsion of the American-sponsored Iraqi National Congress from the US-UK-protected

Kurdish region in September. That brought to a virtual end any serious prospect of his regime being overthrown by US-backed groups, acting singly or jointly.

In December followed the implementation of the UN oil-for-food scheme. However, of the $2 billion worth of petroleum to be sold every six months by Iraq, about a third would be allocated to the UN Compensation Fund, 13 percent to relief in the Kurdish region to be administered by UN personnel, and another 7 percent to cover the administrative cost of the various programs of the United Nations (with its representatives monitoring export of oil and observing distribution of the imported food and medicine), leaving Iraq with about half of the total revenue.

Yet it provided sorely needed relief to Iraqis. Their food ration went up by about a half, raising the daily calorie intake per capita from the miserly 1,350 to 2,000. The increase was greeted with joy by Iraqis, the first truly uplifting news for them in several years. It also provided an opportunity for the state-run media to trumpet that the "steadfastness" shown by an independent Iraq against all odds was paying off. The year ended with the exchange rate for the Iraqi dinar improving to 1,000 dinars to US $1.

On January 17, 1998, the seventh anniversary of the beginning of the Gulf War, in his broadcast, Saddam repeated what he had said before: Iraq had met all its obligations under Resolution 687. To bolster the morale of Iraqis, he alluded to the journey undertaken by Abraham, born in the southern Iraqi town of Ur, to southern Turkey, armed with nothing more than a stick, but possessed of vision: "Prophet Abraham was neither timid nor afraid of the disparity in material resources." In other words, Saddam reassured his audience that their vision and self-righteousness would more than compensate their military inferiority. Nonetheless he decreed the training of one million volunteers to prepare for a jihad if the UN embargo was not lifted within six months as demanded earlier by the Iraqi parliament.[14]

By the time the government organized a martial pageant on Baghdad's Festival and Parade Ground in May, it was able to put on display half a million armed volunteers who had signed up for a jihad against the UN embargo. But the year ended with Iraq being subjected to a hundred-hour blitzkrieg by the Clinton administration, code-named Operation Desert Fox. For this bombing to go ahead, Unscom inspectors had to be evacuated. And they were—by Unscom's executive chairman, Richard Butler.

By so doing, Clinton and Butler handed Saddam a victory. He had wanted Unscom inspectors out because, in his view, they had completed their tasks, and many American nationals among them had engaged in espionage—a subject to be explored in the next chapter—for the United States, which had in turn been used in planning an anti-Saddam coup and in selecting its targets for bombing. The inspectors" voluntary departure handed Saddam a vital card he did not have before. He could now bargain the terms on which they could return.

That is where the situation rested in the spring of 2002 when Iraqi foreign minister Naji Sabri had meetings with UN secretary-general Kofi Annan in New York and Vienna. Pressured by Washington, Annan wanted to limit the talks to the return of UN inspectors according to Security Council Resolution 1284 of December 1999. By contrast, following Saddam's instructions, Sabri, a suave, bespectacled former professor of English literature, wanted to link the issue to the lifting of sanctions and compensation to Iraq for the damage caused by the United States and Britain in the northern and southern no fly zones. The result was a stalemate.

CHAPTER 5

THE OPPOSITION AND ITS FOREIGN LINKS

In the tastefully furnished, wood-paneled office of the caretaker of the over one-thousand-year-old shrine of Imam Ali in Najaf, 120 miles south of Baghdad, there were only three images on the walls: a picture of the shrine with its glittering gold-plated dome—swimming above the desert mirage—with a woman in a black cloak in the foreground; President Saddam Hussein at prayer inside the shrine's inner sanctum; and a family tree of the Iraqi leader. The last image captivated me. I had read about it. Now, there it was—a trunk with roots, branches, and green leaves—in a gilded frame.

It came into existence during the Iran-Iraq War. To counter Tehran's religious propaganda, Saddam had resorted to emphasizing Islam while extending governmental control over religious sites and sponsoring international religious gatherings. In April 1983 the Iraqi minister of Islamic Trusts and Religious Affairs told the First Popular Islamic Conference in Baghdad that all of the nearly 3,200 Muslim religious sites were under total or partial government supervision, and that all 2,300 religious caretakers had become civil servants. Such was the status of the caretaker of Imam Ali's shrine, Dr. Haidar Muhammad Hussein al Kalidar, a thoughtful-looking man in his early middle age in a camel brown cloak, trim of beard, and sporting a neat green turban around his red fez.

After the successful repulse of Iran's March 1985 offensive, Saddam, a Sunni Muslim, offered much-publicized prayers at the Shia shrines in Najaf, Karbala, and elsewhere. Soon after, Saddam ordered a public celebration of his birthday on April 28, which has since then become an annual event. During the holy month of Ramadan (in May-June) he decreed that government officials should hold fast-breaking banquets in public, thus creating a symbiosis between his regime and Islam. He went on to publish his family tree, which showed him to be a descendant of Imam Ali, which entitled him to the honorific of *sayyid* (lit., lord or prince) accorded to the male descendants of Prophet Muhammad. He did so primarily to gain the respect of Iraqi Shias, who formed a majority in the country as well as in the army—due to conscription.

The authorities distributed millions of copies of Sayyid Saddam Hussein's family tree to emphasize his religious credentials.

Rooted in Imam Ali, a cousin and son-in-law of Prophet Muhammad, with its trunk carrying the names of the twelve Shia Imams at the bottom—followed by thirty descendants, ending with Omar Beg (the progenitor of the Begat clan), the governor of Tikrit—the family tree branches out, with Saddam (son of Hussein son of Abd al Majid son of Abd al Ghafur son of Omar Beg) appearing as the only face on one of the outermost leaves. With the last Shia Imam disappearing in c. A.D. 873, the thirty generations after him with an average age of twenty-five would cover 750 years, I calculated, bringing the top of the trunk to c. A.D. 1625, followed by five more generations spanning 125 years, ending around AD 1750—not 1937, when Saddam was born. Well aware that pointing out this numerical discrepancy would be impolite and counterproductive, I merely asked Dr. Kalidar how the president's family tree had been constructed. He replied that it had been prepared by Islamic scholars "specializing in tribal and clan origins."

Certainly this was not the view of the participants in the Shia uprisings in southern Iraq after the Gulf War. They made a point of ripping off Saddam's family tree from all the holy places.

No such incidents occurred during the post–Gulf War rebellion in the North, chiefly because the central government had not bombarded the area, populated by predominantly Sunni Kurds, with Saddam's family tree.

Unlike their Shia compatriots, whose differences with the regime were rooted in religious sectarianism, the alienation of Kurds was rooted in their non-Arab, non-Turkish ethnicity. They had a long history of resistance to their Ottoman Turkish overlords. Later they resisted the Arab-dominated government in Baghdad. During World War II Mustafa Barzani, the founder of the Kurdistan Democratic Party, led a rebellion that was crushed. He fled to Iran, and from there to Moscow via the Azerbaijan Soviet Republic. Following the 1958 coup in Iraq, he returned home and backed the republican regime of Abdul Karim Qasim. In exchange the Baghdad government legalized the KDP, and promulgated a constitution that stated: "Arabs and Kurds are associated in this nation." However, when Barzani advanced an autonomy plan, Qasim rejected it. Fighting broke out between the two sides in September 1961 and continued for nearly five years, at which time an agreement accorded the Kurdish language official recognition, and gave proportional representation to Kurds in the civil service.

The accord failed to dissipate mutual mistrust though. Another round of fighting with the KDP in 1969–70 led to an agreement whereby the Baathist-sponsored constitution of July 1970 recognized Kurds as one of the two nationalities of Iraq, and Kurdish as one of the two languages in the Kurdish region. Iraq thereby gave Kurds an official status they did not enjoy in Turkey, Iran, or Syria. Yet when the KDP failed to get the oil city of Kirkuk included in the Kurdish region or have its nominee for vice president accepted by Baghdad, it withdrew from the accord.

Ignoring this, the Baghdad government implemented the Kurdish autonomy law in March 1974, including the appointment of a Kurd, Taha Muhyi al Din Maruf, a diplomat, as a vice president of the republic; the formation of the Kurdistan Autonomous Region (KAR), comprising the provinces of Dohak, Irbil, and Suleimaniya and measuring altogether 17,000 square miles; and the establishment of the Kurdistan Legislative Council.

The violence that erupted between the KDP and the central government in March 1974 lasted a year, and resulted in 17,000 deaths, civilian and military. At one point, the KDP's 45,000 guerrillas, controlling a third of the Kurdish region, pinned down four-fifths of Iraq's 100,000 troops and nearly half of its 1,400 tanks. Following the signing of the Algiers Accord in 1975 by Baghdad and Tehran, which resulted in the Shah of Iran cutting off military and logistical aid to the KDP, Barzani escaped to Iran.

In the course of the Iran-Iraq War, both the KDP, led by Mustafa Barzani's son, Masud, and its offshoot, the Patriotic Union of Kurdistan (PUK), headed by Jalal Talabani, sided with Tehran. They set up liberated zones along the borders with Iran and Turkey. Once Gen. Ali Hassan al Majid had become the military commander of Kurdistan in mid-1987, he tried to repossess the lost Kurdish territory. His campaign reached a peak with the staging of the seven-month-long Operation Anfal, in which he made frequent use of chemical weapons and emptied 3,800 Kurdish villages, forcing the population away from the liberated zones. More specifically, he decided to reverse the capture of Halabja—a town of 70,000 about fifteen miles from the Iranian border—from Iran and its Kurdish allies, who had seized it on March 13, 1988, and who threatened the dam on the Darbandi Khan Lake, the main source of electricity for Baghdad. He ordered an air strike of the town with poison-gas bombs with the aim of assaulting the occupying Iranian troops. The strike lasted half an hour in the afternoon of March 16, by which time the Iranians had left. Therefore all the casualties were civilian, including 3,200 to 5,000 who lost their lives. The outside world was shocked by the images of men, women, and children, frozen in instant death, relayed by the Iranian media: a dead child lying bent over the steps of his home, a male adult corpse flat on its back in the rear of a cart, a woman clasping her dead baby resting against the wall of her house. In killing its own unarmed citizens with chemical weapons, Iraq did something extraordinarily horrible. Yet this had no impact on Washington's policy of backing Iraq in its war with Iran. Indeed, Britain, its unquestioning ally, granted Baghdad $500 million extra credit after the Halabja atrocity. Having lost their territory to the Baghdad government, the Kurdish leaders escaped to Iran or Syria.

During the crisis created by Iraq's occupation of Kuwait in August 1990, which drew most of the troops away from the KAR, the Kurdish leaders returned to the region. After the Gulf War the uprising led by them spread far and wide in the region, but succumbed finally to the superior force of Saddam's troops.

The Iraqi government then signed a truce with the insurgents as a prelude to negotiations. But a draft agreement reached in June— giving the Kurds predominant military and political authority over the KAR, with joint control of the army and police by the Kurdish authorities and Baghdad, in return for them severing all links with outside powers—failed to win majority approval of the eight-member Iraqi Kurdistan Front (IKF), which included the KDP and the PUK.

Soon the area above the 36th parallel, covering most—but not all—of the KAR, became an air exclusion zone for the Baghdad government as the warplanes of the United States, Britain, and France patrolled the skies. Thus protected, the IKF held Legislative Council elections in May 1992. The KDP shared power equally with the PUK, when the other groups failed to cross the electoral threshold of 7 percent of the vote.

The KDP and the PUK together would become part of Washington's strategy to use Kurdistan as a staging post to oust Saddam, using the CIA-funded Iraqi National Congress as the main instrument. However, the Bush Sr. administration pursued an anti-Saddam coup not as its sole option, but as part of a bigger game plan with diverse but complementary roles assigned to UN sanctions (to further damage Iraq's economy and engender popular discontent against Saddam); the maintenance of a no fly zone in Iraqi Kurdistan (to highlight Saddam's loss of control in part of Iraq); and the upkeep of a US armada in the Gulf (to underscore Washington's commitment to its regional allies).

Following the doubling of his annual budget, Frank Anderson, in charge of the Near East section at the headquarters, expanded his program. By the spring of 1992, he had acquired many Iraqi "assets." Prominent among them was Ahmad Chalabi, a small, rotund, Westernized Shia businessman of some wealth who had been living in London since 1989.

IRAQI NATIONAL CONGRESS
AND IRAQI NATIONAL ACCORD

Born into a rich banking family in Baghdad, Ahmad Chalabi and his parents fled Baghdad in the wake of the republican coup in 1958, when Ahmad was thirteen. After university education in Beirut, Chalabi enrolled at the Massachusetts Institute of Technology, and then obtained a doctorate in mathematics at the University of Chicago. He became a mathematics professor at the American University in Beirut. He stayed there until 1977, when, due to the escalating Lebanese civil war, he moved to Amman. He established Petra Bank there during a time when petro-dollars were aplenty. Within a decade, it became the third largest bank in Jordan, only to be seized by the Central Bank of Jordan in mid-1989 due to shady foreign-exchange transactions. This led to a spate of allegations of embezzlement and fraud against Chalabi. His reported flight in the trunk of a friend's car to Damascus damaged his reputation. The State Security Court in Amman would convict him in absentia in 1992 in two cases, involving the embezzlement of $60 million, and sentenced him to jail terms of three and six years. He denied all charges. From Damascus he moved to London, where he would later acquire British citizenship. In the wake of Iraq's invasion of Kuwait in 1990, he became politically active, carving out a niche for himself in the Iraqi opposition circles.

The CIA found him valuable. As a rich businessman, he was a credible conduit for funding by the agency. Since he lacked any constituency inside Iraq he was the least threatening to other opposition groups, each of which had some sort of following and contacts at home. When he convened an assembly of three hundred opposition delegates in Vienna in June 1992, they all assumed that he was the paymaster. Actually, it was the CIA, which had allocated $20 million to back him.[1] The outcome was the formation of the Iraqi National Congress (INC), an umbrella body that gained the affiliation of nearly twenty groups. These included not only the KDP and the PUK, but also the comparatively new Iraqi National Accord (INA), commonly known as *al Wifaq* (The Accord). Since its inception in 1990, it had focused on staging a coup in Iraq.

In Vienna both Barzani and Talabani concurred with the INC leadership's decision to base the INC in Iraqi Kurdistan and build a liberation army composed of exiled and defector Iraqis. It opened an office in Salahuddin, twenty miles north of the regional capital of Irbil, and began beaming propaganda radio broadcasts into the government-administered Iraq, gathering intelligence from Iraqi military deserters, and building up its own army. The aim was to establish a democratic regime in post-Saddam Iraq, which dovetailed with Washington's professed commitment to democracy and human rights.

But democracy was the last thing that the INA, or its generously funded paymaster, Saudi Arabia's foreign intelligence chief, Prince Turki ibn Faisal, had on its agenda for Iraq. The INA was the brainchild of Adnan Nouri, a former general with an imposing personality and a swaggering manner; Dr. Iyad Alawi, a clean-shaven, moon-faced man of above-average build; and Salih Omar Ali al Tikriti, an elegant, overly ambitious politician-businessman, very much at ease at cocktail parties—all of them defectors. As a former general in the Republican Guard, Nouri was valuable to the anti-Saddam plotters. Based in London, he was in contact with the local CIA station chief.

It was in the early 1970s that Alawi first went to London as a postgraduate medical student. He became president of the Iraqi Students Union in Europe—and an important asset to the Iraqi

General Intelligence Department. He defected in 1975, and concentrated on enriching himself with the help of his Saudi patrons. But when he cultivated British intelligence (MI6) agents, he upset Baghdad. An assassination attempt on him in 1978 in his suburban London house left him injured. After setting up a second home in Amman, he established contacts with the Jordanian intelligence. His business links with Saudi Arabia and his penchant for cloak-and-dagger led him to assist the Saudi intelligence in establishing an anti-Baghdad radio station, Voice of Free Iraq, after Iraq invaded Kuwait. At the radio station, he worked with Salih Omar Ali al Tikriti, who had risen gradually in the Baathist hierarchy to become Iraq's ambassador to the United Nations in the late 1970s. In mid-1982 when Iran marched into Iraq, al Tikriti resigned his post to make himself available as a successor to Saddam. Nothing came of it. He later made his peace with Saddam, who appointed him managing director of Iraqi Freight Services Limited, a government-owned company, in London. As before, he jumped ship when Iraq came under UN sanctions in August 1990. He joined the Iraqi opposition, and moved to Saudi Arabia. As a kinsman of the reputed coup plotters—Minaf Hassan al Tikriti and his brother Gen. Hakim Hassan al Tikriti—soon after the Gulf War, he claimed high-level contacts.

Though nominally affiliated with the INC, the INA had its own office in Kurdistan and maintained direct contacts with the CIA.

MARCH 1995 AND JUNE 1996 COUP PLANS

Sharing power in Kurdistan did not end the rivalry that had existed between the KDP, a tribal-oriented group, and the PUK, led largely by urban Kurds. The use of different dialects—Kermanji in the North, the stronghold of the KDP, and Sourani in the South, the PUK's bastion—was another critical factor setting the parties apart. Their differences were well captured by the turbaned Masoud Barzani, a rotund man dressed in the traditional long shirt and baggy trousers, and the bespectacled, professorial-looking Jalal Talabani, as much at ease in a Western business suit as in traditional garb.

No wonder that a dispute between a pro-KDP landlord and his pro-PUK peasants in May 1994 mushroomed into wide-scale fighting between the two parties. Before a temporary cease-fire, brokered by the INC, came into effect a week later, more than a thousand people were dead, and the PUK had stormed the parliament building in Irbil and ransacked the government treasury. A permanent truce and a peace plan, requiring a reconstitution of the regional government, including the co-option of smaller groups, would not materialize until six months later.

The intra-Kurdish violence reinforced the case of those who argued that if the nationalist Kurds could not close ranks in the face of their mortal enemy, Saddam Hussein, in power in Baghdad, then there was no chance of them doing so once he was gone, and that such a scenario would lead to a breakup of Iraq and create more problems than it solved.

At the CIA's operational level, Frank Anderson conciliated the rival strategies of war of liberation (favored by the INC) and a military coup (advocated by the INA) by subterfuge. While professing to be dealing exclusively with the INC as the sole representative of the Iraqi opposition, he maintained clandestine contacts with the INA.

Little wonder that by late 1993 Salahuddin became a hothouse of intrigue, with the INC and the INA spying on each other, and both of them in turn being spied on by the KDP and the PUK. With the INC employing five to six thousand Kurds and Iraqi Arabs as soldiers and civil servants by mid-1994, there was enough to keep the spies busy. Also active were the intelligence agents of not merely the Baghdad government but also Turkey, Iran, and Syria.

In December 1994 the plans of the CIA—now represented in Salahuddin by a team of five senior operatives, including Robert Baer, whose book *See No Evil*, published in 2002, would provide his side of the story—to overthrow Saddam received a boost when, fearing for his life, Wafiq Jassim al Samarrai, former head of the Iraqi Military Intelligence, defected to the opposition.

Encouraged by al Samarrai's move, the White House decided to accelerate its plan to overthrow Saddam and replace him with a small group of generals, including al Samarrai. Overcoming his suspicion of all former Baathist officers and civilians, Chalabi allied with al Samarrai. Their joint plan envisaged suborning the commanders of the Iraqi forces in nearby Mosul and Kirkuk, and infiltrating these cities with INC partisans with the objective of inciting a popular insurrection and large-scale Iraqi troop desertions following assaults on them by INC soldiers and Kurdish *peshmargas.* By focusing on meeting the INC threat in the North, Saddam would be exposed to the machinations of the Baghdad-based army commanders in touch with al Samarrai. Storming the barracks where Saddam had a residence, they would assassinate him. An amalgam of a popular revolt and a military coup would thus end the bloody Saddam era, and usher in a peace-loving, democratic regime.

While this plan was being devised by Chalabi and al Samarrai in collaboration with the CIA team in Salahuddin, in January 1995 Anderson dispatched a veteran operative with field experience in Afghanistan to Salahuddin with a brief to aid a highly classified INA project, masterminded by Gen. Adnan Nouri, for a pure military putsch, the planning for which had started three months earlier.

In the hothouse of Salahuddin, however, there were very few real secrets. Chalabi knew of the rival INA plan, and part of the reason he had cooperated with al Samarrai was the latter's military rank and experience, which also impressed the CIA. Chalabi and al Samarrai rushed their plan, and fixed March 4, 1995 as the D-day.

The moment Nouri learned of the finalized INC plan, he flew to Washington. In his discussions with his CIA handlers on March 1–2, 1995, he convinced them that a frontal attack by the INC and its Kurdish allies on the Iraqi troops in the North would provoke a massive counteroffensive by Saddam, which would put Washington in a pickle. If it did nothing, Saddam's forces would win. If it decided to intervene, it would have to do so on a large scale and with ground forces. Since the Clinton administration had no intention of getting entangled in a unilateral fight with Iraq, its National Security Adviser, Tony Lake, after consulting the State and Defense departments and the CIA, decided to withdraw Washington's support for the Chalabi-al Samarrai plan. His cable to the seniormost CIA operative in Salahuddin on March 3, stated that the United States would not support this operation militarily or in any other way.[2] With this, the KDP withdrew from the project.

But the INC and the PUK went ahead. On the D-day their forces attacked Iraqi troops. They had some success. The predicted popular uprisings in Mosul and Kirkuk, however, failed to materialize. Nor were there any mass desertions from the Iraqi armed forces, or any subversive moves in the Baghdad region by the military commanders supposedly in cahoots with al Samarrai. In Kurdistan proper, finding PUK partisans busy on the Iraqi front, Barzani tried to recover the territory he had lost earlier to the PUK, particularly Irbil, which had fallen to the PUK in December. This exacerbated the already fraught KDP-PUK relations. The disappointed and discredited al Samarrai left Kurdistan for Damascus, from where he would later go to London.

However, this was not the end of the US endeavors to overthrow Saddam.

Indeed, by October 1995, the INA-nurtured anti-Saddam coup plan had matured enough for CIA director John Deutch to send a new station chief to Amman with a specialist team for the Iraq operation to liaise with a special unit of the Jordanian intelligence. King Hussein addressed the exiled Iraqi opposition groups, including the INA, in Amman, and proposed a federal setup in post-Saddam Iraq to satisfy the Kurds, Shias, and Sunnis. This move by Hussein, who had hitherto kept any anti-Iraq decisions by him secret while professing neutrality in public, alarmed Saddam.

At a high-level meeting of intelligence officials from the United

States, Britain, Jordan, Saudi Arabia, and Kuwait in Riyadh, chaired by Prince Turki ibn Faisal, in January 1996, the Americans committed $6 million, the Saudis the same amount, and the Kuwaitis half as much.[3] Deutch got a go-ahead for an anti-Saddam coup at a top-level meeting at the White House.

In early spring Jordan opened a reception camp for Iraqi "refugees" near Qasr al Azraq, fifty miles east of Amman, as a cover for the base for the INA's Military Council. Since Kurdistan, convulsed by the putative coup attempt a year earlier, had lost its attraction to the would-be Iraqi defectors, they now mostly headed for Jordan. As invariably happens in the world of espionage and counterespionage, some of the defectors were double agents.

Around that time, news reached Chalabi that Iraq's GID knew the names of the coup plotters and that it also possessed the special CIA communications equipment, which the CIA in Amman had ostensibly sent to the prime conspirators in Baghdad, the three al Shahwani brothers—Anmar, Atheer, and Ayead.[4] Chalabi, who had been a persona non grata with the CIA for the past year, saw his chance to rehabilitate himself with the agency. In his meeting with Deutch and his deputy, Steve Richter, he handed over the intelligence he had. But Deutch and Richter viewed Chalabi's action as stemming from his abiding hostility to the INA, implicated in blowing up the INC's Salahuddin office in October. So instead of aborting the well-advanced plan, they brought it forward. They fixed June 26 as the D-day, and activated the CIA operatives working under Unscom cover to contact the vital Iraqi conspirators in the Republican Guard and the Special Republican Guard.

This was the background to Unscom's confrontation with Iraq in early June. Its Baghdad Monitoring and Verification Center (BMVC) team, headed by Goran Wallen, an American, and the Unscom 150 team led by Scott Ritter, a former US Marine intelligence officer, demanded access to two RG and SRG sites in and around the capital. As before, Ritter's team included Moe Dobbs (a pseudonym) and eight other CIA Special Activities Division (SAD) staff. Iraq refused, describing such visits as a threat to its national security. This resulted in a stand-off for five days as negotiations dragged on at the United Nations in New York.

For Iraq, anything to do with the Special Republican Guard was particularly sensitive. Saddam formed it in the wake of two serious assassination attempts on him after the 1991 Gulf War and an ambush of his motorcade the following year. He did so by cherry-picking from the Republican Guard officer corps. Thus the Special Republican Guard emerged as a super-elite force with its officers and ranks receiving higher salaries and better perks than their Republican Guard counterparts. Its missions were to protect the president, safeguard all his facilities, and execute any other job assigned to it.

Despite the June 12, 1996 resolution by the Security Council demanding "immediate, unconditional and unrestricted access to any and all places," the Iraqis stood their ground. Whether they did so to preserve "national security" as they said publicly, or whether they had inside information about the US-sponsored coup—in which the CIA operatives working as Unscom staff were assigned to contact the conspiring Iraqi officers at these Republican Guard and Special Republican Guard bases—remains shrouded in secrecy. What is known, though, is that among those executed later for plotting to topple the regime were many officers of the SRG and the RG—to which the three al Shahwani brothers, the plan's originators, belonged.[5]

On its part, the CIA proceeded as planned, and so did its INA ally. "The uprising should have at its center the armed forces," Alawi told the *Washington Post* on June 23, 1996. "We preach controlled, coordinated military uprising, supported by the people, that would not allow itself to go into acts of revenge or chaos." The interview was a signal for the coup three days later. It turned out to be a nonevent. On June 26, the CIA station at the US embassy received a message from the Iraqi GID, using the CIA-supplied communications equipment: "We have arrested all your people, and so pack up and go home." That is what the special CIA team did.

The Iraqi authorities had started rounding up the plotters in mid-June. During the next fortnight they arrested 120 officers, all of them from the Sunni heartland in central and central-northern Iraq. They held senior positions in the intelligence agencies as well as the army and air force and the elite Special Republican Guard and Republican Guard—and even Unit B32, set up to enable Saddam to communicate securely with military units without using a telephone, an instrument he had shunned on the eve of his invasion of Kuwait to evade detection by high-tech US devices.[6] Many of those arrested would face the firing squad.

The successful recruitment by the CIA-sponsored plotters of many officers of the SRG and the Special Security Directorate—the innermost core of the regime's security-intelligence apparatus—alarmed Saddam. He disbanded the SRG's Third Battalion and the SRG commander issued an order banning contact between SRG personnel and aliens.

Baghdad hardened its stance on Unscom inspections, perceiving them as part of the communications channels for coordinating a coup to be mounted after the Iraqi government's attention had been diverted by US military strikes, which would also create an opportunity for the Jordan-based INA insurgents to enter Iraq to carry out subversive acts.

As if the aborting of the June 1996 coup were not catastrophic enough, a further setback awaited US hard-liners, relentless in their pursuit of Saddam, this time in the mountains of Iraqi Kurdistan.

September 1996 Fiasco

KDP-PUK relations, soured by their opposite stands on the March 1995 coup plans, continued to deteriorate, with Kurdistan virtually divided into two zones, and the KDP and the PUK raising revenue mainly through customs duties on goods moving across either the intra-Kurdish borders or the Kurdistani frontiers with Turkey or Iran.

By September 1995, the intra-Kurdish violence had claimed three thousand lives, with the PUK gaining the upper hand. Having ejected the KDP from half of northern Kurdistan, it had extended its jurisdiction over two-thirds of the 3.2 million inhabitants of Kurdistan. But it lacked the resources to administer the territory under its control. The highly lucrative export of Iraqi oil to Turkey was being conducted through the area under Masud Barzani's control. This trade could be conducted only with the active collusion of Saddam, the supplier of oil. But above and beyond that, Saddam also sold weapons to Barzani.[7]

With six hundred oil trucks using the Iraqi-Turkish crossing daily in each direction, the KDP's customs duties amounted to an estimated half a million dollars. Violating its 1994 pact with the PUK, it refused to share this revenue with its rival. The PUK responded by refusing to meet its obligation of sharing the control of Irbil, a city of more than 700,000, with the KDP. Barzani found this unbearable.

With 12,000–13,000 troops and *peshmargas*, each faction was even in manpower. But due to Saddam's cooperation, the KDP was superior in weapons and ammunition. PUK leader Talabani was alienated from Saddam as well as Iran, whose dissident Kurds received support from him, a position he could not sustain for long because he administered a territory with a long border with Iran. He realized finally that his only source of arms and ammunition was Tehran. So he decided to make peace with it. This disconcerted not only Barzani but also Saddam, who bristled at Iran's renewed involvement in Iraqi Kurds' affairs. The result was a deepening of the secret cooperation between Barzani and Saddam, which encouraged the KDP to attack PUK units in July 1996.

This in turn led to Talabani strengthening his links with Tehran.

Emboldened by Iran's arms supplies, the PUK assaulted the KDP stronghold of Hajj Umran near the Iranian border on August 17. Disturbed by the turn of events, Robert Pelletreau, US assistant secretary of state for the Near East, urged Barzani to confer with Talabani. In response, Barzani requested Pelletreau to "send a clear message to Iran to end its meddling in northern Iraq," adding, "Our options are limited, and since the US is not responding politically . . . the only option left is the Iraqis."[8]

On August 22, Barzani addressed a letter to "His Excellency President Saddam Hussein" via Gen. Ali Hassan al Majid, commander of the northern-based First Corps, requesting military assistance to "ease the foreign threat" from Iran. Saddam complied speedily. He saw a great opportunity to vitiate KDP-PUK relations to an irreparable degree. And he reckoned that since he was blocking the expansion of Tehran's influence in the region Washington would not act against him instantly. [9]

As the situation on the battlefield deteriorated for the Salahuddin-based KDP—facing a military threat from the PUK-controlled Irbil—Barzani again warned the US that he might approach Baghdad for assistance. The Iraqi troops posted about 10 miles south of Irbil—along the de facto border between Kurdistan and the centrally controlled Iraq—were seen to be preparing to march northward.

Early on the morning of August 31, acting in cahoots with Barzani, Saddam sent three Republican Guard armored divisions, armed with four hundred tanks, toward Irbil—located ten miles north of the 36th parallel—while heavy Iraqi artillery targeted the city's suburbs. In the face of such a massive assault, the PUK commander in Irbil, with only three thousand fighters, ordered a hasty evacuation. To set the record straight, Tariq Aziz released Barzani's written invitation to Saddam Hussein on August 22 for military assistance.[10]

The fighting lasted a mere thirty-six hours with direct casualties of less than two hundred. In addition, on their way to Irbil, the Iraqi forces executed two-hundred-plus troops and intelligence agents of the INC. Having captured Irbil, they sealed off its exits to forestall the rise of a refugee problem, and replaced the PUK's green emblem with the yellow flag of the KDP and the tricolor of Iraq at the parliament building, the administrative heart of the region.

In a BBC World Service Radio interview on September 2, Barzani said, "Saddam Hussein is still the president of Iraq. We have not separated from Iraq. We love our Kurdish flag, but there is also [in Irbil] the central [Iraqi] flag. If the Iraqis can meet our demands we can make an agreement."[11]

Along with Iraq's troops came its GID operatives. Working in conjunction with its KDP counterpart, with which the Iraqi GID had long-standing contacts, the Iraqis arrested all opposing activists—including those of the PUK and the Supreme Assembly of Islamic Revolution in Iraq—with especial interest in the INC contingent working with the freshly departed CIA team.

While withdrawing its forces from the area on 2–3 September, Baghdad left behind its GID agents in the KDP-administered territory.

By retaking Irbil with Saddam's open military assistance, Barzani grievously undermined the US administration's strategy of excluding Saddam from Kurdish affairs. Barzani also showed—albeit unwittingly—that Washington's policy was in limbo. It refused to help the quasi-independent Kurdistan graduate to an independent state while vetoing the region's return to Baghdad's jurisdiction. All it wanted was to deploy the Kurds as a lever to keep Saddam down.

Wishing to demonstrate that he was doing something, Clinton announced on September 3 an extension of the southern no fly zone, from the 32nd to the 33rd parallel. That night and the following night, the Pentagon fired forty-four cruise missiles from its warships in the Gulf and B-52 bombers at Iraq's command and control posts and air defense centers near Nasiriyeh, four hundred miles south of Irbil. This elicited ridicule from some commentators, who joked, "The Americans got the Iraqi map wrong way up" by striking targets in the South whereas the problem was in the North.

Of the three Western allies patrolling the North, France argued that by responding to Barzani's request for military assistance on the ground, Iraq had not violated the air exclusion limitation imposed on it and that there was no rationale either for US missile strikes against Iraq, or for extending the southern no fly zone. It ordered its aircraft not to fly above the 32nd parallel.[12]

On the ground in Kurdistan, having retaken Irbil, the KDP was on a roll. By mid-September it expelled the PUK from almost all of Kurdistan, including the latter's bastion of Suleimaniya, with PUK leaders and fighters fleeing into Iran. But this did not last. Within a month, the PUK, freshly armed by Tehran, launched a multipronged counteroffensive from the border zone and recovered within days what it had lost earlier, except Irbil, raising the total human cost to the warring sides to about two thousand. Saddam's lead in warning Talabani not to attempt recapturing Irbil was followed by Tehran and Washington. On October 23 there was a US-UK-mediated cease-fire between the PUK and the KDP, with Barzani and Talabani pledging not to seek foreign intervention. They also agreed to discuss a Temporary Local Administration, sharing of the customs revenue, and a new election. The subsequent negotiations, however, mediated by an American representative got nowhere.

Whatever the rationale behind Barzani's invitation to Saddam to fight on his side, he did irreparable damage to the overarching American strategy in Iraq. The CIA withdrew 2,000 agents immediately, followed by another 3,500, and folded its four-year operation, costing $100 million, to develop Kurdistan as the staging post to subvert and topple Saddam.[13] Satisfied with the collapse of the American strategy, Saddam rewarded the Kurdish leaders by lifting the economic embargo he had imposed on their region almost five years earlier.

The ease with which Saddam's troops marched into Kurdistan highlighted two dispiriting facts to Washington: The Kurdish troops and weapons were no match for Baghdad's soldiers and equipment and, though drastically reduced from its massive strength on the eve of the Gulf War, Iraq was still a substantial military power—with 380,000 troops, including seven RG divisions, equipped with 2,700 tanks, 1,980 artillery pieces, and 330 combat aircraft.[14]

The gravity of the American debacle was aptly captured by the statements of John Deutch to the Senate Intelligence Committee in May and September 1996. During his first appearance he had stated, "Saddam's chances of surviving another year are declining." By contrast, in his second appearance he said, "Saddam Hussein is politically stronger now in the Middle East than he was before sending his troops into northern Iraq in recent weeks," and added that there was "little prospect" of him being removed from power in the near future.[15]

Politically, these major setbacks led to drastically reduced activity by the Iraqi opposition groups and the CIA's involvement with them. This state of affairs held for the first half of Clinton's second term. During the latter half of his presidency, against the background of repeated confrontations between Iraq and Unscom, the popular mood in the US turned strongly anti-Iraq, with Congress taking a lead in shaping official policy, normally the prerogative of the executive branch.

1998 IRAQ LIBERATION ACT

Given the popular dislike of Saddam Hussein in the United States, it was not surprising that in October 1998 the House of Representatives adopted the Iraq Liberation Act (ILA) by 360 votes to 38, followed by a larger plurality in the Senate. It entitled the president to spend up to $97 million for military aid to train, equip, and finance an Iraqi opposition army, and authorized the Defense Department to train insurgents.

Not to be seen as soft on Saddam, the Clinton administration interpreted the enforcement of the ILA as the unveiling of its publicly acknowledged policy of "regime change" in Baghdad. But the prime Iraqi vehicle to achieve this goal was still to be the Iraqi National Congress, a prospect that left those familiar with recent history unimpressed. In its October 20 editorial, entitled "Fantasies about Iraq," the *New York*

Times wrote: "The intended beneficiaries of US support include the Iraqi National Congress, which represents almost no one and has failed to produce results with aid it previously received from Washington."

The military strategy to destabilize Iraq was conceived by Wayne Downing, a retired Special Forces general, and Dewey Clarridge, a retired CIA officer with experience working with the anti-leftist Contras in Nicaragua in the 1980s. Their plan envisaged the CIA, operating jointly with the Pentagon's Special Forces, training Iraqi opposition military officers who would in turn train their Iraqi volunteers. Then, protected by US air cover, they would start seizing lightly defended areas in southern and western Iraq as an opening move to attract defectors from the Iraqi armed forces. Growing guerrilla activity would lead to increased deployment of the Iraqi air force. That in turn would result in intervention by US warplanes to protect the insurgents, and an escalation into conventional warfare in which Saddam's forces would be defeated.

To get the ball rolling, however, the United States had first to designate groups eligible for military aid by the end of January. And for this President Clinton had to be satisfied that a qualifying Iraqi group had "broad-based representation" and "a record of support for democracy."[16]

A warning against following this path came from none other than Gen. Anthony Zinni, commander of the US Central Command, whose writ covered the Gulf region. "I know of no viable opposition to Saddam in Iraq," he said. "Under such conditions any attempt to remove the Iraqi leader by force could dangerously fragment Iraq and destabilize the entire region." He added, "A weakened, fragmented, chaotic Iraq, which could happen if this isn't done carefully, is more dangerous in the long run than a contained Saddam now."[17]

Believing that its Operation Desert Fox had weakened Saddam politically, and encouraged by the Iraqi walkout in protest at the tepid response to the American air strikes by the Arab summit in January 1999, the United States embarked on transforming the divided Iraqi opposition into a united force to become a viable alternative to Saddam's regime.

After the certification of seven Iraqi groups eligible for US military aid, Madeleine Albright named Frank Ricciardone, deputy chief of the US mission in Ankara, as "Special Representative for the Transition in Iraq" to coordinate opposition effort. Besides the INC, INA, KDP, and PUK, the list of the eligible factions included the Tehran-based Supreme Assembly of Islamic Revolution in Iraq (SAIRI), the Halabja-based Islamic Movement for Iraqi Kurdistan, and the London-based Movement for Constitutional Monarchy (MCM), led by Sharif Ali ibn al Hussein, a suave, handsome cousin of the late Iraqi king Faisal, who had been spirited out of Baghdad as an infant at the time of the 1958 antiroyalist coup. Swiftly rejecting the American offer of aid, the KDP, PUK, MCM, and SAIRI attacked the whole enterprise.

Explaining the stance of SAIRI—the single most important Iraqi opposition group, with a two-division-strong army based in Iran—its London representative, Hamid Bayati, a tall, balding man invariably dressed in a well-tailored Western business suit, said: "It is the Iraqi people who should do the job of toppling Saddam and his regime. But they should be able to work independently in their own ways to achieve this objective." Whatever the intention of the ILA, he continued, "it is undermining the Iraqi opposition by portraying them as American agents."[18]

Actually, the inclusion of SAIRI in the American list was a surprise. SAIRI was formed in late 1982 in Tehran by the merger of the Shia Iraqi al Daawa al Islamiya (The Islamic Call), the Mujahedin Movement, and the Islamic Action Organization under the leadership of Ayatollah Muhammad Baqir al Hakim, with the aim of founding an Islamic regime in Iraq. It raised an armed force from among Iraqi exiles and POWs who then fought alongside the Iranians in the Iran-Iraq War.

To rally support for Washington's new policy in the region, Albright took Ricciardone with her on a tour of Egypt and the Gulf states. The exercise was a fiasco. The rulers of these countries argued that any change imposed on Iraq from outside would lead to rifts and civil war, and refused to cooperate in implementing the American plan. With no neighboring country prepared to let the Iraqi opposition infiltrate Iraq from its soil, the Downing-Clarridge plan died a quiet death.

A further setback to Washington came in April when, protesting against his high-handedness, the members of the INC's executive committee demoted Chalabi from chairman to ordinary member of the committee. On top of that, the Kurdish leaders banned him from entering Kurdistan.

The Clinton administration's policy on the subject became confused. After a meeting of the leaders of the certified Iraqi opposition groups, including the INC, with Albright in Washington on May 24, 1999, the State Department spokesman, James Rubin, said that the United States would provide nonlethal assistance to the INC and the newly launched Democratic Centrist Current (critical of Chalabi), thus ruling out military training or weapons. On the other hand Jim Hoagland, a senior columnist at the *Washington Post*, disclosed that during a meeting with National Security Adviser Samuel Berger on May 25 the representatives of the seven Iraqi opposition groups heard him declare "a determination to get rid of the Saddam Hussein regime by the end of Clinton's second term."[19]

None of this impressed Iraq's neighbors. As before they refused to let their soil be used by the Iraqi opposition.

So the reconstituted INC held a two-day conference at the end of October in New York at a cost of $2 million, borne by the Clinton administration. The delegates elected a seven-strong executive committee, including Chalabi, with a member each from the INA, KDP, PUK, and MCM, and two independents. Significantly, they left military matters "for later."

THE BUSH JR. ADMINISTRATION

This was the situation that the George Bush Jr. administration inherited from its predecessor. Its hawkish vice president, Dick Cheney, and defense secretary, Donald Rumsfeld, embraced the INC and Chalabi, who by now had forged friendly contacts with the pro-Israeli lobby in Washington as well as uncritically pro-Israel lawmakers. In contrast the State Department, headed by Colin Powell, remained skeptical of them, aware of their rejection by all the Arab states as well as the European Union, except Britain.

When challenged by the Pentagon to find an alternative to the INC, the State Department toyed with several ideas, including setting up an Iraqi government-in-exile and preparing a dossier for Saddam's trial for committing crimes against humanity. Finally, it opted for approaching various Iraqi exiles not attached to the INC or the INA and urging them to come together.

Out of this emerged the assembly of some sixty former Iraqi military officers on July 12 in London, where most of the high-profile Iraqi exiles are now based. The conferees' statement that they were not funded by the United States was hard to swallow. Various US departments and agencies—including State and Defense, the CIA, and the vice president's office—were represented at the gathering by their officials as "observers." The conference was held in the premises rented by the INC, which is on the US payroll.

Much to the delight of the American hawks, the State Department's strategy of propping up an alternative to the INC failed when the ubiquitous Chalabi, lacking any military or intelligence experience in Iraq, turned up at the conference, acting as a fairy godmother of the new organization, called the Iraqi Military Alliance (IMA), and hogged the media. "We are sending a message to Iraqi military officers that there is life for them after Saddam, and that they should not fear change," he announced.

The "Military Charter of Honor," adopted by the IMA, declared its readiness to join "any effort to establish a new democratic federal regime, based on the rule of law and civil society," welcomed "any foreign help" to rid Iraq of Saddam, and urged all Iraqi soldiers inside and outside the country to work jointly to achieve this objective.

None of the attending former officers had any experience in intelligence. Most of them had left Iraq so long ago (some as far back as 1982) that their contacts were outdated.[20] Moreover, following Iraq's defeat in the Gulf War and the disintegration of most of its military, Saddam re-created the army on the narrow base of those Sunni tribes that stood by him in his hour of need. So the appeals of those attending the London conference were likely to fall on deaf ears.

Not surprisingly, in his television address to the nation on July 17, the thirty-fourth anniversary of the Baathist seizure of power, Saddam declared that "evil tyrants and oppressors" would not be able to overthrow him and his regime. "You will never defeat me this time."[21]

CHAPTER 6

IRAQ, THE UNITED NATIONS, AND THE UNITED STATES

Although the heavily guarded Republican Presidential Palace in Baghdad's Tashri neighborhood is the acknowledged seat of ultimate power in Iraq, it is the Canal Hotel complex five miles to the east of that palace, in the 7th Nisan district, which houses the United Nations, that has been regulating the daily life of ordinary Iraqis since the Gulf War cease-fire.

This three-story, fifty-room building is, or has been, the headquarters of several UN agencies, from the UN Office of Humanitarian Coordinator in Iraq (UNOHIC) to the Baghdad Monitoring and Verification Center (BMVC) to the UN Iraq-Kuwait Observation Mission (UNIKOM). With a large UN sign in English and Arabic atop its front, and a blue UN flag fluttering over its roof, the site is hard to miss. An exceptionally tall transmitter tower and a huge satellite dish in its compound add further to its distinctiveness. With its own electric generator and telecommunications system, the UN head office is free from the vagaries of the erratic local systems. After leasing it from the Iraqi government in 1994, the United Nations equipped it with the latest in countersurveillance technology that US and British intelligence agencies could provide. The building—furnished on one side with a vast, fenced perimeter and erected along the bank of the dried-up Old Nahrawan Canal in Greater Baghdad—stands starkly alone.

Unlike elsewhere in Baghdad, in this complex I found everything working perfectly. It was here, for instance, that I had my best cup of coffee, in the course of my interview with George Somerweil, a pleasant, mild-mannered UN civil servant of long standing, an extremely helpful Briton.

Somerweil's nationality made me muse over the fate of Iraq under the British mandate that the League of Nations awarded in 1920. That political trusteeship lasted twelve years. But the economic mandate that the United Nations, the successor to the League of Nations, acquired in Iraq in the wake of the 1991 Gulf War was very much in place at the beginning of the twenty-first century, and its end was nowhere in sight.

To be fair, the United Nations was not always so severe with Iraq. Indeed, its Security Council was indulgent toward it in 1980 when it invaded Iran. Instead of condemning its aggression, the council treated the aggressor and its victim on a par—thanks to the unanimity on the subject between the two superpowers, the US and the Soviet Union. Baghdad was an ally of Moscow. And Washington was so angered and humiliated by the Iranians' hostage, taking that it had encouraged Saddam to attack Iran by using diplomatic back channels (due to lack of direct diplomatic ties).

Saddam's invasion of Iran, however, did get his country entangled with the UN Security Council. And more than twenty years later, Iraq had failed to set itself free from the bind and become a normal member-state of the international body.

AFTER AUGUST 1990

Within hours of Iraq's invasion of Kuwait, the UN Security Council condemned Saddam's actions, and within days it imposed the most comprehensive sanctions authorized by Chapter VII of the UN Charter against Baghdad.

In its Resolution 687 (April 1991), the council linked the easing or lifting of sanctions to the disarmament of Iraq. This was to be implemented by the Vienna-based International Atomic Energy Agency (IAEA), which had been inspecting Iraq for any possible military use of its nuclear facilities since the late 1970s, and the newly established UN Special Commission under the chairmanship of Rolf Ekeus, a Swedish diplomat, for Baghdad's chemical and biological weapons programs and its medium- and long-range missile projects. In May 1991, Iraq's foreign ministry agreed in writing to grant unhindered access to all sites and facilities that Unscom and the IAEA demanded to inspect.

Resolution 687 required Iraq to submit a list detailing of the locations, amounts and types of weapons of mass destruction (WMD) and proscribed missiles within its borders and to hand over such materials to Unscom within two months for destruction. In the event, the exercise proved long and tortuous. Iraq acted in bad faith and the United States, as the main driving force behind the inspections regime, reciprocated by using the United Nations as a vehicle to further its policy of espionage and subversion of Saddam's regime. It did this by planting its intelligence agents and technicians, trained in handling communications and organizing logistics, into Unscom as early as spring 1992 under George Bush Sr.'s administration, implicating them in its anti-Saddam coup attempts, and getting them to place bugging devices to intercept microwave transmissions used by Iraq's military. The basic flaw lay with the composition of Unscom. Because inspectors and other technical staff were not required to resign their posts in their home countries, they often felt more loyal to their national governments than to Unscom. This was particularly true of Americans and Britons, who were vehemently anti-Saddam, and made no secret of it.

Due to the defection of Gen. Hussein Kamil Hassan in August 1995, Saddam's Concealment Operations Committee (COC) was exposed. Formed in May 1991 under the chairmanship of his younger son Qusay, a quietly efficient and ruthless man with a chubby face and premature paunch, the concealment committee was designed to supervise and safeguard information and material about the core of the military programs proscribed by the Security

Council.[1] In contrast, Washington's clandestine activities remained undisclosed until after Unscom chief Richard Butler had pulled out the inspectors in December 1998 so that the Clinton administration could mount the hundred-hour blitzkrieg against Iraq code-named Operation Desert Fox.

The initial skirmishes between the United Nations and Iraq centered around IAEA inspections, headed by an American national, David Kay. Later, controversy shifted to chemical weapons, followed by biological agents. By the time the white-haired, blue-eyed, aristocratic-looking Rolf Ekeus, a career diplomat, stepped down as Unscom chief in July 1997, to be succeeded by Richard Butler, a heavyset, pugnacious Australian disarmament expert lacking diplomatic finesse, relations between Baghdad and Unscom had become strained. Butler's confrontational personality, and his undisguised collusion with Washington, added to the tension that culminated in Clinton's Operation Desert Fox. For this, Clinton would pay a hefty diplomatic price, with the breach between the United States and its British ally and the trio of France, Russia, and China becoming so unbridgeable that it would take the Security Council a whole year to adopt a virtual replacement for Resolution 687.

Nuclear and Chemical Weapons and Missiles

The first sign of trouble with the David Kay–led IAEA team came in June 1991 when the Iraqis obstructed its access to two sites that they had not listed as nuclear facilities. During the next visit by an IAEA team in July, it discovered several kilograms of highly enriched uranium (twenty-five kilograms are needed for one atom bomb) and large stocks of natural uranium. Iraq explained that it had withheld full information about its nuclear equipment because it feared an attack on it by the Pentagon. Baghdad admitted enriching uranium by the old-fashioned method of electromagnetic isotopic separation (used by the United States in 1945) and producing enriched uranium.

Following its third visit, the Kay-led IAEA team concluded that Baghdad had a nuclear military program, contrary to its assertions of the peaceful nature of its program.

By then Unscom teams had destroyed all but two Iraqi ballistic missiles with ranges above 94 miles/150 km (the limit specified by the UN) and missile launchers. In its submission to Unscom, the Iraqi government admitted possessing 1,005 tons of liquid nerve gas stored in vats, and 11,382 chemical warheads—with 30 fitted for ground-to-ground Scud missiles and the rest for bombs or artillery shells.

On August 15 Security Council Resolution 707 authorized IAEA and Unscom teams to conduct fixed-wing and helicopter flights inside Iraq for all relevant purposes, and use to their own aircraft and Iraqi airfields as necessary. Baghdad objected to such overflights, aware that the Pentagon, acting on Unscom's behalf, had on August 11 flown its U-2 spy planes for high-altitude reconnaissance of Iraq.

A major crisis developed in September 1991 when the Iraqis refused to allow the IAEA team, led by Kay and his deputy Robert Galluci, a former official of the Politico-Military section of the US State Department, to cart away the 60,000 documents it had removed from the Nuclear Design Center. After a four-day standoff —during which Galluci, using a satellite link, sent sensitive information not to the IAEA or Unscom, but to the State Department— a compromise specified a joint review of the documents. The irrelevant ones would be returned to the Iraqis, and the relevant ones listed, with the Iraqis receiving photocopies. This left the IAEA team in possession of five thousand pages, several thousand pictures, and nineteen hours of videotape. According to Kay, the seized material showed how Iraq acquired materials for its nuclear program and the details of its weapons-development program.[2]

This episode had two major elements that would recur over the next several years: well-orchestrated attempts by Baghdad to hide the true extent of its WMD projects, and Washington's misuse of the United Nations as a cover for spying on Iraq to bring about a "regime change."

Overall, periodic hiccups aside, both the IAEA and Unscom forged ahead with their mandates. In his October 1993 report to the Security Council, Ekeus said that substantial progress had been made in getting Iraq to provide information about its programs for producing long-range missiles and chemical and biological weapons, and most of the demands on the nuclear-weapons program had been met.

The next month, after dragging its feet on the subject, Baghdad accepted unconditionally long-term monitoring, as specified in Resolution 715, and formed its own National Monitoring Directorate (NMD) under Gen. Hossam Amin to liaise with Unscom's monitoring and verification department.

Unscom's exceptionally comprehensive monitoring system covered not only the present Iraqi facilities in building and equipment and skilled manpower with experience in the research or production of proscribed weapons and long-range missiles, but also any future introduction of new buildings, plants, or scientists or engineers. Regarding equipment, the focus was on dual-purpose machinery. For example, a fermenter could be used for making beer or biological weapons, and a machine tool for making car components or missile parts. Unscom required the Iraqi government to submit every six months a new list of all dual-purpose equipment in the country.

Unscom used three kinds of sensors as monitoring tools: visual, chemical, and temperature. It linked the visual sensors—cameras—installed at 150 sites through a system of transmitters and repeaters scattered around Iraq to the Baghdad Monitoring and Verification Center and to the United Nations in New York. It linked the video cameras, installed at 150 locations to ensure that dual-purpose machines were not used for military ends, to a central panel in Baghdad. It used chemical sensors—sniffers—to detect the presence of certain compounds signaling proscribed activity. Finally, Unscom staff installed temperature sensors at the sites with potential for use for biological weapons to detect if a factory was operating equipment in a certain heat range. Unscom and the IAEA complemented all this with aerial monitoring done mainly by helicopters, reconnaissance aircraft, and weekly U-2 high-altitude reconnaissance flights by US-owned and -operated aircraft with communications links to the Pentagon. The purpose behind obtaining aerial images was to detect any signs of new construction, power lines, or any other fresh activity.

The overall functioning of this highly elaborate system was illustrated by the (former) laboratories of the General Establishment for Animal Development at Duara in Baghdad. The factory had the capacity of producing annually one million vaccines for animals. But, as its laboratories could be used for producing biological agents, they were shut down by Unscom. Every month Unscom's biological inspectors visited the facility to check the monitoring system installed to record all visitors to the site, ensure that the two Unscom-tagged centrifuges (categorized as dual-purpose machines) had remained untouched, and to check that the hardening foam, pumped through the ventilation system and capped with concrete to seal the main chamber of the laboratories, was intact.

Unscom's remote monitoring system covered three hundred weapons installations and research facilities. Until February 1996, the video images and the logs of the electrical power consumed were recorded onto a magnetic tape at the remote sites, with the Baghdad-based Unscom inspectors periodically collecting the tapes. In March Unscom would start transmitting images from the site cameras to Baghdad using radio signals boosted by relays. This arrangement furnished Unscom with an almost real-time view of faraway facilities in Iraq. But unknown to Unscom's Ekeus (though not to his deputy since 1993, Charles Duelfer, a tall, mustached, lean-faced former US State Department official), the American signals-and-sensors technicians, who installed and maintained the system, were intelligence operatives headed by an exceptionally innovative military intelligence technician. They built boosting stations with covert capabilities. Hidden in their structures were antennas capable of intercepting microwave transmissions used by the Iraqi armed forces. The US agents made a point of planting some of them near important nodes of Iraq's military communications system.[3]

Running in tandem with this system was another. This one used commercial scanners to intercept low-powered VHF radio transmissions purportedly used by the Iraqi government to direct its concealment efforts against Unscom. Both channels were part of the complex "Shake the Tree" operation, which involved staging deliberately confrontational Unscom inspections in order to compel the Iraqis to activate their concealment procedures, which would in turn be identified by a swift synthesis of multifarious intelligence sources, thus arming Unscom inspectors to catch the culprits red-handed as they moved contraband. The US director of the highly classified "Shake the Tree" operation shared his confidential information with a fellow American and a former government official, Duelfer, to ensure the continuity of Unscom's latest procedures. Duelfer's boss, Ekeus, however, and even the openly pro-American Richard Butler, were both kept in the dark.[4]

US SHIFTS GOALPOST

While clandestinely exploiting to the hilt the UN cover to subvert the Iraq government, Washington stiffened its diplomatic stance. In an article in the *New York Times* of April 29, 1994, Secretary of State Warren Christopher said, "The US does not believe that Iraq's compliance with Paragraph 22 of Resolution 687 is enough to justify lifting the embargo." Coming from an eminent lawyer like Christopher, this was truly ironic. His statement flew in the face of the text, which reads, "[The Security Council] Decides that upon the approval by the Council of the program called for in Paragraph 19 above and upon Council agreement that Iraq has completed all actions contemplated in Paragraphs 8, 9, 10, 11,12, and 13 above [concerning Iraqi disarmament], the prohibitions against the import of commodities and products originating in Iraq and the prohibitions against financial transactions related thereto contained in Resolution 661 [1990] shall have no further force or effect." Among those who pointed out that the United Sates had changed the rules unilaterally was the *New York Times*.

By early 1995, having destroyed all known research, development, and manufacturing facilities for nuclear weapons, the IAEA channeled most of its resources into installing and strengthening its monitoring and verification regime.

In his April 1995 report Ekeus declared the Unscom-IAEA verification and monitoring system fully operational, with the Baghdad Monitoring and Verification Center linked directly to its UN headquarters in New York. The BMVC's director, Goran Wallen, an American, had eighty-one subordinates and the backup of a twenty-nine-strong helicopter unit. The five monitoring teams, each two to six strong, working in association with Iraq's National Monitoring Directorate, were: nuclear (with focus on isotope detectors in rivers to detect discharge of any radioactive material); chemical (using chemical monitors in chemical industries to detect key precursors and chemical agents); biological (which was difficult to monitor, but the pharmaceutical industry was put under surveillance); intermediate- and long-range missiles; and aerial inspection. Biological weapons were highly problematic, since most laboratories engaged in medical research in disease control could produce them.

With Unscom and the IAEA having virtually accomplished their disarming missions in chemical and nuclear arms and missiles, Ekeus turned increasingly to biological warfare agents with their production facility at Hakam, thirty-eight miles southwest of Baghdad.

BIOLOGICAL WEAPONS PROGRAM

In March 1995, Ekeus pointed out to the Iraqi officials that they had yet to account for seventeen of the thirty-nine tons of growth media—used for growing bacteria and viruses—bought in 1988–89 for their biological warfare program. Two months later, Iraqi deputy prime minister Tariq Aziz said that Baghdad would provide further information on its biological projects after Unscom had closed the files on Iraq's past missiles and chemical arms programs, and the IAEA, the nuclear file; and after the Security Council had promised to lift sanctions once Iraq had kept its promise. This offer was unacceptable to the United States and Britain. So, accepting the advice of Russia and France, Iraq dropped its conditions. The Iraqi officials meeting Ekeus in Baghdad on July 1 conceded that Iraq had a biological arms program, and that it had produced anthrax (*Bacillus anthracis*) and botulinum (*Clostridium botulinum*) in 1989–90.

This created a suitable environment for the final resolution of the issue of Iraqi disarmament. But any such chance evaporated with the defection of Gen. Hussein Kamil Hassan in August 1995. In his meetings with CIA and British intelligence officials as well as Ekeus in Amman, he said that through UN inspectors had done an exemplary job, the Iraqi government had contrived to retain a certain proportion of banned materials and gave them the specifics of the highly classified military communications systems, which the CIA and the NSA would later exploit to gather intelligence for the US through the American staff in for Unscom.

Having recovered from his initial shock and anger, Saddam singled out Hussein Kamil as the one responsible for all the problems between Iraq, Unscom, and the IAEA. Saddam claimed that it was Kamil who withheld vital information on Iraq's proscribed programs from these UN agencies. To prove the point, Iraqi officials told Ekeus during his August 17 visit to Baghdad that after invading Kuwait, Iraq had loaded biological weapons into 166 bombs and 25 warheads of Al Hussein missiles, with a range of 360 miles.

The Iraqis directed Ekeus to the alleged farmhouse of Hussein Kamil—a villa with a few outhouses—where in a locked chicken shed they showed him forty large boxes containing documents, photos, video film, microfilm, and microfiche—about 650,000 pages of text.

Though later examination of the contents would reveal tampering of the documents—with highly classified material excised—the haul was profuse in detail about the proscribed arms, especially nuclear.

In early September Ekeus announced that the Iraqis had admitted producing larger quantities of anthrax (8,500 liters) and botulinum (19,000 liters) than previously declared. They had also disclosed that they had initiated a crash program in August 1990 to produce one nuclear bomb within a year.[5] (In practice, they failed to obtain the vital triggering device.)

While this ended any chance of Saddam seeing the sanctions lifted, Clinton resolved to crack open the concealment mechanism he had deployed to deceive the United Nations. The administration intensified its use of US nationals working as Unscom staff, with Scott Ritter as a leading actor in the exercise.

US INTELLIGENCE AGENCIES AND UNSCOM

A former colonel in US Marine Corps intelligence who joined Unscom as a chief inspector at the beginning, Scott Ritter, a tall, heavyset man with rimless glasses, was very influential. Once Ekeus had instructed him to concentrate on exposing Iraq's concealment system, he visited Israel, where he proposed that its civilian and military intelligence agencies, Mossad and Aman (which had cooperated with Unscom since October 1994), supply the UN with all-frequency scanners and digital tape recorders to record coded radio communications of Baghdad's innermost military and security apparatus. Israel agreed. At Ritter's behest, Ekeus set up a Concealment Investigation Unit (CIU) with a mandate to conduct Special Information Collection Missions (SICMs). He approached Washington for technology to tap Iraqi security networks on frequencies that could not be picked up by American spy planes and satellites.

Within weeks, the CIA and NSA designed and delivered the appropriate technology to Unscom. By January 1996, Ritter's team had mapped the Iraqi frequencies, and intercepted the communications of Iraq's National Monitoring Directorate, which was in regular contact with the Special Security Directorate, the Special Republican Guard, and the Office of the Presidential Secretary (OPS). Ritter transmitted the intercepts by satellite relay to Bahrain, Unscom's regional headquarters, where a computer filtered conversations for key Arabic words—"chemical," "missile," "biological," etc.—and relayed them to the National Security Agency at Fort Meade, Maryland, for decoding and translation into English.

In mid-March the US undercover "Moe Dobbs" group was part of Unscom 143, led by Ritter, with the inspectors carrying Israeli-supplied radio scanners as part of the highly classified Special Information Collection Mission. This was the first of a series of deliberately confrontational inspection exercises designed to elicit a radio telephone response from the Iraqi Concealment Operations Committee to be picked up by Unscom's radio scanners. Though the Iraqis resisted and delayed access to five sites Unscom demanded to inspect, Ritter's inspections obtained no proof of "Iraqi wrongdoing."[6]

Unscom's next confrontation with Iraq occurred in early June 1996 with its second Special Information Collection Mission, and was linked to the US coup plan to be executed on June 26 (see Chapter 4). But Iraqi officials had an inkling of Washington's plans. "There are two governments, the US and the UK, which officially or formally say they would like to change the government of Iraq," Aziz told Ekeus on June 19, 1996. "Iraq cannot take lightly the fact that Unscom receives information mainly from these two governments, and then you send teams to the Special Republican Guard sites and find nothing. . . .You sent your team, Unscom 150, anticipating a crisis. . . . *I am complaining about the timing of the inspections.*"[7]

After three Special Information Collection Missions by Unscom, contrary to its promise, the CIA-NSA duo failed to furnish Ekeus with any report or conclusion drawn from the field data. In September Ekeus complained about this to CIA director John Deutch.

Yet nothing happened. A disappointed Ekeus approached Britain, with decoding and translation facilities at Cheltenham, and Israel, with its de-encryption facilities at its Unit 8200, to provide the services that the United States was then rendering. Both agreed. They passed on complete transcripts of the SICM intercepts to Unscom.

In his October 1996 report Ekeus noted that during its five-and-a-half-year existence Unscom had dispatched 373 inspection teams, involving 3,574 experts, to Iraq, and that it had spent $120 million, most of it taken from Iraq's assets frozen abroad.

CLINTON'S SECOND TERM, 1997-2000

The reelected President Bill Clinton's promotion of Madeleine Albright to secretary of state in early 1997 signaled to Baghdad that Washington's hard-line stance toward it would continue. Iraq's relations with Unscom became more strained after Unscom's leadership passed in mid-1997 to Richard Butler, who retained as his deputy Charles Duelfer. On the other hand, the entrenchment of the divide at the Security Council between the Anglo-American duo and non-Anglo-American trio encouraged Saddam to demand an end to the UN embargo.

By now the covert cooperation between the United States and Unscom had deepened to the extent that Ritter gave regular briefings to the US National Security Council in Washington before and after his inspection tours of Iraq. During the first half of June, leading Unscom 194, Ritter inspected such extrasensitive premises as the Special Security Department's training institute, and the country's highest military academy, the Al Bakr Military Institute. This alarmed and puzzled the Iraqi authorities. Ritter's team also inspected the headquarters of the Special Republican Guard, followed by three SRG premises the next day, all of them on "no notice" basis. It was only on the following day that the Iraqis denied him access to two more SRG sites he wanted to inspect unannounced.[8]

In retaliation, prompted by the United States and the United

Kingdom, the Security Council suspended the sixty-day sanctions review required by Resolution 687.

Tariq Aziz's efforts to cultivate cordial relations with Butler, who took charge of Unscom on July 1, failed as the latter was intent on using Unscom inspections to lay bare Iraq's concealment mechanism. On their part, Iraqi officials had by now most probably gathered convincing evidence of espionage by some American employees of Unscom.

It was widely known that the Iraqi minders accompanying Unscom and IAEA teams spied for the government. Also, the General Security would have monitored the movements of all Unscom and IAEA personnel, no matter which hotel they stayed at. Such practices, however, yielded scant hard information. The key element in intelligence gathering was the high-technology eavesdropping equipment, where the Anglo-American spy agencies were streets ahead of their counterparts in the Western world, not to mention Iraq. During the Iran-Iraq War, assisted by the West and the Soviet bloc, Baghdad had built up its signals and electronic intelligence (SEINT), code-named Operation 858. Based in Rashidia, twelve miles north of Baghdad, the thousand-strong Iraqi SEINT had half a dozen listening posts throughout the country. But this did not enable it to pick up the conversations of UN inspectors who used scramblers and other secure communications equipment. In any event, SEINT's equipment was designed for the analog system of the 1980s, still in operation in the 1990s, and not for the latest digital system.[9]

Ritter's break came on September 25, 1997. On that day Dr. Diane Seaman, an American microbiologist, conducted a no-notice inspection of the Iraqi Food and Drug Examination Laboratory (IFDEL) in Baghdad. Side-stepping the normal courtesy of having tea with the head of the establishment, Dr. Hilal al Tikriti, on the ground floor, she strode to the administrative office on the second floor. There she noticed two men with briefcases hurriedly heading for a back exit. Giving chase, she cornered them in a laboratory room, where, helped by her three colleagues, she grabbed the brief-cases. Containing documents, biological test kits, and unidentified biological samples, they turned out to be vital catches. Literate in Arabic, she found that many documents bore the letterhead, "Office of the Presidency, Special Security Directorate." A follow-up investigation would reveal IFDEL's involvement in a project involving gas gangrene—*clostridium perfringens*—weaponized in the late 1980s.

During the subsequent meeting that Ritter and Seaman had in the evening with the Iraqi officials at Unscom's Canal Hotel headquarters, the head of the Iraqi side, Dr. Hamza Bilal, explained that the IFDEL had a verbal understanding with the authorities to do "biological testing" for the president and his inner circle. Describing the explanation as unsatisfactory, Ritter informed Gen. Hossam Amin, head of the Iraqi NMD, that he would conduct an inspection of an unspecified site that night and that his team would be ready to leave at 2300 hours. Ritter happened to have a spare "no notice" inspection notification signed by Butler, which the latter permitted him to use.

As the Unscom convoy of fourteen vehicles, accompanied by forty Iraqi minders, left the Canal Hotel, Ritter told Amin that he would name the site on arrival and then he could inform him whether or not it was "sensitive." His (as yet undisclosed) destination was the Special Security Directorate's headquarters, about half a mile from the Republican Presidential Palace. On their way to that office, the first car of the Unscom convoy went past a green traffic light while the rest of the convoy halted when the light turned red. This unexpected situation drew the attention of the SSD sentry and officer near the traffic lights. They stopped all vehicles and ordered the first car to reverse to rejoin the Unscom convoy. Several uniformed Iraqis in the area cocked their guns as tension rose sharply. It was only when Gen. Amr Rashid, a sophisticated British-trained engineer who dealt with Unscom in Iraq at the highest level on a day-to-day basis, arrived on the scene that a semblance of calm returned. By now Ritter, using his satellite phone, was in conversation with Butler at the United Nations in New York. Having consulted Butler, he attempted to negotiate with Rashid a resumption of the journey to the now named site — SSD headquarters — arguing that Unscom had the legal right to inspect it. Rashid disagreed. The Unscom convoy returned to the Canal Hotel.

By then Iraq had denied Unscom access to about a hundred sites — which were usually located inside the perimeter of a presidential palace — during its seventy-seven-month existence, citing "national security." Unscom suspected that the Special Republican Guard were hiding incriminating documents, weapons parts, and biological warfare agents at these sites. If so, this could be viewed as Baghdad's counterresponse to Unscom's strategy, which — in Ritter's words — was to "gradually squeeze retained Iraqi weapons into a few sanctuaries which would then be subjected to no notice inspections."[10]

In his first six-monthly Unscom report on October 6, 1997, Butler noted some progress in the areas of missiles and chemical arms, but described biological warfare agents as a field "unredeemed by progress or any approximation of the known facts of Iraq's program." He also pointed out that the Iraqis had introduced a new classification of "presidential sites" that they had declared out of bounds to Unscom.[11]

On its part, by now Baghdad had evidently concluded that most experts seconded to Unscom by US military and intelligence were, in the final analysis, working for Washington, and would continue finding pretexts to demonstrate Iraq's lack of cooperation with the UN as long as the Clinton administration wanted them to — which would be until Saddam's ouster.

It was no surprise, then, when on October 29 Tariq Aziz told the Security Council that Baghdad would no longer accept US personnel in Unscom teams, since they had shown more loyalty to the United States than to the United Nations, and demanded the end of flights by the Pentagon's U-2 spy plane to monitor Iraq's compliance with the elimination of the WMD. He added that Iraq had the sovereign right to expel aliens it did not want on its territory, charging that under the UN aegis the US government was spying with the aim of changing the Iraqi regime.

On November 3, the Iraqis blocked an inspection of the Al Samoud short-range missile site because the team contained Americans. In response all other UN teams halted work. That day, claiming that the forthcoming U-2 flights on November 5 and 7 were linked to the military strikes that Washington was planning against his country, the Iraqi ambassador to the United Nations, Nizar Hamdoun, urged Butler to cancel the flights, especially when Iraq's air defenses were being activated to meet "the possibility of aggression."[12]

To defuse the crisis, UN secretary-general Kofi Annan sent a team of three senior diplomats led by Lakhdar Brahimi, an Algerian, to Baghdad. Pointing out to the visiting UN team that Americans held 44 percent of the sensitive positions in Unscom in 1996, and 37 percent at present, Aziz called for a change in Unscom's composition.[13] He provided the visiting team with evidence to back up his espionage charges. And the UN diplomats reported this to Annan.

Aziz also complained about the UN inspectors' behavior. This could not have been news to Butler or Ritter. In an interview with Peter J. Boyer of the *New Yorker*, Ritter described how he briefed his team on the eve of an inspection. "When I go into a site I am going to be polite," he began. "I am going to shake their hand, but I am the alpha dog. I"m going in tail held high. If they growl at me, I'm gonna jump on 'em. I'm gonna let 'em know who the boss is here. I'm in charge. They report to me, they do what I say. You work for me, so every one of you are alpha dogs. When you go to a site, they're gonna know we're there, we're gonna raise our tails and we're gonna spray urine all over their walls—that's the equivalent of what we're doing. So when we leave a site they know they've been inspected."[14]

On November 12 Baghdad expelled six US inspectors. Of the remaining eighty-three Unscom staff in the Iraqi capital, Butler pulled out all except seven technicians to safeguard the Unscom headquarters. He contacted the media in New York without informing the Security Council. In Washington, Clinton was furious. "By expelling UN inspectors Saddam has ensured that the sanctions will be there until the end of time or as long as he lasts," he said on November 14.[15] Actually, Iraq expelled only Unscom's American inspectors, not UN inspectors per se. Clinton ordered a military buildup in the region. And the Pentagon assembled two aircraft carriers, seven cruisers, destroyers, and submarines—carrying cruise missiles—as well as three guided-missile frigates.

But an American attack on Iraq was averted by the intervention of Russian president Boris Yeltsin. In return for Iraq's unconditional acceptance of Unscom's return, Yeltsin pledged to get Unscom to finish its task expeditiously, and the Security Council to fix a timetable for the lifting of sanctions. All told, Saddam gained from the crisis he engendered. It exposed deep differences between the five permanent members of the Security Council, with Moscow publicly siding with Baghdad. By acting rashly and without informing the Security Council, Butler drew criticism from several council members. In the region, the Iraq-US standoff compelled the Arab states to take a position. They unanimously opposed military action against Baghdad. They reasoned that, unlike the situation in 1990, Iraq was not occupying another country and had recognized Kuwait as an independent state within its newly demarcated boundaries.

AFTER THE NOVEMBER 1997 CRISIS
The next Unscom team of seventy-five inspectors arrived in Baghdad on November 21–22. They carried Butler's confidential orders for no-notice inspection of the former headquarters of the SRG's Third Battalion, disbanded by Saddam after his intelligence services aborted the US-sponsored coup in June 1996. *"Following a standard procedure that neither Unscom nor Washington officially acknowledges, Mr. Butler's senior staff briefed a liaison officer from the CIA on the target, sources said,"* Barton Gellman of the *Washington Post* would report

later. Albright then telephoned Butler, urging him to delay the operation.[16] Her reasoning was that the Clinton administration wanted to avoid provocative confrontation that would enable Saddam to blame Unscom. Butler agreed. He issued an instruction to his staff banning new inspections until further notice at the Special Security Directorate, Republican Guard, Special Republican Guard, and any other Iraqi sites classified "sensitive" by Baghdad.[17] At the United Nations, an emergency session of Unscom on November 21–22 submitted a report to the Security Council on expediting the task of Unscom.

Nineteen ninety-eight in Iraq started with Unscom 227. Made up of forty-three inspectors, all working under Ritter, it was divided into two operational groups, one headed by Ritter and the other by Dr. Gabrielle Kraatz-Wadsack, a German biologist. On January 12, Unscom 227 carried out seven inspections, including one at the General Security headquarters and another at the Abu Ghraib prison six miles west of Baghdad. The objective was to seize documents showing that the Iraqi government had conducted biological and chemical weapons experiments in 1994–95 on political prisoners arrested by the General Security and detained at the Abu Ghraib jail. According to Ritter, his teams found the records for the period in question missing.

To express their disapproval of Unscom 227's investigation, the Iraqis objected to the unbalanced composition of the team, with two-fifths of its inspectors being American or British. Ritter's operational group had nine Americans, five Britons, one Australian, and one Russian. The Iraqi authorities withdrew permission for Ritter to operate in their country until his team's composition reflected a balanced participation of the permanent members. Accepting any conditions on Unscom was out of the question. And, with nothing to do, Unscom 227 left Iraq on January 15.

On January 17, the seventh anniversary of the Gulf War in Iraq (due to the eight-hour time difference between Eastern Standard Time in the United States and Standard Iraqi Time), in a nationwide broadcast, Saddam ordered the training of one million volunteers to prepare for a jihad if the UN embargo was not lifted within six months as demanded earlier by the Iraqi parliament.

By one of the rare accidents of history, some hours later, a story broke on US television that President Clinton allegedly had an affair with Monica Lewinsky, a young White House intern. The scandal would dog Clinton for a year and culminate in his impeachment by the House of Representatives, but his presidency would be spared due to the failure of the Senate to muster the two-thirds majority required to remove him from office. It would impinge directly on his decisions on Iraq.

The need to act on the issue heightened when Butler, in his report to the Security Council, emphasized the need to inspect "the sensitive and sovereign sites" in Iraq. On January 25, 1998 US sources declared a countdown to a Pentagon-led military action against Iraq, code-named Operation Desert Thunder—named after "Rolling Thunder," under which the United States bombed North Vietnam from the mid-1960s to early 1970s.

To raise the temperature, in an interview with the *New York Times* published on January 27, Butler asserted that Iraq had enough biological weapons and missiles "to blow away Tel Aviv." His statement startled and angered the Security Council, to which he had not presented any evidence of the kind. After reprimanding him, Annan demanded he submit a written apology to the council. He complied.

The prospect of the Pentagon striking Iraq upset the Muslim world on one side, and Russia and China on the other. Clinton asserted that the objective of the Pentagon's strikes would be to degrade Saddam's potential for launching missiles carrying warheads filled with chemical or biological weapons. This failed to convince Washington's Arab allies, as Albright discovered during her tour of the Gulf region. Only Kuwait openly backed military action against Iraq. Of the twenty nations supporting the United States against Baghdad now, only two were Arab (Kuwait) or African (Senegal). By contrast, in the Gulf War, of the twenty-eight countries in the

US-led anti-Iraq coalition, thirteen were Arab, African (Senegal and Niger), or South Asian (Pakistan and Bangladesh).

At the center of the latest crisis were eight presidential sites, which Iraq described as "sovereign." Three were in greater Baghdad: Sijood, Republican, and Radwaniye; the fourth, by the Tharthar Lake, forty-seven miles northwest of the capital. Another three were in Auja, Tikrit, and Jabal Maqbul, with one in Mosul. Whereas Butler, repeating the information supplied by US sources, claimed that these sites occupied 18,000 acres, a visiting UN team of surveyors and cartographers put the total area at 8,160 acres.[18]

To educate the American public, the National Security Council arranged to have CNN transmit worldwide a "town hall" meeting at the Ohio State University stadium in Dayton to be addressed by Albright, Defense Secretary William Cohen, and National Security Adviser Samuel (Sandy) Berger. Reckoning that, given the insatiable popular interest in the Lewinsky scandal, the audience would question him on this awkward subject, Clinton decided to stay away, and sent his three senior most deputies.

The trio faced a vociferous and unruly audience of six thousand—composed of local residents, Vietnam War veterans, and university students and staff. None of them succeeded in convincing the audience that bombing Iraq was the means to rid the country of its WMD, which the administration claimed was the overriding objective. This event, meant to demonstrate the strength of US public support for military strikes against Iraq via CNN—which Iraqi officials, from Saddam down, watched avidly—ended up as a debacle for Clinton.

"The serious threat Mr. Saddam poses was overblown [by the Clinton administration] in the effort to sell the possible [American] attack, some senior US officials now say," Steven Erlanger would report in the *New York Times* nine months later. "Defense secretary William Cohen appeared on television brandishing a bag of sugar in an effort to describe how small a dose of biological and chemical weapons it would take to threaten Americans, but his own chairman of the Joint Chiefs of Staff, Gen. Henry Shelton, expressed serious reservations about the ability of the Pentagon to destroy such easily hidden and reconstituted weapons from the air."[19]

Small wonder that on February 22 a *Newsweek* poll showed backing for military action against Iraq down from 40 to 18 percent.

Meanwhile, Annan's mention of "a personal initiative" on February 13 had led to his intense consultations with the Security Council's permanent members. These continued until he had the backing of all of them. Overcoming its initial reluctance, the United States came on board partly because the momentum for a diplomatic solution had become irresistible and partly because, having asserted repeatedly that the dispute was between Iraq and the United Nations, it had no option but to go along with a trip to Baghdad by the United Nations' highest official.

Annan's talks with Tariq Aziz centered on three Iraqi demands: an unqualified public statement must be made that once UN inspectors had expressed their satisfaction, sanctions would be lifted; senior diplomats must accompany UN inspectors as they inspect the presidential sites; and the composition of the UN teams must reflect a wider range of nationalities than has been the case hitherto.

During a three-hour meeting with Saddam Hussein on February 22, Annan finalized an agreement. The next day Annan and Aziz signed a seven-point Memorandum of Understanding (MOU), which specifically mentioned Security Council Resolution 687, with its statement of a complete lifting of sanctions subject to UN-certified Iraqi disarmament.

Paragraph 3 coupled Iraq's undertaking to accord Unscom and the IAEA "immediate, unconditional and unrestricted access" in conformity with Resolutions 687 and 715 with Unscom's undertaking to "respect the legitimate concerns of Iraq relating to national security, sovereignty and dignity." Paragraph 4 stated that inspection of eight presidential sites would be conducted by a special group and headed by a (special) commissioner, appointed by the UN secretary-general, but who would report to Butler. The last paragraph required Annan to bring the subject of lifting sanctions to the attention of the Security Council.

At a UN press conference, Annan stressed the need for Unscom inspectors to handle Iraq and Iraqis with "a certain respect and dignity," which, by implication, had been missing so far. In a closed session of the Security Council he alluded to some Unscom inspectors acting as "cowboys," throwing their weight around and offending Iraqis. He also conveyed the Iraqi charge that some of them were engaged in hunting down Saddam rather than inspecting.[20]

This turn of events left the Russian, French, and Chinese delegations quietly impressed by Saddam's survival and crisis management skills, while their American counterpart could not hide its frustrated fury. The adoption of the Annan-Aziz Agreement under Chapter VII of the UN Charter by the Security Council validated its authority. It allowed each of the contending sides among the permanent members to claim victory, with the Anglo-American alliance arguing that the statement in Paragraph 3 that any violation by Baghdad of its obligation to accord "immediate, unconditional and unrestricted access" to UN teams would have "severest consequences for Iraq" was tantamount to authorizing military action. This interpretation was vigorously disputed by the rest of the permanent members.

Annan appointed Prakash Shah, a former Indian ambassador to the United Nations, his personal envoy in Baghdad with a brief to monitor the situation firsthand and attempt to de-escalate any future tension between Iraq and Unscom.

Though the immediate crisis was defused, the two contending sides remained basically at loggerheads. Neither Butler (working in collusion with Washington) nor Saddam Hussein had abandoned his respective hidden agenda. The Pentagon, assisted by Britain, maintained its armada in the Gulf at high alert, ready to strike should Baghdad fail to provide "immediate, unconditional and unrestricted access" to all sites other than the presidential ones. And Clinton was itching to strike Iraq, well aware that he would have to do so before the annual Muslim hajj pilgrimage to Mecca, due on March 15.

That meant Unscom insisting immediately on provocative inspections. Much therefore depended on what happened to the latest fifty-strong Unscom team, arriving in Baghdad on March 5, 1998 and headed once again by Ritter. In December, as head of Unscom's Concealment Investigation Unit, he had approached the US National Security Agency for technical support to expedite the processing of Unscom data and relay it back swiftly enough to impact on the ongoing inspection. The NSA agreed, and made rapid progress, with the text decoded and translated into English and relayed back to Unscom's Baghdad office within a short time.

On March 6–7the Unscom team, which included computer analysts and scientists, inspected various Special Security Directorate and Special Republican Guard premises without any problem. The inspected sites included the SSD headquarters, access to which had been denied to Ritter six months earlier. To his delight, Unscom's freshly installed clandestine eavesdropping system worked. He discovered that the SSD was receiving orders from Saddam's personal secretary, Abid Hamid Mahmoud, a young, self-effacing man with an ample mustache and stick-out ears, and that the Iraqis removed documents from one site and delayed the arrival of his team at another until the incriminating documents had been destroyed. He now possessed proof of Mahmoud's direct involvement in Iraq's concealment mechanism.

Ritter knew that the centerpiece of his inspections this time was to be Iraq's defense ministry, as US officials had specified to Butler. The Americans expected that Baghdad would refuse, thus providing them with a rationale for military strikes. On the morning of March 8 Ritter's team inspected the old Defense Ministry in Baghdad and found nothing objectionable. In the afternoon he arrived at the new Defense Ministry with 28 inspectors. A standoff ensued as he and

Gen. Amr Rashid haggled over the number of inspectors to be admitted. "Mr. Ritter, we know that right now your government is kissing our feet to make a crisis," Rashid said. "We have no intention to do so." Sensing that Rashid was aware of Washington's strategy, Ritter agreed to a compromise figure of sixteen. After eleven hours of paper chase across different floors of the building, Ritter's team found nothing.[21]

On top of that, Unscom drew a blank on the presidential palaces. So, to Clinton's regret, the fateful March 15 came and went, with no basis for the Pentagon to strike.

In his six-monthly report on April 28, Butler stated that because of the four-month-long crisis created by Baghdad, there was virtually no progress in verifying disarmament. In response, in his letter of April 22 to the Security Council, Tariq Aziz said, "The report tendentiously ignores everything that Iraq has done over the past seven years." He then dealt with specific disarmament issues. He requested the council put an end to "the false claims which are used [by Butler] to justify intrusive inspections . . . [that] are, in fact, for the purpose of collecting intelligence information for the United States of America, which is determined to launch a new military aggression against Iraq."[22] Few would have surmised then that the targets hit during Operation Desert Fox in December, and the subsequent revelations in the American press about the US infiltration of Unscom, would substantiate Aziz's assertions.

Now that Unscom had installed a monitoring and eavesdropping system in Iraq that worked in tandem with its regional office in Bahrain and that it had found a direct link between Saddam's personal secretary and the SSD to shift or destroy contraband and related documents, Ritter resolved to apprehend the culprits red-handed and pass on the incontrovertible evidence to the Security Council. On their part the Iraqis had fine-tuned their recondite mechanism to the degree that they moved the contraband around every thirty to ninety days and removed or destroyed evidence on fifteen minutes' notice.[23]

Under the circumstances, it was only a matter of time before the two sides would clash again in the open.

Buildup to Operation "Desert Fox"

At the United Nations, Baghdad was helped by the IAEA's six-monthly report on April 13, 1998, which concluded that Iraq had compiled a "full, final and complete account" of its previous nuclear arms projects, and that since its earlier report in October the IAEA's monitoring and verification regime had not revealed "indications of the existence in Iraq of prohibited equipment or materials or of the conduct of prohibited activity."[24] For once, Russia and the United States came together and called on the IAEA to submit a further report to the Security Council. In that document (released on July 4), after reaffirming its earlier conclusion that Iraq did not possess nuclear weapons, the IAEA would bring up the subject of Iraqi nuclear experts, and refer to "Iraq's unwillingness to give the inspectors unfettered access" to them. Describing the issue of Iraq's nuclear specialists as extraneous, Baghdad would demand the IAEA limit itself to long-term monitoring.

The arrival on May 6 of nearly one hundred American peace activists, led by Ramsey Clark, former US attorney general and chairman of the New York–based International Action Committee, in Baghdad, carrying $4 million worth of medicine, including antibiotics and antimalarial drugs, provided a brief cheer for Iraqis.

That there was no light as yet at the end of the tunnel of UN sanctions became apparent to the Iraqi people from the paper, entitled "Necessary Conditions for Resolution of Priority Disarmament Issues," that Butler presented to the Security Council on June 3. It demanded that Baghdad account for special missile warheads and VX, a lethal nerve agent. In the biological field, it must furnish information to enable Unscom to ascertain that the amounts of the ingredients and the final products matched. The paper emphasized that these were "necessary"—not "sufficient"—conditions for Iraq to satisfy in order for sanctions to be eased or ended. Little wonder that Russia, France, and China refused to endorse the document.[25]

To everybody's surprise, Butler's meetings with an Iraqi delegation led by Tariq Aziz in Baghdad on June 13–14 went well. In Butler's words, these resulted in "a measure of agreement" over many issues but not the unaccounted-for five hundred tons of missile rocket fuel and VX. He added that he and Aziz had agreed to a work schedule that could use the road map, outlined in his recent paper to the Security Council, by August, and close Unscom files by October.[26] But there was a caveat. Having addressed the WMD issue fully, Butler then told Aziz that assuming satisfactory progress on all subjects, "we would still need to discuss the Iraqi policy of concealment"—a statement that reportedly infuriated Aziz.[27] Unsurprisingly, Aziz saw Butler, working in collusion with Washington, shifting goalposts in technical and procedural fields—something the US State Department had been doing in diplomatic and political arenas since 1994, first under Christopher and then Albright.[28]

In his report to the Security Council on June 18, Butler noted that Baghdad had refused to deal with VX. Having first denied making VX, Iraq said it produced some for experimental purposes in a laboratory, only to destroy it after having failed to weaponize it or finding a stabilizer for storage. Later, under pressure, it conceded that it had produced 1.7 tons of VX, although not of weapons grade.

Toward the end of the month, Butler informed the Security Council that Unscom had discovered the minutes of an Iraqi meeting at which it was decided to hide evidence relating to mobile missile launchers, and that the files found at the farm of Hussein Kamil Hassan in August 1995 had been put there just before Ekeus's arrival there, rather than previously stored there by the subsequent defector.[29]

When considered together with Butler's earlier insistence on the Iraqi government providing Unscom with details of its concealment policy and mechanism about proscribed weapons, his latest statements showed unmistakably that he wanted to drag out the Unscom mission and thereby hold in abeyance the easing or lifting of the UN embargo on Iraq.

Leaving aside extraneous additions to Unscom's mandate, there was still enough for Butler's teams to do to keep the pot simmering. On July 18 a sixteen-strong team led by Dr. Kraatz-Wadsack inspected Iraqi air force headquarters, a sensitive site, in search of documents to verify the past use of chemical and biological weapons. Having entered the building, she demanded an inspection of the air force command's operations room (an extrasensitive site). She was allowed into the room along with one more inspector and an interpreter. Among the documents stored inside a safe she discovered a file containing a list of four chemical munitions—mustard gas, tabun, sarin, and gas gangrene, *Clostridium perfringens*—used by the air force in the past. She demanded a copy of the document, which her senior Iraqi minder refused, saying she could take notes or have a copy with certain sections censored. When she protested the Iraqi official stopped cooperating. Following several telephone conversations, Butler and Gen. Rashid agreed to seal the document in the presence of Rashid and Kraatz-Wadsack and keep it in the custody of the Iraqi National Monitoring Directorate, pending Butler's visit to Baghdad two weeks later. Meanwhile, assisted by her interpreter, Kraatz-Wadsack discovered that the document listed quantitatively the Iraqi air force's use of chemical weapons during the Iran-Iraq War to a degree not known before.[30]

Complaining that Butler was "focusing on minor issues that make no sense from the angle of disarmament," Aziz told him during their August 3 meeting, "Since this is the wish of the American administration to perpetuate the situation—as long as this is the American wish, you are serving American policy." At their second meeting later that day, Aziz told him, "There is no further work to be done, nor is there any additional information for Iraq to provide concerning its past programs of weapons of mass destruction."

CHAPTERS
Great Books Are Just The Beginning
Chapters Store 964
Chinook S.C. 6455 MacLeod Trail S.#178
Calgary, Alberta T2H 0K9
(403)212-0090 Fax: (403)212-0109

127239 Reg 3 ID 100 3:04 pm 24/02/03

R KING RALPH	-1 @	29.95	-29.95
R 1552634698			
S IRAQ IN THE EYE O	1 @	21.50	21.50
S 1560254777			
SUBTOTAL			-8.45
TAX: GST - 7%			-.59
TOTAL SALES TAX			-.59
TOTAL			-9.04
CASH REFUND			-9.04

Book in mint condition can be returned
for exchange, credit or refund, with
receipt, within 14 days of purchase sale
books, magazines, & opened music
are not returnable GST#R987152666

Butler replied, "You have refused to give us the evidence required to support your claim."[31]

The next day, following a call by the Iraqi Revolutionary Command Council and parliament to end cooperation with Unscom, Saddam decreed that cooperation with Unscom and the IAEA be suspended. But he exempted Unscom's monitoring activities, and so the cameras and sensors installed at suspected weapons sites remained intact. He demanded that Unscom be led by a new Executive Bureau representing equally the permanent members with a chairman chosen on a rotation basis; that Unscom's offices in New York, Bahrain, and Baghdad be reconstituted on the same principle; and that Unscom's headquarters be moved from New York to Geneva or Vienna to insulate it from direct American influence.[32]

Reversing its past policy, the Clinton administration played down the Iraqi move. Describing the latest crisis as "a confrontation between Iraq and the UN," Albright left it to Annan and the Security Council to secure Saddam's turnaround on the subject. Other US officials rationalized Clinton's restraint by describing Unscom as "one tool among many for containing Iraq" and, more significantly, one that had "outlived much of its usefulness."[33] Thus the implication was that Unscom had achieved virtually all that it had set out to do. Yet, for domestic reasons, US policy makers refrained from saying so unambiguously, well aware that being perceived to be soft on Saddam was a political liability.

A highly convincing instance of US home politics impacting on Washington's policy on Iraq was recorded by Scott Ritter in his book, *Endgame*. While he, Charles Duelfer, and Butler were discussing the Annan-Aziz Agreement in Butler's office at the UN in February 1998, denouncing it as a betrayal of Unscom, the phone rang. Butler lifted the receiver. Taking their cue from him, Duelfer and Ritter departed. When they returned, Butler said, "Madeleine [Albright] is very nervous. The heat coming down from [the Republican Senate majority leader] Trent Lott is upsetting the administration. She wants me to hold a press conference and endorse the Kofi Annan agreement [with Aziz]."[34] He did, and it undoubtedly blunted Lott's attack.

It was this direct impingement of US domestic politics on Unscom that would so appall Ritter that he would resign his post on August 26, 1998. He did so in protest of the cancelation of his Unscom 255 by Butler under pressure from Washington, which thought it too confrontational. He claimed that between November 1997 and early August 1998 the Clinton administration had made at least seven attempts to stymie Unscom investigation. "The United States has undermined Unscom's efforts through interference and manipulation, usually coming from the highest levels of the administration's national security team," he said.[35] Ritter's revelations damaged US standing at the Security Council. What had earlier been guessed and expressed privately now emerged as a fact—Washington's interference in and manipulation of Unscom to suit its domestic agenda.

In his six-monthly report on October 6 Butler asserted that, having prevented the disarmament phase of Unscom's mandate from being achieved, Baghdad was now planning to hamper Unscom's monitoring function. His censorious tone was in line with the feelings of the council president of the month, Sir Jeremy Greenstock of Britain. During that month, following a debate on the comprehensive review of sanctions (as promised in the Annan-Aziz agreement), the council asked the Briton to draft a letter to Baghdad, summarizing the discussion. He did so. In it he crucially omitted the timetable for lifting sanctions, repeatedly canvassed by Iraq, on the grounds that council members could not prejudge the outcome of their review in advance of the experts' reports on which it was to be based. This angered Baghdad, which had set its sights on getting the embargo lifted by year's end.

Its chances dimmed when its officials failed to accord full cooperation to a Unscom inspection team in late October 1998. The

Security Council threatened to ban foreign travel by the Iraqi officials interfering with Unscom activities. In return Baghdad decided to expel those ten of the forty Unscom inspectors who were Americans. On October 31 it stopped cooperating with Unscom and the IAEA both in inspecting and monitoring, and demanded a swift comprehensive review of its compliance in disarmament linked to a timetable to lift sanctions.

When the mid-term US congressional elections on November 3 resulted in Clinton's Democrats improving their strength in the House of Representatives, and the Lewinsky cloud having lifted temporarily, Clinton abandoned the stance of downplaying Saddam's defiance he had adopted over the past many months on the basis that he did not want to dance to the Iraqi dictator's tune. Now he raised the temperature and escalated the crisis to the boiling point quickly by not repeating the strategy of educating the American public to win its approval for bombing Iraq, as he had done in February. What further helped him was the fact that the presidency of the Security Council in November rested with the US ambassador to the United Nations, Peter Burleigh.

As before, while the crisis deepened Clinton ordered a military buildup in the Gulf. Only this time he faced a factor that did not exist earlier: a disgruntled Scott Ritter. Since his resignation from Unscom in August, Ritter had regaled the world media with sensational revelations. In an interview with the Israeli newspaper *Ha'aretz* he mentioned Unscom sharing information with Israel, a fact that deeply embarrassed Butler, who now asked Ritter, a *former* Unscom inspector, to shut up.[36] Earlier the same Richard Butler had taken no action against *serving* Unscom inspectors who had made public the information gathered in the course of their work tendentiously in a CNN documentary, "High Noon in Baghdad: The Inspectors' Story," which aired on March 1. This was a blatant violation of the legal agreement between the United Nations and Iraq, which prohibited publication of material collected during inspections or monitoring and despite the fact that Iraq lodged a complaint about the matter with Annan.[37]

In an interview with CNN on November 13, Tariq Aziz repeated his earlier charge that Unscom inspectors were spying for the United States and Israel.

That evening, following deliberations at the Security Council, Annan sent a letter to Saddam, outlining what he had to do to avoid an attack by the United States and Britain, and promising him that once Iraq had resumed its cooperation with Unscom, the council would settle the issue of a comprehensive review of Iraq's disarmament. Other diplomatic sources, meanwhile, told Saddam that the Pentagon would stage its strikes against Iraq within the next twenty-four hours if he failed to back down.

Saddam and Aziz jointly drafted a reply to Annan that was finely balanced between "surrender" (as the US-UK alliance would term it) and "defiance" (as the Iraqis would call it), and attached a nine-point memorandum on a comprehensive review as an annex.

The aim of Iraq's decisions of August 5 and October 31, 1998 was, said the Iraqi letter, signed by Aziz and addressed to Annan, "to end the suffering of its embargoed people and to see the implementation of Paragraph 22 of the Security Council Resolution 687 as a first step for lifting the other sanctions." As regards the initiative on a comprehensive review of the matter, the deliberations of the council "did not result in a clear picture. . . . America objected to the presentation of any clarity in regard to the objective of the comprehensive review." However, in view of Annan's letter, and in order "to give further chance to achieve justice by lifting sanctions, commencing with the implementation of Paragraph 22 . . . the leadership of Iraq decided to resume working with Unscom and the IAEA."

But before Aziz's letter reached the White House, he announced on CNN that his government had decided to let UN inspectors back into Iraq. By then the Pentagon's B-52 bombers, which had taken off from the bases in Louisiana, were within an hour of unleashing their cruise missiles. Informed of Aziz's CNN statement by Sandy Berger, Clinton aborted the mission instantly. Iraqis danced in the streets of their capital.

By November 14 Clinton had unilaterally listed five conditions—including "unfettered access" to inspectors and all relevant documents to be submitted—for accepting Aziz's letter, and warned that if Baghdad did not abide by its latest agreement, the US military would strike Iraq without warning. The next day the Security Council accepted Iraq's various statements as constituting a reversal of its earlier decisions to withdraw cooperation from Unscom and the IAEA.

"Sandy Berger . . . immediately met with Butler to coordinate inspection schedules in the framework of all-but-inevitable military strike[s]," noted Ritter in his book *Endgame*. "Butler had the customary test ready to go, one that he knew would be confrontational. It was a reworking of the Unscom 255 inspection [under me] that had been canceled in August on the grounds that it was too confrontational. Now, however, Butler and Berger knew what they wanted, and the newly numbered Unscom 258 delivered in spades. Delays, blockages, evacuated buildings—the classic pattern of Iraqi obstruction—were all provoked and catalogued. . . . Butler appeared to have forgotten that he was a servant of the Security Council, not the United States. The Butler-Berger hand-in-glove relationship during Unscom 258 was too cozy. Prior coordination, daily Butler-to-Berger situation updates during the inspection, and a mutual review of Butler's report before its submission to the [UN] secretary-general infringed on the Security Council's powers."[38]

Unscom 258, arriving in Baghdad, was headed by an Australian, Col. Roger Hill. Between November 18 and 25, it undertook twenty-five inspections. On November 19 the Iraqis refused to hand over unconditionally certain documents that were demanded. The following day, Butler released a list of twelve demands for documents and the responses of Riyadh al Qaisi, an Iraqi foreign ministry official.

The list included (a) the minutes of the meetings of the Iraqi High Level Committee on the Retention of Banned Weapons and Materials formed in June 1991; (b) a report on Iraq's investigation of Gen. Hussein Kamil Hassan and his concealment of banned weapons capabilities and documents; and (c) the document detailing the Iraqi air force's use of chemical weapons during the Iran-Iraq War that Kraatz-Wadsack had seen in the air force command's operations room on July 18, 1998. Regarding (a), al Qaisi replied that the IAEA had earlier made this request and had been told that "there was no such committee in the technical sense of the word." On (b), he said that the Iraqi government did not formally investigate Hussein Kamil Hassan's defection. On (c), he expressed Iraq's readiness to disclose "relevant portions" of the said document in the presence of Prakash Shah, the special envoy of Annan in Baghdad.[39]

At the Security Council there was a growing consensus among the Russian, French, and Chinese diplomats that Iraq's disarmament was practically finished, and that the comprehensive review should be completed by Christmas and the embargo on oil lifted, leaving only financial sanctions in place. Their view was shared by Annan's senior advisers. "You can never have 100 percent proof disarmament because it is too easy to develop, manufacture and hide biological weapons, so at some point technical exercise gives way to political judgment," an adviser to Annan told Barton Gellman of the *Washington Post* on November 21. "At some point it becomes impossible to prove the negative."[40]

Pressured by Russia, France, and China at the Security Council, Butler began submitting weekly reports, starting December 4, the day Unscom initiated a series of inspections in Iraq. Between December 4 and 9, the Iraqis barred Unscom 261, a biological team, from inspecting one site, and a chemical weapons team from taking pictures of a bomb. They blocked the inspection of the headquarters of the Iraqi Baath Party, which was suspected of harboring missile parts.[40] Butler canceled the inspections due on December 12–13, after handing over his second weekly report to the Security Council on December 11.

That day Butler had a meeting with Berger at the American mission to the United Nations near the UN headquarters. Their common aim was to manipulate the fast-moving situation in a way that would provide the United States with a credible basis for bombing Iraq against the background of imminent impeachment proceedings against President Clinton. Berger then joined Clinton and his entourage on their way to Israel and the Palestinian Territories. Having collected highly confidential information about the inner workings of Saddam's regime—most of it by infiltrating Unscom—the Clinton administration was eager to use it to impress on Saddam his vulnerability, and to warn him of more punitive action if he threatened afresh the neighboring states. On Sunday, December 13, Butler handed over the first draft of his report on Iraq (meant for the Security Council) to senior American diplomats at the UN, who communicated it immediately to Clinton, then in Israel. Finding it weak, Clinton advised that it be stiffened. At a midnight meeting with Berger he revived the US strike plans against Iraq that were to be code-named Operation Desert Fox. The next day the *Washington Post* reported that US officials had played "a direct role in shaping Butler's text during multiple conversations with him at secure facilities at the US mission to the United Nations."

On December 15 Peter Burleigh, the US ambassador to the United Nations, "advised" Butler to withdraw all UN inspectors, monitors, and support staff from Iraq immediately.[42] Butler did so, without bothering even to inform the Security Council. At 6 P.M. EST, he delivered to Annan his ten-page report—prepared in close consultation with US officials from Clinton downward—which concluded that Iraq was not cooperating with Unscom. Three hours later, news agencies put out a summary of his report. Aside from the United States, the council members saw the news agencies' story *before* receiving their own copies of the Butler report.

On the morning of Wednesday, December 16, all US television news bulletins led with the Iraqi story just as the national interest was focused on the impeachment debate in the House of Representatives due the following day. House Democrat leaders urged their Republican counterparts to postpone the impeachment debate as long as the US commander in chief, President Clinton, was leading a war with Iraq. Conscious that the bombing could be an open-ended operation, extending beyond Christmas and the official end of the tenure of the House in January, and anxious to wind up the House business a week before Christmas, Republican leaders agreed to a deferral of just twenty-four hours. Later that day, the bombing of Iraq started at 3:12 P.M. EST, with Clinton addressing the nation on television on the subject a few hours later.

On Friday, December 18, the two-day debate on impeachment started in the House of Representatives. After sunset the Muslim holy month of Ramadan began, with no respite in the nighttime bombing of Iraq. The following day the House impeached Clinton at 1:30 P.M. EST on the first article—perjury before a Grand Jury—and again on the third article—obstruction of justice—half an hour later, thus preparing the ground for the case to go to the US Senate, which had the final authority to dismiss him.

At 4:30 P.M. Clinton stopped the bombing of Iraq after one hundred hours. By then the Pentagon had fired 415 cruise missiles, 90 more than in the Gulf War, and dropped 600 laser-guided bombs.[43]

Once Clinton's wily strategy to manipulate the Butler report to get the House Republicans to postpone the impeachment debate failed, the House vote went against him against the background of sharply rising anti-American sentiment in the Middle East. With anti-American demonstrations in Cairo, Rabat, Tripoli, Amman, Beirut, and Damascus—and even in Muscat, the first such event in the history of Oman—he halted the strikes within three hours of the impeachment ballot.

The Pentagon claimed to have struck seventy-five of the one

hundred targeted sites, including the headquarters of the Military Intelligence, the Special Security Directorate, the Special Republican Guard and the Baath Party National (i.e., Pan-Arab) Command. However, the local authorities had evacuated all likely targets, including Baghdad University's science laboratories and the SSD headquarters, in the hours preceding the bombardment as soon as Saddam ordered immediate "evasive action" and devolved power to four trusted deputies in as many regions as Iraq was divided. "The initial [US] assertions of significant damage inflicted on Iraq appears to be an awkward combination of propaganda and complete rubbish," said Anthony H. Cordesman, an American military analyst. "No change in Iraqi politics or Saddam's behavior should be expected. He has shown the Iraqis, the Gulf and the world that he can survive another US attack."[44]

While Operation Desert Fox lent credibility to Clinton's repeated threats of force, and showed once more the superiority of the US military-intelligence apparatus, which accomplished its objective of striking enemy targets without causing many civilian casualties, he lost considerable political-diplomatic ground in the region and the Security Council. This was aptly encapsulated by the public approval that Kuwait, the most pro-American of the Gulf monarchies, gave to the end of the bombing.

The end results of the Washington-led air strikes (with token participation by London) were to end the Unscom regime; reinforce divisions among the permanent members; alienate Annan from the US-UK axis; precipitate damaging revelations of the American intelligence agencies' infiltration of Unscom in the US press; highlight the diminishing backing in the region for military action against Baghdad, making it harder for Washington to claim in the future that its unilateral actions are taken on behalf of the world community; sharpen anti-American feelings in the Arab world; and move the issue of anti-Iraq sanctions to the top of the Security Council's agenda.

SECURITY COUNCIL RESOLUTION 1284 (1999)

The division that Operation Desert Fox caused among the permanent members was so deep that it took a whole year to draft and debate a follow-up resolution to replace inter alia Unscom. Even then, France, Russia, and China abstained when Resolution 1284 was put to a vote in December 1999. Gone was the P5 unanimity that the permanent members had shown so far on Iraq on major issues.

When Britain and the Netherlands presented a draft resolution, prepared in collaboration with the United States but without any consultation with Iraq, to the Security Council on December 11, 1999, the objections raised by Russia, France, and China were so vehement that the council's British president, Jeremy Greenstock, fearing a veto by one of them, thrice postponed the vote. Considering the concessions made by the drafters as marginal, the non-Anglo-American trio among the permanent members, backed by Malaysia, abstained in the vote taken on December 17.

Like its all-inclusive predecessor 687, the thirty-nine-clause Resolution 1284 was passed under Chapter VII of the UN Charter. Section A, dealing with disarmament, replaced Unscom with a new UN Monitoring, Verification, and Inspection Commission (Unmovic), charging it with setting up and operating "a reinforced system of ongoing monitoring and verification . . ." and addressing "unresolved disarmament issues" and identifying "additional sites in Iraq to be covered by the reinforced system of ongoing monitoring and verification." From the day they started operating in Iraq, Unmovic and the IAEA were to be given sixty days within which to produce a work program for the discharge of their mandates, which would include "the key remaining disarmament tasks to be completed by Iraq," and it was stipulated that "each task shall be clearly defined and precise." Also, Unmovic staff were to become international civil servants, to be recruited from the broadest possible geographical base, and to be different from their Unscom predecessors, personnel who were loaned temporarily by member-states.

Section C dealt with economic sanctions and the related oil-for-food scheme. It authorized member-states to "permit the import of any volume of petroleum and petroleum products originating in Iraq," thus removing the ceiling on Iraqi oil exports immediately. It also eased procedures for Iraq to "import foodstuffs, pharmaceutical and medical supplies, as well as basic or standard medical and agricultural equipment and basic or standard educational items."

The final section outlined conditions and modalities for suspending sanctions. On receiving reports from the heads of Unmovic and the IAEA that "Iraq has cooperated in all respects with Unmovic and the IAEA in particular in fulfilling the work programs in all the aspects referred to in Paragraph 7 above . . . [and] the reinforced system of ongoing monitoring and verification is fully operational," the Security Council expressed "its intention" to suspend sanctions for 120 days—so read Paragraph 33. And Paragraph 35 stated that if the Unmovic or IAEA chief reported that Iraq was "not cooperating in all respects with Unmovic or the IAEA" or if Iraq was "in the process of acquiring any prohibited items," the suspension of sanctions shall terminate on the fifth working day following the report. Paragraph 38 reaffirmed the Security Council's intention to "act in accordance with the relevant provisions of Resolution 687 (1991) on the termination of prohibitions," which *inter alia* included a satisfactory outcome regarding Kuwait's missing personnel and property.

For Iraq, Resolution 1284 was a mixed bag. On the positive side, on disarmament, an open-ended search for banned weapons was to be replaced by specific demands on Iraq. While oil exports were delinked from disarmament, the sales were still to be administered by the United Nations, which curtailed Iraq's economic and political sovereignty. The Security Council's wish to see Iraq's petroleum industry recover fully from the ravages of the Gulf War and sanctions had to do with the rising global demand for oil, particularly in the United States. On the negative side, since 1284 was adopted under Section VII of the UN Charter, it gave the member-states the option of using force to implement it. Also, Iraq had to readmit Unmovic and IAEA inspectors, agree to "a reinforced system of ongoing monitoring and verification," address "unresolved disarmament issues," and "identify additional sites in Iraq to be covered by the reinforced system of ongoing monitoring and verification." Most significantly, the latest document mentioned only a temporary suspension of the embargo. And the basis for that—Iraq cooperating "in all respects"— was far too vague. It compared unfavorably with Paragraph 22 of Resolution 687, which stated that once the council had agreed that "Iraq had completed all actions contemplated in Paragraphs 8, 9, 10, 11, 12, and 13 above, the prohibitions . . . contained in Resolution 661 (1990) shall have no further force or effect."

Not surprisingly the Iraqi government repeated in essence what the ruling Baath Party organ, Al Thawra (The Revolution), had said earlier: "We cannot tolerate the impact of the sanctions and the spies at the same time. But unjust sanctions are easier to tolerate than spies and their recurrent and concocted crises to prolong sanctions."[45] Saddam had no illusions about an end to economic sanctions. "We have said that the embargo will not be lifted by Security Council resolution but will corrode by itself," he said in his address on the seventy-ninth anniversary of the country's Army Day on January 5, 2000. "The corrosion has already started."[46] As the year progressed, his statement would be taken seriously at home and abroad.

Among those who were unimpressed by 1284 was Hans von Sponeck. Considering it insufficient to address the humanitarian needs of Iraqis, he resigned his post in mid-February. "My commitment is for the Iraqi people as a group of deprived people whose tragedy should end," he told the Doha-based Al Jazeera Television. He repeated his earlier remark that deprivation in Iraq was also partly due to "a tightly controlled state with many limitations."[47]

In Washington, seventy members of the US Congress addressed an open letter to Clinton, asking him to do "what is right: lift the economic sanctions." They cited the UN estimates that over one million civilians, mostly children, had died due to sanctions, and added, "Morally it is wrong to hold the Iraqi people responsible for the actions of a brutal and reckless government." They urged the president "to delink economic and military sanctions against Baghdad." But Clinton ignored the plea.

In July 2000 Unmovic boss Hans Blix, former IAEA director-general, announced that Unmovic's forty-four inspectors from nineteen countries were to undergo a monthlong training at New York's Columbia University to familiarize themselves with the historical, legal, administrative, and political aspects of inspections and monitoring, and become "sensitive" to Iraqi culture. As the end of this course neared—and with it the scheduled date for the deployment of a small Unmovic team in Iraq—Tariq Aziz said, "Iraq will not receive any person who has a relationship with Resolution 1284 and its results; Iraq will not cooperate."[49]

When Blix presented his draft report for the Security Council to his College of Commissioners for review, four of the five permanent members—including the United States—advised him to change his conclusion. They suggested that instead of saying that Unmovic was "now in a position to start activities in Iraq," he should say that "the arms experts could plan and commence preliminary tasks to prepare for future inspections." Explaining this, a senior US official stressed that Unmovic was not yet ready to mount a full-scale program in Iraq. In an astounding reversal of roles on Iraqi disarmament, Washington lined up with Moscow. "The US and Russia agreed that it was not appropriate to give the impression that Mr. Blix and the Commission were ready to go back into Iraq [as] this might create a climate of confrontation at an inappropriate time," explained a Security Council diplomat. So half of the forty-four trained inspectors went home.[50]

From the Clinton administration's viewpoint, the timing was inopportune to confront Saddam for the following reason: a shortage of oil in the global market provided the Iraqi president a leverage he did not possess before, and any face-off with him would highlight the fact that there had been no inspections for banned arms in Iraq since December 1998, which would hurt Democrat Al Gore's electoral chances on November 7, 2000.

Though Gore obtained half a million votes more than George Walker Bush, he secured fewer electoral college votes than his rival, and lost the election. With Dick Cheney, who had served as defense secretary during the Gulf War, becoming the new vice president, and Colin Powell, who had been chairman of the joint chiefs of military staff during the Gulf War, appointed secretary of state, it seemed Saddam was being revisited by the old ghosts.

Within weeks of assuming the presidency, Bush Jr. authorized the Pentagon to strike targets outside the southern air exclusion zone on the basis that the Iraqi government was about to link parts of its air defense system with the freshly installed fiber-optic network, thus improving its chance of hitting the US and UK aircraft patrolling the two no fly zones. On February 16, 2001 the Pentagon struck five Iraqi air defense targets above the 33rd parallel, killing three people. In their briefings the defense ministries in Washington and London first accused Iraq of having upgraded its air defense system, and then said that it was on the verge of doing so.

Criticism of the United States came from all Arab states, except Kuwait, with Saudi Arabia adopting an equivocal stance. The popular belief among Arabs was that Bush Jr. had manufactured the pretext of the upgrading of Iraq's air defenses to punish Saddam for the vocal and material support he was providing the four-month-old Palestinian intifada. By conferring on Saddam the image of a victim, Bush unwittingly boosted his already high standing among Palestinians. "A youthful countenance of Mr. Saddam smiles from posters pasted on walls, taped to store windows and waved aloft at funerals," reported Molly Moore of the *Washington Post* from the West Bank city of Ramallah. "In public opinion polls, Mr. Saddam . . . has consistently outpolled the Palestinian leader, Yasser Arafat."

CHAPTER 7

IRAQ AND THE REGION

Traveling along the Amman-Baghdad highway through the Badiyat al Shama Desert for several hours in the heat of a summer day can play tricks with one's vision, and make one susceptible to seeing a mirage. What else could have explained that as the Qadisiya complex of the border town of Traibeel came within my view, I saw an enormous portrait of Shaikh Jaber III al Ahmad al Sabah in a white robe and an Arab headdress suppressing a smile under his luxurious mustache. I rubbed my eyes. Was I on my way to Kuwait? No, I was en route to Iraq. As my Jordanian taxi neared the Iraqi frontier, however, I realized that the giant figure adorning the border post was none other than President Saddam Hussein dressed in traditional Arab garb. Why he had chosen to present himself as a nomadic Arab to the travelers approaching his country from the west puzzled me.

Perhaps he wanted his portrait to fit the surrounding desert and its nomadic bedouin. Or maybe by projecting the traditional Arab image he wished to highlight the fact that Iraq is the easternmost boundary of the Arab world stretching as far west as Mauritania on the Atlantic. Beyond Iraq's eastern frontier lies Iran, a Persian-speaking country. And to its north is Turkey, another non-Arab state. Such a geographical position has made Iraqis more imbued with Arab nationalism than virtually any other Arab nation.

It has also made Iraq more strategically important than most other members of the Arab League, with common borders with four Arab countries and two non-Arab. On the other hand, of all the littoral states of the Gulf, Iraq has the shortest shoreline, a mere fifty-four miles, a grave handicap to Iraqi leaders" ambition to be regarded as a major player in the Gulf region.

One of the goals behind Saddam's invasion and occupation of Kuwait and its offshore Warba and Bubiyan Islands in 1990 was to elongate Iraq's meager shoreline. The dispute between Kuwait and Iraq, however, had a long history. Indeed, the 1990 crisis was the second during the latter half of the twentieth century, the first occurring in 1961. Both were centered around the identity of Kuwait vis-à-vis Iraq. So long as both Kuwait and Mesopotamia (meaning Baghdad and Basra provinces) were part of the Ottoman Empire, the status of Kuwait as a subprovince of Basra was fairly clear. In 1913, yielding to pressure by the British, who maintained an important trading post in Kuwait, the Ottomans recognized Kuwait as "an autonomous administrative unit" of their empire. But this arrangement fell victim to the 1914–18 world war, and this allowed the British to declare Kuwait to be "an independent shaikhdom under British protectorate."

The disintegration of the Ottoman Empire in 1918, followed by the emergence of Iraq as an independent state in 1932, briefly revived the issue of Kuwait's status when the nationalist King Ghazi occupied the throne in Iraq. After the overthrow of the pro-British Iraqi monarchy in 1958, differences between the Arab nationalist Baghdad and the British-protected Kuwait were accentuated. When Kuwait became independent in June 1961, Iraqi leader Abdul Karim Qasim demanded that it revert back to being part of the Basra province. To meet this threat, Kuwait appealed to the Arab League and also sought Britain's help. The immediate arrival of British troops, who were soon succeeded by the Egyptians, forced Qasim to back down.

Within two decades the situation had changed so radically that Kuwait lined up with Iraq in its battle with the newly emergent Islamic Republic of Iran, which regarded monarchy as un-Islamic.

That enabled Baghdad to claim that it was fighting for "the Arab homeland," meaning all of the Arab world, and claiming that Iranians were foes of all Arabs.

The bankrolling of Iraq's war effort came not only from the governments of the Gulf monarchies but also their subjects. The kingdom most generous to Iraq was Saudi Arabia. It parted with $20–25 billion in cash and oil during the Iran-Iraq conflict. Unlike Kuwait, it did not demand a return of the money after the war. In 1989 it went on to sign a Non-Aggression Pact with Iraq, which stipulated the principles of "non-interference in the internal affairs of the two sisterly countries" and "non-use of force and armies between the two states."

Following Baghdad's invasion of Kuwait in August 1990, when the United States warned Riyadh of Iraq's aggressive designs on the Saudi kingdom, Saddam continually referred to the 1989 Non-Aggression Pact but to no avail.

Indeed Saudi Arabia provided multifaceted facilities to the US-led coalition, which stationed the bulk of its troops on Saudi soil, and without which the Gulf War would have lasted much longer. Besides the Gulf monarchies, Syria and Egypt joined the coalition. So did Turkey. Unlike Egypt and Syria, Jordan maintained neutrality in the conflict, with a pro-Baghdad tilt. This had partly to do with economics. During the long Iran-Iraq War, when the Iraqi ports in the Gulf became inoperable, the Jordanian port of Aqaba became the main sea outlet for Iraq. Jordan's economy became integrated into Iraq's. Before and during the Gulf War, open backing for Saddam came from the Palestine Liberation Organization (PLO) and Yasser Arafat. The Iraqi Baathists had all along been strong supporters of the Palestinian cause, and (as was shown in chapter 2) the history of independent Iraq had been molded by the events in Palestine and then Israel. The Baathists were such anti-Zionists that they persisted in refusing to call Israel by its name, choosing instead "the Zionist entity." Israel reciprocated. In a daring act, Israel destroyed the two

French-built nuclear reactors at Tuweitha on June 7, 1981. This left a deep scar on the psyche of Saddam and his government. They resolved never to let such a thing happen again, and directed much of their military strategic thinking toward that end. This explains why Iraq was able to withstand almost continuous bombing for forty-three days by the Pentagon during the 1991 Gulf War.

During that conflict, while staying out of the Washington-led alliance, Tehran complied strictly with the UN resolutions against Iraq.

After the war, as the UN embargo impoverished Iraqis, the anti-Iraq front that Riyadh had forged in the Arab Gulf broke down in the spring of 1995, with Qatar, Oman, and the United Arab Emirates calling for an easing of sanctions against Baghdad to alleviate the suffering of the Iraqi people. Sympathy for Iraqis remained high in Jordan, which, with UN permission, continued to receive its oil needs of 75,000 barrels per day from Iraq, half of it free, and the rest at the fixed price of $18 a barrel. Turkey's stance toward Baghdad revolved around the issue of the Kurdish problem that existed within its boundaries and also in Iraqi Kurdistan. With most of its 12 million Kurds concentrated in the southeastern sector and agitating for autonomy, Ankara was loath to see Kurds in neighboring Iraqi Kurdistan progress toward autonomy, much less independence, which in their view would encourage irredentism among Turkish Kurds. As part of the Gulf War coalition, Turkey allowed its Incirlik air base to be used for strikes against Iraq. The base was later used as the staging post for American, British, and French warplanes to keep Iraq above the 36th parallel under constant aerial surveillance and enforce a no fly zone for the aircraft of the Baghdad government.

Ankara noted, with deep concern, the holding of elections to the regional parliament in May 1992 independent of Baghdad, viewing it as a first step toward the founding of an independent Kurdistan in northern Iraq. The intra-Kurdish violence that erupted two years later in Iraqi Kurdistan pleased Turkey—as did the failure of the Kurdish leaders to conduct fresh elections due in May 1996. Regarding the continued sanctions against Iraq, Ankara considered the contraband sale of much-needed Iraqi oil to the Turkish traders as poor compensation for the damage done to its economy due to the loss of lucrative trade with Iraq, which until then had been its largest trading partner. It would estimate its loss at $38 billion by the end of the decade.

In August–September 1996, Turkey quietly welcomed another bout of intra-Kurdish bloodletting. The five-year-old autonomous Iraqi Kurdish area had inspired the separatist Turkish Partiye Karkeran Kurdistan (PKK, Kurdistan Workers Party), which had been conducting an armed struggle against Ankara since 1984 and using the Iraqi Kurdistan as its rear base. Small wonder Turkey refused to let the Clinton administration use its air bases to hit targets in northern Iraq, compelling it to do so in the South.

Once the UN oil-for-food scheme was under way in December 1996, Jordan became even more closely integrated into the Iraqi economy. Having actively cooperated with Washington in planning an anti-Saddam coup for nearly a year, King Hussein of Jordan did a U-turn just before the UN program got going by holding a much-publicized meeting with Iraqi foreign minister Muhammad al Sahhaf in Amman. He thereby pleased the local business community keen to have a share of the increased Iraqi trade.

In Turkey, after having renewed the six-month mandate for the Western "Operation Provide Comfort" ten times, the parliament allowed it to lapse on December 31, 1996. It then adopted a six-month mandate for the foreign Reconnaissance Force (*Keshif Gucu*, in Turkish), which Washington and London renamed "Operation Northern Watch." By then France had withdrawn from the surveillance exercise out of disgust at the endemic intra-Kurdish violence.

According to Turks and others, there was much difference between Operations "Provide Comfort" and "Northern Watch." The former had both aerial and ground components—with US, British, and French ground forces and intelligence agents posted at the

Turkish border town of Zakho, and a publicly acknowledged aim of overthrowing Saddam's regime. But the US evacuation of several thousand Iraqi Arabs and Kurds—who had collaborated with the United States, Britain, and France—from northern Iraq in September 1996 meant an end to any ground presence. The aerial freedom that the three Western powers had enjoyed under Operation "Provide Comfort" was reduced. Turkey's new rules of engagement required that the Reconnaissance Force be led jointly by US and Turkish commanders, and that the US-UK aircraft refrain from any offensive action and deploy arms only in self-defense and only after the identity of the threatening plane had been confirmed and its pilot warned to turn back.[1] While the northern air surveillance operation was conducted by the US European Command based in Stuttgart, Germany, the southern one was staged by the US Central Command (Centcom) based at MacDill Air Force Base near Tampa, Florida, which maintained the Fifth Fleet headquarters in Bahrain, and had 24,000 troops in the Gulf, with almost half of them stationed on Kuwaiti and Saudi soils. Its planes took off from the US aircraft carriers and the bases in Kuwait and Saudi Arabia.

By the spring of 1997 the balance of power had shifted gradually in Saddam's favor after the failure of the several attempts by the CIA and Iraqi opposition to overthrow him. This had discouraged the United States' regional allies to let the Pentagon use their territory for military strikes against Iraq. Well aware that they shared the same region as Iraq, they did not want to stoke up Baghdad's hostility by participating in covert or overt actions against its regime. The Gulf rulers were also conscious of the growing sympathy for impoverished Iraqis shown by their subjects, who compared unfavorably the United States' uncompromisingly harsh treatment of Iraq with its indulgent stance toward Israel, which over the past decades had ignored or flagrantly violated a series of Security Council resolutions with impunity.

Having concluded by the fall of 1997 that many military and intelligence officials seconded to Unscom by Washington would persist in finding reasons, however specious or extraneous, to show Iraq's non-cooperation to suit the Clinton administration's agenda, Saddam focused on reducing the pro-US bias of Unscom in personnel and equipment, and demanding that lifting of sanctions should be decided within the context of Resolution 687, and that alone.

Simultaneously, to highlight the damage done to Iraqis by the economic embargo, he attempted to bring the issue out of the Security Council portals and into the streets and bazaars of the Middle East—an aim he would realize to the full, he calculated, if the Pentagon were to attack Iraq. Furthermore, he correctly reckoned, Washington's military action would jeopardize what it was keen to save—an ongoing monitoring regime. In this he was helped—albeit inadvertently—by the report published by the World Health Organization (WHO) in the fall of 1997. It said that over 500,000 Iraqi children under five had died as a result of malnutrition and lack of medicine caused by the UN embargo. (The Iraqi health ministry's statistics were twice as high.) This weighed heavily on the consciences of the Arab publics and governments. The warmth with which Tariq Aziz was received in the capitals of Morocco, Egypt, Jordan, and Syria, en route to Baghdad after a diplomatic trip to Moscow, showed Arab opinion shifting in favor of Iraq, a worrisome prospect for the Clinton administration.

Small wonder that when Baghdad-Washington tension rose in November 1997, Kuwaiti foreign minister Shaikh Sabah al Ahmad al Sabah told his US counterpart, Madeleine Albright, that his country was opposed to any military action against Baghdad as it would harm the Iraqi people. His stand was shared publicly by Egypt, Syria, and Bahrain. Earlier, Saudi Arabia had announced that it did not want its air bases to be used for bombing Iraq.[2]

Had Clinton ignored the disunity among the permanent members at the Security Council as well as official advice from his Arab allies, and acted unilaterally against Iraq, he would have ended up confirming Saddam's claim that the dispute was between Baghdad and

Washington, and not between Baghdad and the United Nations. So, when Russian president Boris Yeltsin offered to mediate in the dispute, Clinton gave him a green light. Yeltsin managed to defuse the crisis.

The next month Saddam was invited by Iran, chairing the fifty-four-member Islamic Conference Organization (ICO) in Tehran, to attend the summit. He chose not to go, and sent Izzat Ibrahim, his deputy at the Revolutionary Command Council. The Iranian invitation implied an important step toward normalization between the two onetime foes.

When a fresh crisis arose between Iraq and the United States in February 1998, the ICO, based in the Saudi port city of Jiddah, warned, "Military action against Iraq will bring a new catastrophe with incalculable consequences for the region."

So it came as no surprise when Albright drew a blank in Riyadh in her effort to gain support for US military action against Iraq. "There are those in Saudi Arabia who would grant the US use of Saudi facilities; there are also those who would refuse; and still others who want to see all Americans leave the kingdom," Crown Prince Abdullah, the effective ruler of the kingdom since late 1995 (when King Fahd fell seriously ill), reportedly told Albright. "Since I represent all these people, I am obliged to say 'no' to the use of Saudi facilities for attacks on Iraq." He also asked why the United States was all set to deploy force against Iraq for failing to implement a few Security Council resolutions when Israel not merely violated with impunity many Security Council resolutions but also refused to honor its internationally guaranteed treaty commitments to the Palestinians. "Saudi Arabia will not allow any strikes against Iraq under any circumstances from its soil due to the sensitivity of the issue in the Arab and Muslim world," said the official communiqué after the meeting.[3] Later, on the eve of the arrival of US defense secretary William Cohen in Riyadh, Saudi defense minister Prince Sultan told the Jiddah-based *Arab News*, "We are against striking Iraq as a people and as a nation."[4] This happened against the backdrop of resumption of commercial links between the Saudi kingdom and Iraq, with Saudi companies signing up $100 million contracts with Baghdad for supplying food and medicine within the UN framework.[5]

The position of the United Arab Emirates had been reaffirmed earlier by its president, Shaikh Zaid ibn Sultan al Nahyan, who had proposed that a decision on accepting Iraq's return to the Arab League as a normal member be reached by a majority vote rather than the customary consensus. "Let us tell this man [Saddam Hussein] that you have erred towards us," he said, "but we now tell you 'Welcome back as a faithful brother.' "[6]

Little wonder that the UAE did not figure in the predominantly Western list of 20 countries that sided with Washington against Baghdad. Nor did Syria, which had joined the anti-Iraq coalition in the Gulf War, appear on the list.

In fact, in May 1998, a Syrian trade delegation visited Baghdad, the first sign of a thaw between the two neighbors, who had broken off diplomatic ties seventeen years earlier at the start of the Iran-Iraq War when Damascus sided with Tehran. Three months later Syria and Iraq signed agreements to reopen the Kirkuk-Banias pipeline with 1.4 million bpd capacity, once the UN sanctions had been lifted, and to build a new pipeline with an enhanced capacity. Because of the shorter distance, using this pipeline was half as costly as using the Kirkuk-Yumurtalik line.

When, in October 1998, encouraged by the freshly passed Iraq Liberation Act, the Clinton administration announced plans to bring about "regime change" in Baghdad, a word of caution came from one of its leading longtime allies, Egypt. Alluding to the anti-Baghdad activities of the US and UK intelligence agencies, President Hosni Mubarak said, "These projects won't get anywhere. Anyone who knows Iraq knows no action will succeed if it isn't led from the inside, by people living in Iraq."[7]

In late January 1999 on her visits to Cairo and Riyadh to spell out to the Egyptian and Saudi leaders the details of the new, proactive US policy on Baghdad, Albright took along Frank Ricciardone, the newly appointed "Special Representative for the Transition in Iraq" to coordinate Iraqi opposition efforts. Her hosts' response was not publicized. But the London-based Arabic newspapers *Al Sharq al Awsat* and *Al Hayat*, owned by senior Saudi princes, said that Saudi Arabia opposed any foreign role in changing the Iraqi regime and that any change "should take place from within Iraq and by the people themselves."[8]

Later, senior officials from Qatar, Oman, and the UAE were not so diplomatic after being briefed on the subject by Martin Indyk, assistant secretary of state for the Near East. Fearing rifts and civil war in Iraq in case a regime change was imposed on the country from outside, they told Indyk that any external interference would not be in the interests of anybody.[9]

After his meetings with Albright and Cohen, UAE president al Nahyan made public his refusal to join Washington's campaign to overthrow Saddam. "The present US policy of containment is harming the Iraqi people without weakening Saddam Hussein," a source close to al Nahyan told the London-based *Middle East International*. "There is even evidence that sanctions are strengthening the regime. Iraq is too central, too powerful and too important to be treated this way."[10]

Iran's position was outlined by Hamid Bayati, the London representative of the Tehran-based Supreme Assembly of Islamic Revolution in Iraq, when he said that the task of overthrowing the Saddam regime should be left to the Iraqi people working "independently in their own ways."[11]

Another issue on which regional sentiment ran against the United States was the imposition of the air exclusion zones on the government in Baghdad. The subject came up for debate when, in February 1999, Iraq decided to challenge the no fly zones, which led to periodic firing of Iraqi antiaircraft guns at the US and UK warplanes in both zones, and at least one air duel. The last time the South had witnessed such a confrontation was in 1993.

Opposition to the air exclusion zones in Iraq was aired by some members of the six-strong Gulf Cooperation Council (GCC). Appearing along with William Cohen during his visit to Doha in March 1999, Qatari foreign minister Shaikh Hamad ibn Jassim al Thani criticized the Pentagon's strikes in the Iraqi no fly zones. Later that month the Arab League called for "an immediate halt to all military activity against Iraq which is only worsening the situation."[12]

Washington took no notice. In fact, in mid-August 1999 US and UK warplanes went on to strike Iraqi targets outside the air exclusion zones. This led France, still basking in the glory of its participation in the successful US-led NATO campaign in the Kosovo region of Serbia, to protest vehemently. It worked, and the Anglo-American alliance quietly reverted to the original parameters of its operation. To mask its embarrassment at the turn of events, the Pentagon revealed that over the past eight months the Anglo-American air forces had fired over 1,100 missiles at 359 Iraqi targets—more than three times the number during Operation Desert Fox in December 1998.

The United States cited Security Council Resolution 688 (April 1991) to rationalize its behavior. But there was no mention of air exclusion zones in that document. Indeed, as the resolution was not passed under Chapter VII of the UN Charter, it did not authorize use of force by a UN member-state to implement it. When challenged on the specifics, the United States argued that its action was "derivative" of Paragraph 6 of Resolution 688, which appealed "to all Member States and to all humanitarian organizations to contribute to these humanitarian relief efforts" for the Kurdish refugees caused by the failure of the Kurdish uprising after the Gulf War. How humanitarian relief was furthered by stretching an air umbrella over a region remained unclear.

In any case, even that sort of reasoning could not rationalize "Operation Southern Watch," which was imposed in August 1992— sixteen months after Resolution 688 was adopted. After consulting the British and French leaders, George Bush Sr. had decided to impose an air exclusion zone in the South to safeguard the Shias there. This had more to do with Bush punishing Saddam for his long standoff with Unscom on disarmament in the previous month than it had to do with protecting southern Shias.

The Pentagon's standard statement that "the purpose of the no fly zone [in southern Iraq] is to ensure the safety of Coalition aircraft monitoring compliance with United Nations Security Council Resolution 688" was a typical example of a circular argument. The fact that enforcing an air exclusion zone in the South did not stop Baghdad's ground-based attacks on the southern marshes, which were providing refuge to Iraqi fugitives, underlined Washington's lack of concern for civilians.

"International law as created and interpreted through the Security Council is an approximate process," noted Sarah Graham-Brown, a British specialist on Iraq, in her book *Sanctioning Saddam*. "The fact that there was no challenge to the use of force, some argue, constitutes de facto international acceptance that the terms of the resolution allow for it. Essentially, as one informed source put it, by dint of political power the main Coalition states (the US, the UK and France) won the day and established a precedent."[13] Of the two air exclusion zones, the southern one, costing four-and-a-half times more than the northern, had nothing to with protecting civilians.[14] But it had proved strategically valuable to Washington. The Pentagon perceived it as a means of denying Baghdad the opportunity to train its pilots in the southern Iraqi airspace and as a source of intelligence input in its early-warning system. In patrolling this zone, it had the support of Riyadh and Kuwait, which footed the bill for the aircraft fuel and accommodation for the pilots and the ground staff, and which earned them Saddam's continuing ire.

But most of the Iraqi sites that the US air force kept striking were in the North, and almost all of them near Mosul, the third largest city in Iraq. A glance at a map explained why this was so and underscored the illogic of the Western decision to impose a no fly zone above the 36th parallel to protect the Kurds. Whereas almost half of the territory and the population of the predominantly Kurdish Kurdistan Autonomous Region were below this parallel, the area above it contained a vast swath of the overwhelmingly Arab sector of Iraq, with Mosul as its main city. This territory was administered by the Iraqi government, which maintained a large military garrison and many air defense sites in and around Mosul.

That the real reason for maintaining the air exclusion zones in the North and the South was political, rather than humanitarian, became public when Albright said in November 1999, "I believe that through our . . . continued patrolling of northern and southern no-fly zones, we are able to keep Saddam Hussein in his box."[15] This admission came at a time when the US State Department was actively engaged in helping draft a Security Council resolution to be sponsored by Britain and the Netherlands, which would pass as Resolution 1284 in December 1999. It was found to be so unsatisfactory from a humanitarian viewpoint that it led to the resignation of Hans von Sponeck of the UN Office of Humanitarian Coordinator in Iraq. The Arab League in Cairo demanded that the Security Council discuss the suffering imposed on the Iraqi people by sanctions in light of von Sponeck's resignation, but nothing came of it.[16]

Ironically, it was a bold step taken by a non-Arab leader that would weaken the sanctions against Iraq. President Hugo Chavez of Venezuela, the current chairman of OPEC, was an ideologically oriented partisan of the Third World in general, and a friend of China and Cuba in particular. In August 2000 he became the first foreign-elected leader to visit Baghdad since 1990. He arrived in Baghdad (where OPEC was founded) in the course of a tour of OPEC member-states, inviting each head of state personally to attend the organization's summit in Caracas in late September to celebrate the organization's fortieth anniversary. His two-day visit to the Iraqi capital was hailed as historic in Iraq and most other Arab countries. "Who is the next hero?" asked *Babil*, run by Uday Hussein, rhetorically. "Chavez knows the true meaning of independence as other thrones tremble when the American administration waves its big stick at them."[17] Chavez's trip set the scene for air flight-busting—a process that started with a Russian plane arriving in mid-August from Moscow at the newly reopened Saddam International Airport near Baghdad, the first such flight since Iraq's invasion of Kuwait, which had resulted in the imposition of UN sanctions.

Within two months this trickle turned into a flood, aided by the Israeli-Palestinian violence that erupted in late September and that caused the Arab countries to close ranks. The flare-up in Israeli-Palestinian hostilities followed the failure of Clinton-mediated talks between the two parties on the final status of the Palestinian Territories including East Jerusalem in July, and the provocative visit to the Muslim Noble Sanctuary (*Haram al Sharif*) in the Old City of Jerusalem, the third holiest shrine of Islam, by Ariel Sharon, the hard-line leader of the right-wing Likud bloc, two months later.

For Iraq, the big regional boost came in late September when a Jordanian plane carrying a large delegation of cabinet ministers, parliamentarians, trade unionists, politicians, businessmen, and medical personnel—along with medical supplies—arrived in Baghdad from Amman. Jordan's lead was followed by Yemen.

During the next four weeks the Baghdad airport received one foreign flight daily. Excluding the small or geographically peripheral countries like Comros Island, Djibouti, Mauritania, Somalia, and Sudan, almost all members of the twenty-two-strong Arab League participated in flight-busting. The notable exceptions were Kuwait and Saudi Arabia, both involved in assisting the United States and the United Kingdom in their patrolling of the southern air exclusion zone in southern Iraq.

Among the flight-busters, the most noteworthy was Syria, which reopened its rail link with Iraq in August after an interruption of nearly two decades. The plane from Damascus that arrived at the Baghdad airport on October 8, with a thirty-four-member delegation of high-level officials and famous personalities, led by Muhammad Mufdi Sifo, minister for cabinet affairs, along with food and medicine, was the first such aircraft since 1980. "The flight shows the total support of the Syrian people for the Iraqi people to ease their suffering caused by the embargo," said Sifo.[18] The flight took place after the meeting of Tariq Aziz with Syrian president Bashar Assad in Damascus. "Syria supports the call for the lifting of sanctions imposed on Iraq," said Syrian foreign minister Farouq al Shaara. "We expressed this position during the recent meetings of the UN General Assembly and the Arab League."[19] Moreover, instead of waiting for the end of the UN embargo, the two neighbors announced that they would reopen the Kirkuk-Banias oil pipeline in November.[20]

By early October 2000 the Arab world was shocked by the excessive force the Israeli military used against the stone-throwing Palestinians, who rioted in the West Bank and Gaza in protest at the visit on September 28 to the Noble Sanctuary by Ariel Sharon. With a death toll of Palestinians rising above eighty, on October 7 the UN Security Council condemned Israel for "the excessive use of force against Palestinians" by fourteen votes to none, with the US abstaining.

Against this background the need for uniting Arab ranks was so urgent that Egyptian president Mubarak, in consultation with Saudi crown prince Abdullah, decided to close the chapter on the Arab division rendered by the Iraqi occupation of Kuwait, and invite Iraq to the emergency Arab League summit in Cairo to discuss the grim situation prevailing in the Palestinian Territories and its impact on the Israeli-Palestinian peace process. This marked the formal end of a decade of Baghdad's ostracism by the Arab League. It was the latest example of the continued linkage between the fate of the Palestinians and the history of Iraq.

However, Saddam did not attend the summit on October 21–22, partly because he could not be sure of the security that the Egyptian authorities could provide for him, and partly because he thought that his health would become a focus of attention, not least by the intelligence agents attached to the US and Israeli embassies in Cairo. A report in early September in the London-based, Saudi-owned *Al Sharq al Awsat* had quoted an Arab doctor "with an excellent reputation" saying that a team of five European doctors was treating Saddam with chemotherapy for lymph cancer after he had suffered from inflamed joints, breathing difficulties, poor vision, and temporary loss of memory. As Saddam did not show any loss of hair—an unmistakable consequence of chemotherapy treatment—the report lacked credibility.

Izzat Ibrahim, vice chairman of the Iraqi RCC, attended the summit, and repeated the essence of the communiqué issued by the Iraqi government on the eve of the Arab conference: "Iraq is calling [for] and working to liberate Palestine through jihad because only jihad is capable of liberating Palestine and other Arab lands [from Israel]." He added that Iraq could provide a plan for a jihad if Arab leaders decided to follow that course.[21]

At the summit Ibrahim was pleased to hear King Abdullah II of Jordan say, "Our [Arab] nation can no longer stand the continuation of this suffering, and our people no longer accept what is committed against the Iraqi people from [UN] embargo."[22] A day earlier, responding to Baghdad's request, his government had announced that it would remove the Lloyd's of London inspectors from their posts overseeing Iraq-bound shipments arriving at the Jordanian port of Aqaba as part of the UN oil-for-food scheme.

While the Arab summit gathered in Cairo, Saddam sent a convoy of forty trucks of food and medicine to the Palestinian Territories via Amman. The next week a Palestinian plane brought many wounded Palestinians to Baghdad for medical treatment. These gestures boosted Saddam's already high standing among young Palestinians, accelerated his rehabilitation among Arabs, and helped create a symbiosis between him and the Arab street that, he hoped, would pressure the Arab rulers to break the UN sanctions on Iraq. But this scenario of his remained unrealized.

An area in which Saddam had clear success was in improving relations with Iran. Iranian foreign minister Kamal Kharrazi arrived in Baghdad from Tehran on October 13 by an Iran Air carrier—a participant in the flight-busting exercise—for a three-day trip. He became the most senior Iranian official to visit Iraq since the 1979 revolution. His visit had been arranged by President Muhammad Khatami during his meeting with Iraqi vice president Taha Yassin Ramadan, a bull-necked, large-faced Saddam loyalist, on the fringes of the OPEC summit in Caracas in late September.

After his meeting with Saddam, Kharrazi announced that both sides had agreed to reactivate the joint commissions on border demarcation, economic cooperation, the pilgrimage to the Shia holy places in Iraq by Iranians, and security cooperation that they had formed under the 1997 accord to resolve their differences. The long-running issue of the exchange of POWs was virtually settled.[23] While Saddam expressed his "willingness and determination to normalize relations with Iran," Kharrazi said, "We have decided to activate the 1975 [Algiers] agreement in order to set up balanced and good-neighborly relations."[24] So twenty years after Saddam's invasion of Iran following his tearing up of the Algiers Accord during a television address, the two neighbors were returning to the status quo ante.

With President George W. Bush labeling both Iraq and Iran as part of the "axis of evil" in his State of the Union speech in January 2002, the relations between the two countries would grow closer.

CHAPTER 8

OIL, THE DEFINING ELEMENT OF IRAQ

Exactly at 10 P.M., lights went out. "Power cuts remind us daily of sanctions," said Abdul Razak, my urbane, articulate, bespectacled host with a shock of gray hair and a salt-and-pepper mustache, as we sipped black tea in his walled garden in central Baghdad on a warm August night.

Within minutes diesel engines came to life next door and started the generators. Lights returned there. "That's a French oil company," Abdul Razak told me. He was referring to Elf Aquitaine, then on the verge of acquiring Total Société Anonyme to become ElfTotal, a behemoth French oil corporation. Interested in developing the richly endowed Majnoon and Nahr Omar oil fields in southern Iraq, each of the two companies had signed contracts that would become operative once the UN sanctions ended.

"Across the street is a Russian oil company," he continued as I turned my eyes in that direction and saw the light there banish the surrounding darkness. He meant the giant Lukoil corporation. "And over there is a Chinese oil corporation," he concluded. It could only be the China National Petroleum Corporation, a state-owned company, I figured.

In those fleeting minutes, surrounded by the fragrance of bougainvillea, I discovered the prime motive that had informed the stances that these three permanent members of the Security Council had adopted on Iraq since the mid-1990s: the foul-smelling petroleum.

The significance of oil, however, goes far into the history of modern Iraq, even preceding its inception, with the potentially oil-bearing Mosul province being snatched from the defeated Turkey by the Allied-dominated League of Nations in 1925 and attached to the provinces of Baghdad and Basra to create the Kingdom of Iraq. Two years later, it was the discovery of petroleum in northern Iraq that led Britain, then exercising the League of Nations mandate in Iraq, to moderate its staunchly pro-Iran policy, where it had discovered the precious mineral nearly two decades earlier.

Petroleum provides the leitmotif to explain many diverse phenomena in independent Iraq and abroad. Among them are the driving motive behind Britain's counterattack on the nationalist Rashid Ali Gailani's regime in 1941; the unprecedented prosperity of Iraqis during the mid- to late 1970s, which enabled the Baathist regime to consolidate its power; the financial crippling of Iran at war by Saudi Arabia's and Kuwait's flooding of the oil market in 1986, which would two years later compel Tehran to accept a truce; the leverage exercised by Kuwait to pressure Saddam on the boundary demarcation that in turn would lead to its being overrun by Iraq; the prime reason for the uncompromising policy on Saddam's aggression by Bush Sr., alarmingly aware that by appropriating Kuwait Saddam would double his enlarged country's oil reserves and vie with Saudi Arabia as a swing producer of oil; the dynamics of the internal Kurdish politics in the post–Gulf War period; the humanitarian relief for Iraqis from 1997 onward; the shifting attitudes of the Clinton administration to the severity of United Nations inspections in Iraq, and the rapid releasing of blocked contracts at the UN to help Baghdad rehabilitate its run-down petroleum industry against the backdrop of rising demand for oil worldwide; and the efforts of Bush Jr.'s administration to manipulate the price of the Iraqi petroleum—required to be determined by the UN Sanctions Committee—in such a way as to deprive the Baghdad government of any chance of receiving directly even a tiny fraction of the oil money. Finally, in the debate on invading Iraq, the easy access to its oil for US corporations at the expense of their French, Russian, and Chinese rivals would become an increasingly important argument in the armory of the hawks. They and North American oil experts were depressingly aware that at 64 billion barrels, the *aggregate* oil reserves of the United States, Canada, and Mexico amounted to only three-fifths of Iraq's 112 billion.

Tempted by the rich oil prospects of Iraq, the United States showed great interest in the country right from its birth in 1921. Its importance shot up when the Turkish Petroleum Company (TPC), owned largely by the Anglo-Persian Oil Company (APOC) after World War I, struck oil in commercial quantities in the Kirkuk area. Under Washington's pressure, the TPC was reconstituted in 1931 as the Iraq Petroleum Company (IPC)—a 23.5 percent share each was held by the government-owned British, French, and Dutch companies and two US corporations, with the remaining 6 percent held by Partex, owned by C. S. Gulbenkian, a Portuguese businessman.

The oil output had reached such proportions by the start of World War II that Britain intervened militarily to overthrow the nationalist regime of Rashid Ali Gailani in 1941. After the war, when the government realized the enormous profits the Iraq Petroleum Company was making, it passed a law that required it to pay half of its profit as tax, thus making oil income an important part of the public treasury, a continuing fact of life in Iraq.

Following the 1958 revolution, nationalist leader Abdul Karim Qasim, pursuing a nonaligned policy in international affairs, developed friendly relations with the Soviet Union that would blossom in coming decades and benefit inter alia Iraq's oil industry. In 1961 he issued a decree that deprived the Iraq Petroleum Company of 99.5 percent of the 160,000 square miles originally allocated to it for prospecting, covering almost the whole country, including the oil-rich Rumeila in the south. His government set up its own Iraq National Oil Company (INOC). The Iraq Petroleum Company challenged the law. But it was not until 1969 that a partial compromise was reached. Meanwhile the official decrees of August and October 1967 gave the Iraq National Oil Company wide powers and the exclusive right to develop the Rumeila oil field. Here Soviet petroleum experts helped Iraq develop its industry independently of Western oil companies, and this gave the Iraqi government growing confidence to challenge the Iraq Petroleum Company. To pressure Baghdad to reverse its hard-line policy, IPC halved the output of the Kirkuk oil fields in March 1972.

The tactic boomeranged. Iraq warned the Iraq Petroleum Company that it would end the ongoing negotiations if its demands were not met within a fortnight. They were not. So the government nationalized IPC in June, and became the first Arab country to take over a Western-owned oil corporation. The event also marked the end of an era that had begun with the Turkish Petroleum Company in 1912 under Ottoman rule.

Since oil nationalization had the backing of almost all Iraqis, it resulted in raising the prestige and popularity of the four-year-old Baathist regime, which could now rightfully claim to be truly anti-imperialist and revolutionary. Furthermore, possession of Iraq's most precious resource provided the authorities with unprecedented economic clout and independence.

Moscow helped to develop Iraq's petroleum industry in exploration and extraction—as in the Rumeila oil fields—as well as in refining. It was on this economic foundation, and their common opposition to Western imperialism and Zionism, that in 1972 the Soviet Union and Iraq signed a twenty-year Friendship and Cooperation Treaty, agreeing to "develop cooperation in the strengthening of their defense capacity."

Having consolidated its acquisition of the Iraq Petroleum Company's assets, Iraq nationalized the American and Dutch interests in the Basrah Petroleum Company operating in the South. It did so during the October 1973 Arab-Israeli War, when feelings in the Arab world were running high against the United States and the Netherlands, which openly and materially sided with Israel.

The fivefold increase in revenue from petroleum exports between

1973 and 1974—with Iraq producing 2.26 million bpd—provided an unprecedented boost to the Baathist regime. Investment in all economic sectors trebled or quadrupled, and grew steadily during the rest of the decade. The government raised the salaries of its civil servants and military personnel dramatically. Its ambitious five-year plan for 1976–80 promised a prosperous future for all. To save for the rainy day, a three-member Committee for Strategic Development, chaired by Saddam Hussein, and set up in 1975, began depositing clandestinely into a secret Swiss bank account, named the Fund for Strategic Development, 5 percent of Iraq's oil revenue before it was credited to the Iraqi treasury as well as commissions received on large contracts.[1] This fund would help Saddam to resist compromising the economic sovereignty of his country for five years in the 1990s while his government procured sorely needed food and medicine for its citizens by dipping into it.

In 1979 and 1980, when the national population was less than 13 million and the oil output 3.5 million bpd, the exports of 3.3 million bpd provided income of $21.3 billion and $26.3 billion respectively to the public treasury. Unlike in the Gulf monarchies and in Iran under the Shah, petroleum revenue filtered down to ordinary citizens in Iraq with a strong public sector, extensive free public services, and a large body of small landowners.

It was during this period, when Baghdad was flush with US dollars and was modernizing and expanding its economic infrastructure rapidly, that it developed close economic and military links with France, which came to rely increasingly on oil supplies from Iraq. This state of affairs did not last long, though. Iraq got mired in two major wars—first with Iran and then with the US-led coalition over its invasion of Kuwait.

The first economic casualty of the conflict with Tehran was the petroleum industry. Its output sank to a quarter of its prewar level. Then it rose steadily to 1.75 million bpd in 1986. But with the price plummeting to below $10 a barrel in that year, the country's oil income fell to $7 billion. It was able to withstand the price crash because of the large grants it received from Saudi Arabia and Kuwait. During the war Iraq built a pipeline that connected with a Saudi pipeline leading to the Red Sea port of Yanbo, thus supplementing its earlier outlet to the Turkish port of Dortyol.

Except for the first two years in the 1980–88 Iran-Iraq War, when, protesting Baghdad's aggression against Tehran, Moscow stopped shipping weapons to Iraq, Soviet arms supplies to Baghdad continued unabated. By the time the war ended, Iraq owed the Soviet Union $8 billion in unpaid bills.

During the conflict, among the Western nations, France openly backed Iraq, arguing that its defeat would lead to the spread of Islamic fundamentalism in the region, which would hurt Western interests. Its involvement in running the two nuclear reactors near Baghdad continued until the June 1981 bombing of the facilities by Israel. By 1983 about a thousand French companies were active in Iraq, and between six to seven thousand French specialists were based there. As much as 40 percent of total French military exports were destined for Iraq. Military cooperation between the two states had developed to the extent that the French government decided to lease to Baghdad five Super-Etendard warplanes originally meant for use by the French air force. Little wonder that during the years 1970–89 France became the second largest supplier of military hardware (after the Soviet Union) to Baghdad, with contracts worth $6 billion. With civilian and military contracts worth FF 130–150 billion (i.e., $22–25 billion) during the period 1973–89, France became Iraq's third largest trading partner. In 1989 Baghdad owed Paris $4.5 billion in unpaid bills.[2]

In the course of its war with Tehran, Baghdad's relations with OPEC soured when the latter refused to grant Iraq's demand of parity with Iran in its export quota in October 1986. Baghdad ignored OPEC's quota altogether. And it was not until its request was granted in the summer of 1988, following the truce in the Iran-Iraq War, that it returned to the OPEC fold.

With the end of the hostilities, Iraqi oil production surpassed the 3 million bpd mark in the first half of 1990. But its oil export income suffered when flooding of the market by Kuwait and the UAE depressed the price from $18 to $11 a barrel, causing it to lose $20 million a day, a loss it found debilitating given the urgent demands of postwar reconstruction.

In August 1990, an oilman-turned-politician, President George Bush Sr., understood immediately the consequences of Saddam raising petroleum reserves under his control from 11 percent of the world total to 20 percent by incorporating Kuwait into Iraq, and thus rivaling Saudi Arabia's 26 percent and challenging its role as the ultimate fixer of oil prices. All other Western nations and Japan shared his assessment, and backed him diplomatically and militarily in his confrontation with Iraq.

Saddam's invasion of Kuwait, which led to an immediate ban on petroleum exports, resulted in the output falling steeply to 400,000 bpd, just above the domestic demand. During the next three years production crept up to 455,000 bpd, of which 65,000 bpd were exported to Jordan under a special UN dispensation.

Following its aggression against Kuwait, Iraq fell foul of Moscow, which condemned its action. With the disintegration of the Soviet Union in December 1991, Russia inherited the Soviet legacy of close and multifarious ties with Iraq, including an estimated $8 billion credit accorded to Baghdad. With the Russian economy going into a tailspin following the collapse of the Soviet Union, this sum acquired more importance than before. At the same time, Russia was intent on maintaining an ally in the strategic Gulf region. And the gravely isolated Iraq was willing.

Baghdad realized that one way to fend off Moscow's pressure to pay up was to give Russian oil companies a stake in its petroleum industry. It was with this aim in mind that the Iraqi oil minister visited Moscow in October 1994 to negotiate contracts with Russian companies to rebuild his country's oil industry once the UN sanctions ended or eased. Lukoil, the Russian petroleum giant, was keen to exploit Western Qurna and the North Rumeila oil fields in the South—the region where, earlier, Soviet oil experts had been involved.

By now, both Russia and France knew that the only way they would be able to recover the $8 and $4.5 billion that Baghdad owed them respectively was to see at least the oil embargo on Iraq lifted. That partly guided their stance on UN inspections.

China had no such direct economic interest. But considering itself the only (unofficial) representative of the Third World on the Security Council, it had all along taken a moderate line toward Iraq. It had abstained on Resolution 678 (November 1990), authorizing UN members to use "all necessary means" to expel Iraq from Kuwait. Because of its threat to veto a Western-sponsored resolution regarding Baghdad's oppression of Kurds if it were put under Chapter VII of the UN Charter, the Western powers refrained from doing so. China then abstained on Resolution 688 as well.

As the 1990s progressed, Beijing developed interest in oil-exporting countries worldwide. With industrialization gaining unprecedented momentum in China, the country became a net importer of oil in 1993. Its modest imports of 25,000 bpd in 1993 would rise eighteen-fold during the next three years.[3] This turned Beijing's attention increasingly to petroleum-rich countries like Iraq. The China National Petroleum Corporation (CNPC) began courting the Iraqi oil ministry for development contracts in the future.

In short, the Chinese-French-Russian axis on Iraq that had emerged at the Security Council was by early 1995 underpinned by economic interest, present and potential, as much as by ideological and strategic factors.

In the coming months, as the divide between the Anglo-American duo and the non-Anglo-American trio became sharper, the Anglo-Americans would accuse their detractors of being guided solely by the prospect of picking up lucrative contracts in Iraq. In return their rivals would refer to the indecent haste with which the US and UK corporations had signed massive contracts for weapons and infrastructure projects in Kuwait and Saudi Arabia after the Gulf War. They would argue that the staunch opposition by the United States and Britain to easing sanctions on Baghdad had more to do with the Kuwaiti and Saudi ability to pay for the huge arms and other deals they had contracted with US and British companies than with the provisions of the Security Council resolutions, since the reentry of Iraqi oil into the world market would depress the price and reduce the petroleum revenues of Kuwait City and Riyadh.

At home, oil had become the center of Saddam's relations with the Kurdish leaders. Starting in late 1992 and early 1993 Iraq began selling petroleum and petroleum products—especially diesel oil—at bargain-basement prices to Masud Barzani of the KDP, most of them for resale. There was much demand in Turkey for these products. So Barzani benefited enormously even when he sold them just below the international market prices to Turkish truckers who carried them overland to Turkey through the KDP-controlled sector.

This was the foundation on which Barzani forged military links with Saddam, buying Iraqi arms and ammunition from Baghdad with the profits he made on the contraband trade. After the debacle of September 1996, when Washington had to pull out its intelligence operatives from the Kurdish area, Barzani severed his military links with Saddam under US pressure but maintained his economic ties with him.

Washington was well aware of this, but turned a blind eye to this breach of UN sanctions for two reasons, one of which had to do with Turkey and the other with the Iraqi Kurds. At 50,000–60,000 bpd, these imports amounted to about 10 percent of Turkey's fuel market, and its purchase at prices below the international rates helped the Turkish economy, albeit marginally. So, now US officials explained that Turkey had suffered so heavily as a result of UN sanctions on Iraq (with Ankara claiming an annual loss of $4 billion in two-way trade with Baghdad) that it would be churlish to object to the small benefit it derived from the Iraqi oil smuggling.[4] But by offering this rationale, the United States provided ammunition to its critics, who charged it with being selective in its application of the UN embargo against Baghdad.

The implementation of the UN-administered oil-for-food scheme in December 1996, allowing Iraq to sell $2 billion worth of petroleum in six months to buy food and medicine, left unaffected the contraband sale of Iraqi oil and oil products to Turkey. Indeed, by the fall of 1997 the estimate was that this trade earned the KDP $800,000 a day, up 60 percent form the previous figure. And customs duties and service charges yielded a further $250,000 daily. The cash was deposited in the regional bank in Irbil, and controlled by the Kurdistan parliament with a KDP majority. This deprived the PUK of cash, and embittered Jalal Talabani.[5] He demanded that a joint committee or a neutral body be set up to collect and distribute the customs revenue, but to no avail.

In Washington, following the start of the oil-for-food scheme for Iraq, the Clinton administration announced that US companies were free to buy Iraqi oil. And they did—until Saddam Hussein, angered by Operation Desert Fox, banned direct sales to the US oil companies or traders.

In mid-February 1998, ignoring the rising tension between Baghdad and the United Nations on weapons inspections, at the initiative of Kofi Annan, the Security Council raised the six-monthly ceiling for the oil-for-food scheme from $2 billion to $5.26 billion. This was welcome news for Iraqis. The only problem was that at $15 a barrel, Baghdad would have to raise its crude oil exports from the current 900,000 bpd to 2.34 million bpd to earn $5.26 billion in six months. This and the domestic consumption of 450,000 bpd meant an aggregate production of 2.8 million bpd. But such was the state of Iraq's run-down oil industry that its total output could not exceed 2 million bpd. Despite this, at the UN 661 Sanctions Committee, the United States insisted on adding conditions on passing the $300 million requested for Iraqi petroleum industry repairs over the next six months.[6]

Due to continuing low petroleum prices in 1998, the partially upgraded productive capacity of Iraq's oil industry failed to fill the public treasury by the allowable $10.52 billion a year, the actual total being over $3 billion short of this figure. Prices rose in 1999, but not sufficiently to enable Baghdad to reach its permissible level of income, much less make up, even partially, for the previous shortfall. The continued disrepair of its petroleum industry was the problem. In October, backed by Annan, France proposed doubling a $300 million budget over the next six months for Iraqi oil repairs. Washington refused to endorse the French proposal. This was a way of getting even with Saddam, who forbade Iraqi oil sales to US corporations and UK companies and traders in retribution for Operation Desert Fox. That forced the American oil traders to buy the commodity from the Russian, French, and Chinese intermediaries, who resorted to loading their tankers at the Iraqi oil terminal in the Gulf destined for non-American ports, and then diverting them to US destinations and charging extra for the arrangement. Saddam thereby deprived the US companies of their trading profits, which were diverted to the middlemen from the countries friendly with Baghdad—Russia, France, and China.

Yet in 1999, according to the Washington-based Petroleum Industry Research Foundation, Iraq emerged as the fastest-growing source of US petroleum imports, with the American companies buying more than a third of the 2 million bpd exported by Baghdad. "The Chevrons and the Exxons of this world have to buy [Iraqi oil] from the Russians, the French, and the Chinese traders," said Larry Goldstein, president of the Petroleum Industry Research Foundation.[7] Part of the reason for American companies to seek out Iraqi crude was the Clinton administration's 1995 blanket ban on trade with Iran, OPEC's second largest producer, whose output was on a par with Iraq's.

The position of the US administration became morally untenable when it emerged in early 2000 that American corporations and their foreign subsidiaries were purchasing Iraqi oil on a large scale and selling petroleum-related equipment and spare parts to Iraq. "While the US and Britain carry out almost daily air strikes against military installations in northern and southern Iraq, executives and even some [former] architects of American policy toward Baghdad are doing business with Saddam's government and helping to rebuild its battered oil industry," reported Colum Lynch of the *Washington Post*. Citing diplomats, industry officials, and UN documents, he said, "Placing bids through overseas subsidiaries and affiliates, more than a dozen [US] companies have signed millions of dollars in contracts with Baghdad for oil-related equipment since the summer of 1998." According to the State Department, US citizens had received licenses to export only about $15 million worth of oil-related spare parts to Iraq, a minuscule part of the total. But this figure excluded the parts and equipment Iraq bought from US subsidiaries abroad. Though this indirect trade was monitored by the UN 661 Sanctions Committee, it kept this information under wraps. "The UN helps both countries avoid embarrassment by treating the business arrangements as confidential," reported Lynch.[8]

When it came to repairing the run-down oil industry of Iraq, the European subsidiaries of the American oil equipment corporations such as Halliburton, of which present US vice president Dick Cheney was then the chief executive officer, were in the forefront. Placing bids through their foreign subsidiaries and affiliates, more than a dozen US companies signed up tens of millions of dollars' worth of contracts with Iraq for oil-related equipment between mid-1998 and the end of 1999. With the United Nations now allowing Baghdad to spend an average of $1.2 billion a year on repairing its oil industry, the pickings were rich.

In addition, at Washington's behest, the British and Dutch drafters of UN Security Council Resolution 1284 ensured a fast track for putting the Iraqi petroleum industry on its feet again. Paragraph 18 of the resolution requested that the UN 661 Sanctions Committee appoint a group of experts to "approve speedily contracts for the parts and the equipments necessary to enable Iraq to increase its exports of petroleum and petroleum products."

When 2000 began with an increasingly tight oil market, impacting positively on Baghdad's economic and diplomatic standing, Saddam grew more confident—as did China, France, and Russia at the Security Council. On March 24, at the council, they delivered stinging attacks on the United States and the United Kingdom for subjecting Iraqi purchases unrelated to its oil industry—such as equipment required to upgrade Iraq's old analog telecommunications system to the digital system (see chapter 1)—to nitpicking scrutiny at the UN 661 Sanctions Committee, and staging frequent air strikes against Iraqi targets in the no fly zones.[9]

Whereas the United States had ignored such strictures previously, this time it behaved differently as the oil crisis deepened as the year unfolded. Reversing its past policy of insisting on UN inspectors conducting their task with utmost severity, it greeted with undisguised embarrassment the announcement of Hans Blix, the head of the freshly created UN Monitoring, Verification, and Inspection Commission, in August that its newly trained inspectors were ready to travel to Iraq, which had yet to accept Resolution 1284. To the surprise of many, US secretary of state Madeleine Albright said that Washington would not use force to compel Iraq to accept Unmovic inspectors. She then lined up with the UN ambassadors of China, France, and Russia in urging Blix not to force the issue.

Thanks to the thriving world economy, the global demand for petroleum exceeded supply despite OPEC's decision to raise output twice, and any interruption in Iraq's oil output, running at 3.6 million bpd in August 2000, the highest ever, would spike up the prices even further—so calculated US policy makers, and rightly so. In addition, given Baghdad's exemption from the OPEC quota (an arrangement made to help Iraq recover from the devastation of the Gulf War), the United States was now eager to see it increase output to the maximum to ease the market and help lower prices. With Baghdad's oil shipments running at 3 million bpd, equaling the two recent OPEC increases, it was in a strong position.

On the other side, President Clinton was dejectedly aware of growing American dependence on oil imports. The country was importing 60 percent of the 19 million oil barrels it consumed daily—a twofold increase since 1983—and the trend was up. In the 1990s oil output in the United States fell by 15 percent while consumption grew by 11 percent.[10] With less than 5 percent of the world population, the United States consumed 25 percent of the global oil output. It sucked up all the petroleum exports of Canada, Mexico, and Venezuela. And it was becoming increasingly dependent on imports from the Gulf region, including Iraq. That no interest was higher or more important in America than to keep gas-guzzling cars running, and homes and offices heated in winter, was such a glaring fact of life in the United States that no politician could afford to overlook it.

When OPEC's decision on September 11, 2000 to increase production by 800,000 bpd failed to calm oil traders and prices remained firm, Iraq's petroleum minister, Gen. Amr Rashid, reflecting Saddam's thinking, threatened that the government would postpone its plans to raise output if the United States continued to put holds on Iraq's contracts for food, medicine, and economic infrastructure before the UN 661 Sanctions Committee. With Baghdad's oil export revenue at an impressive $7.1 billion during January–June 2000, Saddam was keener than before to deploy whatever leverage he could muster to gain the upper hand, and he had this time found himself armed with an instrument that could not fail: oil.

The Clinton administration softened its policy toward him considerably. On September 12 Albright repeated that the United States would not use force if Baghdad failed to comply with Security Council Resolution 1284, which had led to the establishment of Unmovic. But that failed to pacify oil traders, who noted nervously that inventories of home heating oil in the six New England states were 60 percent below last year's, and the crude oil inventories in the country were 10 percent lower than that of the past year's. On September 20 the West Texas crude futures rose to $37 a barrel. It caused panic in the White House. Two days later Clinton announced that his administration would release one million bpd for thirty days from the US Strategic Petroleum Reserve in November, an unprecedented step to take in peacetime. That calmed the market. On September 25, Monday, the oil futures in London dropped by $3.

For the first time since the Gulf War, Saddam became proactive, rather than reactive, in his foreign policy. His government alleged that by carrying out slant drilling near the Kuwaiti-Iraqi border, Kuwait was stealing 300,000 bpd of Iraqi oil. It addressed a letter to the UN Security Council holding Saudi Arabia responsible for the losses that Iraq suffered when the Saudi kingdom closed the oil pipeline from southern Iraq to its Red Sea port of Yanbo in August 1990.[11] Saddam's intent behind putting Kuwait and Saudi Arabia, major petroleum producers, on the defensive was to destabilize the oil market and spike up prices, the opposite of what Clinton was attempting to accomplish.

For once, in his dealings with Saddam, Clinton found his area of maneuver limited. His hands were tied further by the impending US presidential vote on November 7, which made him wary of even threatening to use force against Saddam for fear of the Iraqi leader retaliating by reducing or cutting off Iraqi exports running at a hefty three million bpd.

It was this state of the oil market that George W. Bush inherited from the preceding administration in January 2001.

Iraq's income from petroleum supplied outside the UN-supervised oil-for-food scheme became a source of concern to Washington. It alleged that Saddam was using these funds to finance his program for weapons of mass destruction. Besides the well-documented contraband sale of oil and oil products to Turkish traders, the other known outlet was the pipeline to Syria, which became operational in late 2000. Then there were clandestine sales to the Iranian public sector organizations at heavily discounted rates where, after loading oil at Iraq's terminal in the Gulf, the tankers used the protected sea lanes within the twelve-mile-wide territorial waters of Iran to navigate the Gulf, and then sailed out to the high sea. The total annual income to Baghdad from these sources was put at $1.5 billion—a fraction of what it earned from legitimate exports, but enough to make the hawks in Washington feel agitated.

As yet there was another petroleum-centered element that was a possible source of contraband income to Saddam. According to the oil-for-food program, it was the UN 661 Sanctions Committee that had to approve the price at which Iraq sold its petroleum. As a rule, the commodity is sold for delivery in a certain month in the future. Depending on the destination of the oil, its wholesale price for a primary lifter is fixed against a benchmark, and expressed as plus or minus the benchmark. Then there is the retail price that the actual lifter—often an oil refiner—pays. Naturally, the retail price is higher than the wholesale. It is the difference between these two figures that Iraq tries to exploit. It specifies a low wholesale price, and advises the primary lifter to pay a surcharge (of, say, 50 cents a barrel) into its own bank account. The United Nations, on the other hand, prefers a high wholesale price in order to reduce the profit margin of the primary lifter and dissuade it from depositing a surcharge into Iraq's account. To pressure Baghdad to desist from gaining direct access to foreign money, the UN Sanctions Committee resorted to putting on hold its oil contracts, and specifying the wholesale price only after the trading month had passed. This left the buyers in limbo, and reduced the demand for Iraqi oil.

Always sensitive to the Palestinians and their cause, Saddam lost no time in demonstrating his backing for them when Israeli prime minister Ariel Sharon ordered a military reoccupation of the West Bank in late March 2002 in response to a particularly lethal suicide bomb attack in Israel. The Iraqi leader suspended his country's oil exports for 30 days from April 8, or until Israel withdrew its forces from the West Bank, and invited other oil-exporting Arab states and Iran to follow his example. They failed to do so, thus highlighting his gesture. It was only after Israel had pulled back its troops by the end of April that Iraq resumed its shipments. Saddam's act won wide-scale Palestinian acclaim.

Such actions once again underscored the vital significance of petroleum, impinging as it does on assorted elements of Iraq's policies—from armament to domestic politics to relations with major foreign powers like the United States, Russia, France, and China.

CHAPTER 9

IRAQ AFTER 9/11

On September 11, 2001, two passenger jets smashed into the twin towers of the World Trade Center in Lower Manhattan, causing their collapse. Mayhem gripped the area below Canal Street, with thousands of ash-covered people running away from the scene of devastation. Foreign diplomats and their staff sixty-four blocks north, at the thirty-eight-story UN headquarters along the East River, were overcome by the smell and ash that would envelop the island. The next day, with the smoke from the devastated WTC site still shrouding the city, the UN Security Council members unanimously adopted Resolution 1368. It called on "all States to work together urgently to bring to justice the perpetrators, organizers and sponsors of the terrorist attacks." These attacks were soon attributed to Osama bin Laden, the Saudi fugitive in the Taliban-controlled Afghanistan, and his Al Qaeda (The Base) network.

Iraq was one of the three countries that refused to fly their flags at half-mast at their UN missions in New York, the others being Libya and China. Baghdad went beyond this gesture. Declaring that "America is reaping the thorns planted by its rulers," Saddam Hussein warned Washington against using retaliatory force, and cited the example of Iraq, where, in his view, such force had failed. Iraqi foreign minister Naji Sabri recalled American "crimes against humanity"—from Hiroshima, hit by an American atom bomb in 1945, to Vietnam; from Central America to Palestine—a bloody trail littered with millions of dead going back more than fifty years. "All Muslim and Arab people consider America the master of terrorism, the terrorist power number one."[1] In his address to the UN General Assembly, Iraqi ambassador Muhammad al Douri said that Iraq had sent messages of condolence to individuals in America. However, he added, "It would have been hypocritical to condemn the bombings, given the sanctions and bombings against Iraq."[2]

Among the top US policy makers who assembled in Washington, Colin Powell stood out as he had after Iraq's invasion of Kuwait eleven years earlier, when he was the youngest chairman of the military joint chiefs of staff to serve. Then he had successfully argued for full mobilization of men and materials—and against incremental increases—before embarking on military action against Iraq. This time, as secretary of state, he applied this doctrine to diplomacy. Before undertaking an extensive foreign tour, he explained to his cabinet colleagues that his mission would advance smoothly only if bin Laden and the Taliban remained the United States' sole targets. He argued against the idea of "eliminating" terrorism-sponsoring states, as advocated by deputy defense secretary Paul Wolfowitz: "It is not just simply a matter of capturing people and holding them accountable, but removing the sanctuaries . . . ending states that sponsor terrorism," he said.[3] Diplomatically, US actions should be multilateral—part of a broad coalition including Western allies and moderate Arab and Muslim countries, Powell reasoned.

In contrast, the hawks, led by Donald Rumsfeld, advocated striking Afghanistan swiftly, eliminating bin Laden and overthrowing the Taliban regime, then extending the war to Iraq to topple Saddam and targeting the training camps run by such non–Al Qaeda factions as Hizbollah in Lebanon and Syria. Diplomatically, they argued, the US should operate unilaterally when necessary, and as part of a revolving coalition—in which some nations help with certain operations and others with other operations—and eliminate the states harboring terrorists. Powell prevailed in this round partly because the hawks could not prove that the groups like Hizbollah had "a global reach," a qualification laid out earlier by President George W. Bush.

In the end, Iraq and Hizbollah were put on the back burner while Powell got on with cobbling together a coalition to attack Afghanistan.

The bombing of Afghanistan started on October 7. On that day, Bush had hardly stepped out of his Oval Office after addressing the nation on television, when his aides told him that the popular Arabic-language Al Jazeera satellite TV had just broadcast a 20-minute statement by bin Laden:

> Here is America, struck by God Almighty in one of its vital organs, so that its greatest buildings are destroyed, said bin Laden.
>
> [W]hat America is tasting now is only a copy of what . . . [o]ur Islamic *umma* (nation) has been tasting for eighty years—humiliation and disgrace, its sons killed and their blood spilled, its sanctities desecrated. God has blessed a group of vanguard Muslims . . . to destroy America. . . . When they stood in defense of their weak children, their brothers and sisters in Palestine and other Muslim nations, the whole world went into an uproar, the infidels followed by the hypocrites.[4] We hear no denunciation . . . from the hereditary [Muslim] rulers. . . . Israeli tanks rampage across Palestine, in Ramallah, Rafah, Jenin and Beit Jala and many other parts of the Land of Islam, and we do not hear anyone raising his voice or reacting. . . . The least that can be said about those hypocrites is that they are apostates. . . . Americans have been telling the world they are fighting terrorism. . . . A million children [killed] in Iraq, to them this is not a clear issue.[5]

Bin Laden's reference to the suffering of Iraqis was not an afterthought. In February 1998, amid the deepening Baghdad-Washington crisis on UN inspections, which resulted in the Pentagon assembling an armada in the Gulf, bin Laden and other Islamist leaders had published an assessment that applied to the Middle East as a whole, including Iraq. And it was in the aftermath of Operation Desert Fox in December that bin Laden called on Muslims worldwide to "confront, fight and kill" Americans and Britons for "their support for their leaders' decision to attack Iraq."

On February 23, 1998, on the eve of the formation of the International Islamic Front (IIF) against the Crusaders and the Jews, bin Laden and four other extremist Islamist leaders from Egypt, Pakistan, and Bangladesh issued a communiqué laced with the kind of vehement language they had used earlier against the Soviets in Afghanistan. "For more than seven years America has been occupying the lands of Islam in the holiest of places, the Arabian Peninsula, plundering its riches, dictating to its rulers, humiliating its people, terrorizing its neighbors and turning its bases in the Peninsula into a spearhead through which to fight the neighboring Muslim peoples," the communiqué stated. "Despite the great devastation inflicted on the Iraqi people by the Crusader-Zionist alliance . . . the Americans are once again trying to repeat the horrific massacres."

Now, in early October 2001, at the start of the Afghanistan War, Americans were nervous, with anthrax-related deaths in Florida triggering a nationwide alarm that became shriller when the FBI issued a general warning on October 10, saying that "attacks may be carried out during the next week on US targets at home or abroad." The hawkish US officials claimed immediately that Iraq was the instigator behind the anthrax attacks, embellishing their claims with illustrative diagrams and graphics, showing the source (Iraq) and the links leading to the United States, but providing no evidence. Later the Bush administration's own investigators would dismiss this claim.

The American hawks were angered by Saddam's statement on the US-led Afghan campaign. "The true believers cannot but condemn this act, not because it has been committed by America against a

Muslim people but because it is an aggression committed outside international law," said Saddam. "These methods will bring only greater instability and disorder in the world. The American aggression could spread to other countries."[6]

The Iraq mania reached fever pitch in November when, during his visit to Washington, Czech prime minister Milos Zeman told Powell that Muhammad Atta, one of the ringleaders of the September hijackers, had visited Prague in April 2001 to confer with Iraqi intelligence officer Ahmad Ani—posted as a diplomat at the Iraqi embassy—to plan an attack on Radio Free Europe's head office for beaming anti-Saddam programs to Iraq. After 9/11, a Middle East informant told the Czech intelligence that he had seen Atta meeting Ani in April.[7] The anti-Baghdad frenzy did not lead to a precipitate action against Iraq because the Pentagon was focused on defeating the Taliban, and capturing or killing bin Laden.

But once the Taliban were expelled from power Bush's top officials began discussing the second phase of the war on terror. As expected, the hawks advanced their case for attacking Iraq even though the investigation of Baghdad's complicity in the September 11 attacks, ordered earlier by Bush, had yet to be completed. The doves remained skeptical of the wisdom of an anti-Iraq military campaign to overthrow Saddam's regime.

Iraq was the particular obsession of Wolfowitz and Richard Perle, chairman of the eighteen-member Defense Policy Board, a group of national security experts that advises the Pentagon.[8] However before the hawks could gather momentum, Powell said in an interview with the *Washington Post* on December 21: "Iraq and Afghanistan are two different countries with two different regimes and two different military capabilities. They are so significantly different that you cannot take the Afghan model and immediately apply it to Iraq."[9] Also, in contrast to the Northern Alliance, with twenty years of experience in insurgency and conventional fighting in Afghanistan, the weak, fractured Iraqi opposition lacked combat experience, and was in no state to lead a victory march to Baghdad on the back of American tanks.

Unlike the predominantly rural Afghanistan, where the government barely touched the lives of most people living in villages, an urbanized Iraq has been a strong centralized state ever since the overthrow of the monarchy in 1958. Governed by the Baathist Party since 1968, it has been administered—as has been shown in previous chapters—with an iron rod by Saddam since 1979. By the end of its eight-year war with Iran in the 1980s, he had armed more than a million men. And within a few years of the humiliating defeat in the 1991 Gulf War, he rebuilt the shattered military to 350,000 troops. By contrast, the Taliban were created chiefly by Pakistan in 1994. At the height of their power seven years later, when they controlled 95 percent of Afghanistan, their ragtag army, maintained by Pakistani subsidies, was only 45,000 strong. Furthermore, unlike Afghanistan, Iraq was part of the Arab world, where most political-diplomatic issues revolve around the Israeli-Palestinian conflict. So Washington's policy toward Baghdad could not be devised in isolation from the latest state of play between Israelis and Palestinians. This axiom seemed to have escaped those hard-line presidential advisers who won the latest argument, which Bush, still enjoying an approval rating of 80-plus percent, reflected in his State of the Union address to Congress on January 29, 2002.

"My hope is that all nations will . . . eliminate the terrorist parasites who threaten their countries and our own," Bush said. "Our second goal is to prevent regimes that sponsor terror from threatening America or our friends and allies with weapons of mass destruction. . . . North Korea is a regime arming with missiles and weapons of mass destruction, while starving its citizens. Iran aggressively pursues these weapons and exports terror. . . . Iraq continues to flaunt its hostility toward America and to support terror. . . . This is a regime that has something to hide from the civilized world. States like these, and their terrorist allies, constitute an axis of evil, arming to threaten the peace of the world."[10]

Bush's remarks about the "axis of evil" were received with disdain not only by most Europeans and Arabs but also by many Americans, including Bill Clinton. "They may all be trouble, but they are different," he said. Support for sanctions against Iraq had fallen apart. "Iran has two governments now, progressive elements that the US can work with and hard-liners whose every move must be watched." On North Korea, he added, "I have a totally different take. . . . I was ready to go to Pyongyang to close a deal on North Korea's missile program but had to stay in Washington on a last-minute Middle East peace initiative which fell apart."[11] In a television interview, Madeleine Albright said that Bush had made "a big mistake" by conflating Iran, Iraq, and North Korea. The Clinton administration had a "potentially verifiable agreement" with North Korea to stop the export of missile technology.[12]

Comparing Iraq, Iran, and North Korea to the fascist axis of World War II was spurious. These countries had not forged any pact of aggression against the West. Indeed, Iran and Iraq had warred long and hard in the 1980s. Bush's new doctrine inadvertently increased dangers facing the United States by upsetting the European Union, which was pursuing a policy of constructive engagement toward Iran.[13]

In the coming weeks and months European opposition to Bush's hawkish stance built up. The criticism by French foreign minister Hubert Vedrine was echoed by a senior British politician, Chris Patten, the European Union commissioner for external relations. In an interview with the London *Guardian*, he attacked the United States for its "absolutist and simplistic" approach, and said, "There is more to be said for trying to engage and to draw these societies [of the "axis of evil"] into the international communities than to cut them off." He called on EU leaders to raise their voices before Washington went into "unilateralist overdrive."[14]

At home Democrat senator Tom Daschle, the Senate majority leader, combined his caution on a military action against Iraq with sharp criticism of Bush on his "axis of evil" statement, rebuking his administration for its incautious rhetoric and warning against alienating allies and friends.[15]

Daschle's stand on Iraq, expressed in February, had a constitutional ramification. Though the congressional resolution on the terrorist attacks on the United States on September 14, 2001 gave wide powers to President Bush constitutionally, only Congress could declare war—something it had done only five times: 1812 (against Britain), 1845 (against Mexico), 1898 (against Spain), 1916 (World War I), and 1941 (World War II). On the other hand, US presidents have sent troops abroad at least 120 times. Congress passed the War Powers Act in 1973, requiring the president to notify it in a timely fashion when troops are dispatched abroad. The troops must be withdrawn within ninety days unless Congress approves the mission. President George Bush Sr. sought and won congressional approval for military operations against Iraq in January 1991, with the Senate voting for it by a margin of only three. Democrat senator Robert C. Byrd pointed out that though the president was the commander in chief, it was Congress that had the power to "provide for the common defense and general welfare, to raise and support armies, and to declare war," and therefore it had "a constitutional responsibility to weigh in on war-related policy decisions."[16]

Like other critics of Bush, Daschle was aware that after a thorough investigation, the US intelligence agencies had concluded that Iraq was not involved in the September 11 terrorist attacks—a conclusion that would be confirmed in March in London by a report by John Scarlett, chairman of Britain's Joint Intelligence Committee, which stated that there was no evidence to link Baghdad with the 9/11 attacks or to the Al Qaeda network.[17] By then, after months of investigation, the Czech authorities, the original source of the Saddam–Al Qaeda connection, said that they were no longer sure. After examining thousands of documents, FBI and CIA analysts failed to find any proof that Atta left or traveled to the United States in April 2001, when he was supposed to be in Prague. "We ran down literally hundreds of thousands of leads [and found nothing]," said FBI director Robert Mueller in a public speech in San Francisco in April 2002.[18]

According to the longtime Saudi intelligence chief Prince Turki, who possessed volumes of intelligence on Iraq and bin Laden, "Iraq does not come very high in the estimations of bin Laden. He thinks of Saddam Hussein as an apostate, an infidel or someone who is not worthy of being a fellow Muslim."[19] Jamal al Fadl, a key Al Qaeda defector, said there were individual Iraqis in Al Qaeda but there was no specific Iraqi group that Al Qaeda was backing. He told the US authorities that bin Laden criticized Saddam "sometimes for attacking Muslims and killing women and children, but most importantly for not believing in 'most of Islam,' and for setting up his own political party, the Baath."[20] The Baath was a secular party, and Tariq Aziz (aka Mikhail Yahunna), Iraq's deputy prime minister and chief spokesman for the Western media, was Chaldean Catholic. For eight years Iraq fought the Islamic regime of Iran. So the idea of an alliance between Saddam and Al Qaeda seemed outlandish.

Yet Bush and his hawkish advisers remained intransigent, buoyed by the opinion polls that showed 88 percent support for military action against Iraq, up from the previous 78 percent. They saw Bush's remarks about the "axis of evil" as setting out markers for the future. "All the three countries I mentioned are now on notice that we intend to take their development of weapons of mass destruction very seriously," reiterated Bush.

Elaborating on the theme, administration officials argued that the United States needed to plan to prevent the possibility of a terrorist group obtaining WMD from Iraq, which retained the possibility (even probability) of acquiring them. This threat, founded on *two* preconditions, was offered as something novel. But it was not. The Clinton administration had considered this possibility and appointed an advisory panel—the Gilmore Commission—to examine it. In its report published in December 1999, the Gilmore Commission concluded: "The rogue states would hesitate to entrust such weapons to terrorists because of the likelihood that such a group's action might be unpredictable even to the point of using the weapon against its sponsor." Regarding the rogue states themselves, they would be unlikely to use such weapons due to "the prospect of significant reprisals."[21] Nearly three years later, in his *Wall Street Journal* article entitled "Don't Attack Iraq," Brent Scowcroft, the national security adviser under Presidents Bush Sr. and Gerald Ford, would offer the same argument in the debate on Iraq.

What those "significant reprisals" would mean in reality became abundantly clear by the end of 2001 with the defeat of the Taliban in Afghanistan by the US-led coalition—as well as by the rigorous regime that the UN Security Council's Committee on Counterterrorism was in the process of establishing in accordance with Resolution 1373, adopted on September 28, 2001. Given this, no leader of Iraq or any other member of the "axis of evil" would be so foolhardy as to commit political suicide by passing on WMD to a terrorist organization if and when it came to acquire them.

Behind these exaggerated scenarios, however, was an unexpressed plan to advance the neoconservative agenda of Bush and his inner circle of hawks: increased spending on defense under the rubric of enhancing national security, the prime argument articulated during the forty-five-year-long Cold War. Little wonder that the $213 billion federal budget for October 2002–September 2003 that Bush presented to Congress on February 4 showed a 13.7 percent rise in defense expenditure—taking it to $379 billion—compared to a 2 percent raise for education spending, an area Bush had emphasized in his election campaign.[22] Most of the extra funding for the Pentagon was earmarked for developing and producing advanced conventional and nuclear weapons. It remained unclear as to how such weapons would advance the fight against terrorists engaged largely in guerrilla attacks more often on property than persons—as demonstrated repeatedly by the State Department's annual reports on the subject. Its "Patterns of Global Terrorism, 2001" showed that of the 346 terrorist attacks on American targets, one-half were directed at the oil pipelines in Colombia owned by US corporations— low-level bombings—by the members of the left-wing Fuerzas Armadas Revolucionrias de Colombia (FARC). In the previous year, two-fifths of the 426 terrorist attacks on American targets were directed at these pipelines.[23]

US HAWKS VS. ARAB STATES

In mid-March Vice President Dick Cheney, a leading hawk, undertook a tour of the Middle East to create a "new agenda" for the region—constructing an anti-Iraq coalition and fighting terrorism— to replace the old agenda of resolving the Israeli-Palestinian conflict that has been at the center of Israeli-Arab relations since 1948.

The timing had to do with the administration's plan to invade Iraq with 70,000 to 250,000 troops in the fall, a timeline that would later be postponed to early 2003 in order to avoid combat in bulky chemical suits during hot weather and to prepare for the anticipated oil price shock. Cheney failed in his mission. At a joint press conference with Cheney, when asked whether Bahrain would back action against Iraq, Bahraini foreign minister Salman ibn Hamad al Khalifa said: "In the Arab world the threat is perceived quite differently. The people who are dying today on the streets are not a result of any Iraqi action. The people are dying as a result of an Israeli action. And likewise people in Israel are dying as a result of action taken in response [by the Palestinians]."[24]

That this was a collective Arab view became apparent when the Arab League summit, held in Beirut in late March, resolved to reject "exploitation of war on terrorism to threaten any Arab country and use of force against Iraq," and coupled it with praise for the eighteen-month-old Second Palestinian intifada against Israeli occupation. It also adopted the peace plan proposed by Saudi crown prince Abdullah, offering peace and recognition by the entire Arab world to Israel in exchange for its total withdrawal from the Occupied Arab Territories, including the Golan Heights of Syria.

Abdullah won backing for his peace plan from Iraq, the most anti-Zionist state, in return for his support for the summit's opposition to Washington's threatened war against Baghdad, and his promise to conciliate Iraq and Kuwait. By embracing Iraq's Izzat Ibrahim, vice president of the Revolutionary Command Council, dressed in traditional Arab dress, before television cameras—to the enthusiastic clapping by the audience—Abdullah paved the way for normalization of relations between Riyadh and Baghdad. Saudi Arabia reopened its border with Iraq at Arar, and Saudi companies became more active in trading with Iraq within the framework of the UN oil-for-food scheme. (Saudi Arabia's publicly announced refusal to let the Pentagon use its state-of-the-art command center at the Prince Sultan air base at Al Kharj for war against Iraq followed.) Ibrahim and Kuwaiti foreign minister Sabah al Ahmad al Sabah shook hands in public after the former had signed a document recognizing Kuwait's sovereignty and security. Responding to the summit's call to both sides to end negative media campaigns and find a prompt solution to the missing Kuwaiti POWs issue, Iraqi foreign minister Sabri said, "We have instructed our media to avoid any references which may annoy the State of Kuwait."

However, Sabri's smooth, sophisticated manner (in contrast to the confrontational style of his predecessor, Muhammad Said al Sahaf) failed to overcome the continuing differences between Baghdad and the United Nations. Whereas Kofi Annan's agenda for a meeting with Sabri in March focused on readmission of UN inspectors to Iraq and the missing Kuwaiti POWs, Sabri wanted to discuss the lifting of sanctions, no fly zones, the compensation to be paid by the United States and Britain for the damage they had caused, and lack of any progress on "establishing in the Middle East a zone free from weapons of mass destruction" as specified by Paragraph 14 of Security Council Resolution 687. While the technical experts of both sides had a useful exchange, the talks between Annan and Sabri got nowhere. During their meeting Sabri also sought answers to twenty questions he posed. These included "Do threats to invade Iraq and to change the national government by force violate UN Security Council resolutions and rules of international law?" and "Is it possible to normalize relations between the Security Council and Iraq when calls are made for invading Iraq and overthrowing its national government?" Annan promised to pass the list on to the Security Council. During their next meeting in May, Annan explained to Sabri that the questions about an invasion of Iraq or the regime change there were "political" and should be addressed directly to the countries concerned. Though their technical experts once again had long sessions, the talks between the principals in New York proved sterile.

Further meetings in early July in Vienna too ended without any agreement. Yielding to Washington's pressure, Annan insisted on limiting the talks to the return of the UN inspectors to Iraq, refusing to discuss any disarmament issue before their readmission. By contrast, Sabri, intent on having a comprehensive deal, wanted the UN to acknowledge at the outset what had been achieved until December 1998 (when chief inspector Richard Butler withdrew his inspectors from Iraq); spell out up front what remained to be done and specify the time frame; and state that sanctions would be lifted fully if the inspectors found nothing objectionable. In reply Annan referred to the provisions in Security Council Resolution 1284: The inspectors would take sixty days to produce a work program *after* they had been let into Iraq, etc. (see chapter 6). The basic problem was that Annan was referring to a resolution that Iraq had *not* accepted. "We are opposed to merely agreeing to the return of UN inspectors," Sabri told the *Financial Times* on July 31, "because they will come just to update the information [on Iraqi targets] and provide it to the US military and intelligence bodies to use in bombing Iraq." Also Baghdad was seeking assurances from the Security Council that the United States would abandon its regime change plans if inspectors returned to Iraq. But no such assurance was forthcoming because it was not a prerogative of council members to direct Washington's foreign policy.

THE INTERNATIONAL DEBATE ON IRAQ

While the Sabri-Annan talks were in progress in early July, the *New York Times* published the outline of a five-inch-thick dossier on the "concept" of war on Iraq, which specified air, land, and sea-based forces to attack Iraq from three directions, with the use of warplanes from the bases in the six Gulf monarchies, Turkey, and Jordan (subsequently all of them would publicly oppose an invasion of Iraq). The document had precise details of Iraqi bases, surface-to-air missile sites, air defense networks, and fiber-optics communications. The target list was so long that one military expert described it as "almost flagrant." This proved to be the first in a series of leaks about the battle plans that followed. Another serious option was to mount a proxy war against Baghdad by using US Special Forces, the CIA and Iraqi dissidents, and selective American air strikes—a pet project of (Retired) Gen. Wayne Downing of the Special Forces, who held an important post at the National Security Council. His plan was dismissed as insufficient to topple Saddam by Gen. Tommy Franks, commander in chief of the Central Command, whose beat included the Gulf region as well as Afghanistan. He estimated that at least 200,000 US troops would be required for the job. Missing from these leaks was a crucial element: what Saddam would do during the US military buildup around Iraq.

These leaks aside, in early spring the Bush administration had sent US Special Forces units to Iraqi Kurdistan, and the British government had dispatched its Special Air Services (SAS) units to the area, despite the ambivalence of Masud Barzani and Jalal Talabani. During their secret meeting with US officials in Frankfurt, Germany, in April, they were asked to host two full-time CIA missions in their territories. They demanded secure guarantees of protection from Saddam for agreeing to such a provocative step against him, and their interlocutors carried the message to Washington. As soon as Saddam got wind of this, he dispatched delegations to Kurdistan to berate Barzani and Talabani, and moved tanks and infantry in offensive positions on the border of Kurdistan.

As for the exiled Iraqi opposition groups, the Iraqi National Congress and its leader, Ahmad Chalabi—by now nursing warm relations with the pro-Israel lobby in the United States—were cordially embraced by the Defense Department and Cheney. But, aware of their rejection by all the Arab states and the European Union (except Britain), the State Department kept its distance from them. When challenged by the Pentagon to find an alternative to the Iraqi National Congress, the State Department sponsored a high-profile meeting of five dozen former Iraqi officers in London in mid-July 2002.

"American policy makers believe that if you scare Saddam and threaten him, he will yield," said an independent-minded Iraqi commentator based in London. "They think this high-profile meeting in London will ruffle his feathers. It also gives a military dimension to the predominantly civilian INC." In other words, this was part of the psychological warfare against Saddam that the Bush administration had launched, unannounced, while keeping alive the threat of military action to overthrow his regime.

The net effect of this policy was to channel the debate on the subject to "how to topple Saddam" while skipping the more basic "why?" Among the early critics of this strategy was Senator John Kerry, a veteran of the Vietnam War, who accused Bush of allowing his "rhetoric to get ahead of his thinking." Only by delving on the "why" aspect of the issue could Bush expect to carry with him not only the reluctant and skeptical Europeans and Arabs but also the American public and Congress. For the task was not just overthrowing Saddam's regime with force but also to maintain a large body of peacekeepers in Iraq for many years and invest in the country's reconstruction. "If we are to achieve our strategic objectives in Iraq, a military campaign very likely would have to be followed by a large-scale, long-term military occupation," wrote Scowcroft in his August 15, 2002 *Wall Street Journal* article.

Oddly, at the Pentagon, while the debate was being led by Wolfowitz and Douglas Feith, undersecretary of defense for policy, their military chiefs preferred the option of achieving the regime change through Saddam's assassination or deteriorating health. The top soldiers opposed the military option on several counts. The policy of containment, applied on the military and economic fronts—naval enforcement of sanctions, no fly zones, continuous presence of 24,000 US troops in the region, rigorous UN administration of Iraqi oil sales, and continued UN supervision of Iraq's imports—had proved effective in severely reducing Baghdad's military threat, and should continue. These restrictions had stopped Saddam from upgrading his armor and air force, two-thirds of which had become obsolete.[25]

Regarding the WMD, Hans Blix, the Unmovic chief, said in late August 2002 that there was "no clear-cut evidence" that Iraq possessed them. Nobody was claiming an Iraqi breakthrough in the nuclear field in the near future, least of all the IAEA, or even British prime minister Tony Blair, who had failed to make public the long-promised dossier on Iraq's WMD.

In the case of biological agents—where Unscom had described Iraqi disclosures as "incomplete, inadequate and technically flawed"—the major problem was maintaining them in a stable condition. The potency of any such agents, weaponized around the time of the 1991 Gulf War, would have by now expired. The only statistic that the Bush administration could provide was the CIA's analysis that Baghdad possessed 2,650 gallons of anthrax. If possessing WMD was a sufficient cause for a country to merit an invasion by the Pentagon, then certainly Israel—possessing an arsenal of two-hundred-plus nuclear arms, produced since 1968, and vast quantities of chemical and biological warfare agents at its Nes Tziona facility south of Tel Aviv, established in 1952—should have been invaded by Washington a long time ago, especially when Israel also had missiles and aircraft to deliver its WMD.

Baghdad, on the other hand, lacked means of delivery. Of the 819 medium- and long-range missiles that it once had, all except two were accounted for and destroyed by the UN inspectors. The Pentagon's worst-case analysis was that Iraq had at most two dozen Al Hussein Scud-B missiles, with a three-hundred-sixty-mile range, but they were not assembled. It was ironic that while the Bush administration had failed to find the domestic source of the anthrax that killed five Americans and created nationwide alarm, it succeeded in engendering a wellspring of hatred toward Iraq based on conjecture peddled by the hawkish officials.

Their overarching case was rooted in the doctrine of a preemptive strike—early unilateral action against a foe suspected of posing a future threat to the United States, a radical departure from the traditional policy of a defensive war sanctified by international law as set out in the United Nations Charter. In a speech in June, Bush declared that "Iraq poses a continuing, unusual and extraordinary threat to the national security of the United States."

Two months later, addressing war veterans in Nashville, Tennessee, Cheney declared that he had "no doubt" that Saddam had chemical and biological warfare agents, and that "many of us are convinced that Saddam Hussein will acquire nuclear weapons fairly soon." His statement contradicted that of Hans Blix made a day earlier on NBC TV. Having ignored facts on the ground as reported by a technocrat who had been in the disarmament business since 1971, Cheney built up an apocalyptic scenario. Armed with nuclear, chemical, and biological weapons—and the power that came from possessing 10 percent of the world's oil reserves—Saddam, he said, "could be expected to seek domination of the entire Middle East, take control of a great portion of the world's energy supplies, directly threaten America's friends throughout the region and subject the United States or any other nation to nuclear blackmail." If Saddam, flush with the funds that Saudi Arabia and Kuwait—not to mention the United States, the Soviet Union, France, and Japan—provided him during the Iran-Iraq War, had failed to produce nuclear arms, how could an Iraq now reduced to the poverty of a sub-Saharan African state after the 1991 Gulf War, acquire such weapons now?

Such simple logic seemed to escape the Cheneys and Rumsfelds, itching to invade Iraq. "We should not mortgage our security to the false promises of wishful thinking and appeasement," said Tom Delay (R—Texas), the House majority whip. It was foolish to use the term "appeaser," applied to British premier Neville Chamberlain in his dealings with Adolf Hitler in the late 1930s. Unlike Hitler, Saddam was not threatening territorial expansion, having tried it in Kuwait with catastrophic results. Battered, deindustrialized Iraq in 2002 had little in common with the militarist, industrialized Germany on the eve of World War II. Finally, no politician in the West or the Arab world was proposing to buy off Saddam by making concessions.

There were other items in the hawks' charge sheet against Saddam. He was a terrorist. But the last instance of his alleged involvement in such action went back to 1993, when a plot to assassinate Bush Sr. during his trip to Kuwait was quashed by the Kuwaiti authorities. Two, Iraq gave $25,000 each to the families of Palestinian suicide bombers. After the eruption of the Second Intifada by the Palestinians against the Israeli occupation in September 2000, the Palestinian Authority (PA) handed over a $2,000 check to the family of the Palestinian killed in the struggle to compensate it for the loss. Following the PA's lead, the Arab Liberation Front (ALF), a pro-Iraq Palestinian faction, gave a $10,000 check to the family of the latest Palestinian "martyr," and a $1,000 check to the family of an injured Palestinian.[26] Later, when Palestinian militants resorted to suicide bombings, the ALF raised the compensation to their families to $25,000. Of the 1,500 Palestinians killed during the first two years of the intifada, only 70 were suicide bombers. So it was not that Saddam was singling out Palestinian suicide bombers. His government had started to compensate *all* the Palestinians who died in the intifada, almost invariably at the hands of the Israeli military or Jewish settlers in the Palestinian Territories—as had the PA.

Three, Saddam had violated human rights. Appalling though his record in this field was, it was not worse than those of several other surviving despots. There is Kim Jong Il, the dictator of Communist North Korea, who succeeded his equally ruthless father Kim Il Sung, the two of them together exercising power since the end of World War II. For the past four decades, a military junta has been ruling Burma under their iron heels, and the original coup leader, Ne Win, who overthrew the popularly elected government in 1962, though too old to govern, is still around. Crucially, was there any UN Security Council resolution that said that Saddam should be overthrown because of his violations of human rights?

Given Baghdad's recent successful overtures to mend its fences with its neighbors, including Iran, Kuwait, and Saudi Arabia, the hawks' fourth charge, that Saddam was a threat to his neighboring countries, lacked evidence. All of Iraq's neighbors had come out against a military attack on it. And on August 27 Egyptian president Hosni Mubarak reiterated that all Arab League members were opposed to an invasion of Iraq, thus reiterating the position taken by the Arab summit five months earlier.

Finally, the hawks argued that Iraq was in breach of several UN Security Council resolutions. But, as detailed in chapter 6, in each case the council had responded. So the matter had evened out. It was noteworthy that the all-important Resolution 1284 (December 1999), which virtually rewrote the earlier Resolution 687 (April 1991), did not get the backing of three of the five permanent members of the council. Moreover, as the administration's tougher critics noted, Israel had been in breach of more Security Council resolutions than Iraq. Had Washington gotten around to even pointing out this simple fact?

Moreover, by threatening to invade a sovereign state without a UN mandate, without showing a just cause, and without exhausting all avenues of a peaceful resolution—a prerequisite for a just the United States was making a much bigger mockery of international law than Iraq. "If we try to act against Saddam Hussein without proper provocation we will not have the support of other nations," warned Republican representative Dick Armey, the House majority leader.

To argue that Saddam's possession of WMD was a breach of the 1991 cease-fire did not authorize the United States to invade Iraq to overthrow Saddam. As James Baker, secretary of state to George Bush Sr., said in his August 25 *New York Times* article, Washington needed a Security Council resolution requiring that "Iraq submit to intrusive inspections anytime, anywhere" and authorizing "all necessary means to achieve it" and that during the debate the US should make clear that if Saddam resorted to "cheat-and-retreat tactics" it would apply "whatever means are necessary to change the regime." Saddam's acceptance of no-notice inspections would keep him "off balance and under close observation, even if all his weapons of mass destruction capabilities were not uncovered," argued Scowcroft in his August 15, *Wall Street Journal* op-ed. "And if he refused, his rejection could provide the persuasive casus belli which many claim we do not now have."

In contrast to Baker and Scowcroft, the hawks in the Bush Jr. administration made no mention of the law in their argument. The White House seemed to consider itself exempt from the laws of war and the traditional norms concerning just and unjust wars. In London, however, government lawyers pointed out to Blair in March that destroying Saddam's WMD was "one thing" since it could be covered by a Security Council resolution, but invading Iraq to oust him was "totally illegal under international law."[27] In the past, they pointed out, there was the specific Security Council Resolution 678 on Kuwait authorizing UN member-states to "use all necessary means" to expel Iraq from the emirate, and that Resolution 1368, passed on September 12, 2001, recognized the inherent right of individual or collective self-defense for the United States. Dealing with the question of legality in his *Washington Post* article in early August, Samuel Berger, the national security adviser to Bill Clinton during the years 1997–2001, said: "The fact that America can do it [overthrow Saddam] alone does not mean it is wise to do so. *Power by itself does not confer legitimacy.*"[28]

Intent on attacking Iraq, the Bush administration had taken to downgrading the significance of UN inspections and monitoring while pressuring the United Nations to stick to discussing with Baghdad only the modalities of the return of UN inspectors. That explained the rejection of Iraq's invitation to Blix and his experts in early August to Baghdad "to discuss outstanding disarmament issues and to establish a solid basis for the next stage of monitoring and inspecting activities, and to move forward to that state." However, Blix put a different spin on it. "My visit to Baghdad would only raise expectations and potentially create a crisis if talks between him [Blix] and Iraqi officials broke down," he told the London-based *Al Hayat* (The Life). Small wonder that the invitation to US Congress leaders by Iraqi speaker Sadoun Hamadi to visit Iraq for three weeks along with disarmament experts "to see the true facts for yourself through direct dialogue and then reach your own conclusions" went unacknowledged. While the Iraqi gestures were dismissed out of hand by US officials and media, they played very well in the Arab world, convincing the public there that the talk about the WMD allegedly possessed by Baghdad was merely a pretext and that Washington was out to invade Iraq no matter what Saddam did or did not do.

THE RISKS

While thundering that "the risks of inaction are far greater than the risks of action," Cheney did not even mention briefly what the hazards of invading Iraq were. These risks—military, diplomatic, political, and economic—were grave at best and catastrophic at worst. Unlike in

1991, when the Iraqis faced the US-led coalition forces in Kuwait, a foreign country, they would now fight to defend their homeland on familiar terrain. Iraqis are known as staunch nationalists. They mounted a yearlong popular uprising against the British mandate in 1920, and were never properly pacified until their country became independent twelve years later. References to their successful resistance to Western imperialism in the recent past will form the core of the official propaganda to inspire Iraqis, military and civilian, to fight to preserve their country's independence and freedom—an aim they would take all the more seriously when they find the traditional Arab allies of the United States staying out of the war.

In this conflict Saddam is unlikely to repeat the blunder of exposing his armed men and material in the desert as he did in the Gulf War. Indeed, he is reported to have planned urban warfare and instructed the provincial officials accordingly. "If Crusaders attack us," he told George Galloway, a British member of Parliament, in August, "we will fight on the streets, from the rooftops, from house to house." This will likely result in the death of thousands of American soldiers and Iraqi civilians.

Consequently Anthony Cordesman told the Senate Foreign Relations Committee hearings that "Iraq might be a far easier opponent than its force strength [of 380,000] indicates. But it also is potentially a very serious military opponent indeed. . . . Only fools would bet the lives of other men's sons and daughters on their own arrogance, and call this [Iraqi] force a cakewalk or a speed bump or something you can dismiss."[29] Military experts estimate that, allowing for the efficacy of the smart weapons used by the Pentagon in Afghanistan, a successful war against Iraq would require the further destruction of Iraq's towns and cities, resulting in a toll of civilian lives on a scale not witnessed in Afghanistan, or the Federal Republic of Yugoslavia in 1999 during the Kosovo campaign.

Then there is the process of transmitting war news by image and word. The key difference between now and the Gulf War is that in

1990–91 the Arab governments had a monopoly over the broadcasting channels and most of the print media. That was how King Fahd of Saudi Arabia managed to suppress the news about Iraq's invasion of Kuwait in the kingdom's print and broadcasting media for one hundred hours.

Today, with Al Jazeera and twenty other Arabic-language satellite channels in business, such a scenario is unthinkable. This became clear when Al Jazeera brought the images of carnage caused by the US bombing in Afghanistan into millions of Arab homes, thus hardening anti-American sentiment.

Were the Bush administration to repeat its Afghan military performance in Iraq—deploying up to 250,000 troops on land, sea, and air—with the concomitant loss of thousands of civilian lives and massive damage to Iraqi public and private property, it would daily provide hours of visual record of the carnage to tens of millions of Arabs and Muslims. One can well imagine the inflaming of popular feelings in the Arab and Muslim states and the destabilizing consequences if that sentiment escalated into street rioting and attacks on Western targets in those countries.

Saddam's statement to Galloway indicated that he would depict Washington's invasion of Iraq as aggression against a Muslim country and therefore against Islam. It is worth noting that on the eve of the 1991 Gulf War he decreed that the slogan "*Allahu Akbar*"— God Is Great be inscribed on Iraq's tricolor flag, a step that went down well in the Muslim world. In other words, though heading the government run by the secular Baath Party, Saddam is quite adept at invoking Islam when he finds it expeditious.

This time, by invoking Islam, he will aim to co-opt the majority in the Arab and Muslim world that is passionately interested in the fate of the Palestinians and East Jerusalem, which is the site of the Dome of the Rock, the third holiest shrine of Islam. "The obsession of the [Middle East] region is the Israeli-Palestinian conflict," wrote Brent Scowcroft in the *Journal*. "If we were seen to be turning our backs on that bitter conflict—which the region perceives, wrongly or rightly, to be within our power to resolve—to go after Iraq, there would be an explosion of outrage against us. We would be seen as ignoring a key interest of the Muslim world in order to satisfy what is seen to be a narrow American interest." That will inflame the already rancorous relations between the pro-American Israelis and pro-Iraqi Palestinians, and threaten the stability of Jordan, with three-fifths of its population being of Palestinian origin, and also Saudi Arabia, which is regarded as the prime state in the Muslim world because it contains Islam's two holiest shrines in Mecca and Medina, and whose ruler is expected to further the interests of Muslims in the Palestinian Territories and elsewhere. The destabilization of the Arab regimes, and the rise in militant anti-Americanism in the region, will increase Israel's isolation, not decrease it, thus defeating one of the US hawks' strategic aims and, inadvertently, abetting Saddam's agenda. Furthermore, the negative repercussions will also be felt in Turkey, Afghanistan, and Pakistan, where a dramatic upset might put the country's nuclear arsenal in the hands of fundamentalist generals. At the very least these developments will curtail foreign governments' cooperation with Washington to counter terrorism as well as swell the terrorist ranks.

By invading Iraq, Washington will initiate a conflict the course of which is very hard to predict. The best scenario projected by the US hawks shows Iraqi soldiers defecting in droves and civilians welcoming the Americans as liberators. Such an eventuality is based on the information and expectations of the exiled Iraqi opposition. History shows that exiles are the last people to have a correct grasp of the current situation in the country they have left. Washington faced a fiasco when it mounted its Bay of Pigs operation in Cuba, based on information provided by Cuban exiles, in January 1961. More recently in Iraqi Kurdistan, the scenario visualized by the Iraqi National Congress and the Patriotic Union of Kurdistan in March 1995 failed to materialize (see chapter 5).

To imagine that a people who have suffered grievously at the hands of the United States for twelve years, and have grown deep hatred for it, would turn out in thousands to greet American soldiers and their Iraqi cohorts as liberators seems unrealistic. The United States has been generally wrong both in gauging popular feeling in Iraq and in devising policies likely to turn Iraqis against Saddam and his regime. Leaving aside the immediate aftermath of the Gulf War, what has actually happened in Iraq is the opposite of Washington's scenarios, often conceived in consultation with the Iraqi opposition. The United States has failed to grasp a basic element of popular psychology. When a country is attacked, its citizens rally around the leader. This is what happened after the September 11 terrorist attacks on New York and Washington. Americans turned to President Bush Jr. for leadership and succor. His popularity ratings soared from 50 percent to 90 percent. In Iraq this is precisely what happened after the Pentagon's bombings of Iraq—in January and June 1993, September 1996, December 1998, and February 2001. They stoked feelings not against Saddam, but the United States. Also, far from causing Saddam's ousting or destabilization of his regime, the US policy of maintaining punishing sanctions against Iraq has ended up—albeit inadvertently—aiding him to tighten his grip over society by a most effective instrument of rationing.

Besides urban warfare, the other major risk was that, facing the prospect of losing power, Saddam would have no qualms about deploying chemical or biological agents if he possesses them, rather then let the invading Americans seize them. In that case, the Pentagon's worst scenario estimates 35,000 US casualties. Simple logic tells us that the chance of Saddam using nonconventional arms rises with the imminence of the fall of his regime. Also, with the strict control of the country by Saddam gone, there is a strong chance of the existing chemical or biological agents falling into the hands of a renegade Iraqi general, thus increasing, rather than decreasing, the chance of their proliferation. The task of locating Saddam and/or his close associates and/or renegade generals will be long and hazardous. It took the United States a fortnight to find President Manuel Noriega in Panama, a tiny state where the Pentagon maintained military bases.

By opening a new and, potentially, very messy military front, Washington will end up diluting and complicating its commitment to pursue its war on terrorism as well as causing a diminution in the cooperation other nations have been offering it in the counterterrorism war. Among those who pointed out this danger were Scowcroft and Berger, with the latter warning that any alienation of the United States' traditional European and Arab allies caused by its unilateral invasion of Iraq would be hard to repair.

In the economic field, the disruption of oil supplies from the region will hurt the economies of the United States, the European Union, and Japan at a time when the economic picture is far from bright. On top of this will come the financial demands of postwar Iraq, ranging from $50 billion to $150 billion, the cost of maintaining 75,000 peacekeeping troops for one year alone being $16 billion.

Politically, unlike in Afghanistan or Yugoslavia, there is no Iraqi leadership waiting in the wings to fill the vacuum left by Saddam's overthrow and initiate a democratization process. The conquering army of the United States would need active cooperation and participation by the European Union, Russia, and Iraq's neighbors. All of them (with the possible exception of an ambivalent Britain) are against an American preemptive strike. That vastly increases the chance of anarchy and the breakup of Iraq. If that happens, it will create fresh anti-US regimes and terrorist havens in the region. If and when peace is restored, the oil-rich southern zone, dominated by Shias and close to Iran, politically and geographically, will be less amenable to US oil corporations. Neither Iran nor Syria will take kindly to the pro-US regime that is installed by Washington. Since both countries nurture political constituencies in Iraq, they will not be averse to destabilizing the post-Saddam regime.

Assuming Washington's best-case scenario, that post-Saddam Iraq will be peacefully transformed into a federation of its Arab and Kurdish parts, both Ankara and Tehran will view the new arrangement as transient, expecting Iraqi Kurdistan to secede from Baghdad at the earliest opportunity to become an independent state. This will encourage Turkish and Iranian Kurds to relaunch their secessionist movements. To counter this threat to their territorial integrity, neither Turkey nor Iran will shy away from attacking, singly or jointly, the fledgling independent Kurdistan.

If the risks are high, so are the rewards, argue the hawks. Ousting Saddam and replacing him with a democratic regime in Baghdad will open Iraq's rich oil fields to US corporations, thus releasing the United States from its dependence on petroleum from Saudi Arabia, a fundamentalist kingdom that provided the bulk of the hijackers for the 9/11 attacks. Furthermore, they claim, Washington will introduce democracy in Iraq, from where it is bound to spread to the rest of the region.

Interestingly, several weeks before the debate on Iraq took off in the United States in early August—when neoconservative hawks in Washington were preaching democracy across the Arab world, with the "regime change" in Baghdad as the starter—Bush had called for the removal of Yasser Arafat as the Palestinian leader. "These pro-democracy strategies are part of a 'neo-imperialist' school expressed powerfully by former US officials such as Robert Kagan, Richard Perle and William Kristol," wrote David Ignatius, senior columnist of the *Washington Post* and executive editor of the *International Herald Tribune*.[30]

Everybody in the West agrees that a democratic change in the Arab world is overdue. The question is: how is this transformation to be effected. Should it be imposed by a foreign conquering army or should it come from within?

If democracy is delivered to Iraqis by the Americans arriving in tanks and helicopter gunships, then the local people and other Arabs will perceive it as a consequence of a defeat inflicted on them by their nemesis, the Israeli-American nexus. That would unveil a new and bloody chapter of US military occupation of humiliated and resentful peoples.

The other alternative is to encourage the trend toward a representative government that is already in train in the oil-rich Gulf states. Since 1999 direct elections for municipalities and the national Consultative Councils on the basis of adult franchise have been held or scheduled in Bahrain, Oman, and Qatar. Since Kuwait has had parliament elected on a limited franchise since its independence in 1961, all that is required is an expansion of its electoral base.

The major exception is Saudi Arabia. There the Consultative Council remains fully nominated by the monarch. Bush and his team should be advising Crown Prince Abdullah, the de facto ruler, to have the council members elected by popular vote and be given legislative and budgetary powers they now lack. But US officials are not doing so. For they know well that in a free and fair election Saudi voters will choose those who want to remove the kingdom from under the wings of the American eagle.

No wonder that the support for war against Baghdad by US forces fell from 88 percent in November to 53 percent in August, according to the Gallup Poll. More worryingly for the hawks, only 20 percent backed an attack if the US mounted it unilaterally, with 75 percent opposing it.[31] In a way the American public was catching up with its European counterpart.

"America may be just rattling a saber to persuade Saddam Hussein to allow the return of UN inspectors," said a former German minister of culture in February. "But the experience of two world wars on its soil has taught Europe to be wary of anything that raises the prospect of uncontrollable military escalation."[32] The general European consensus was that President Bush had frittered away the moral leadership that he was granted after 9/11 by opting for unilateralism in the aftermath of a surprisingly swift victory in Afghanistan. This in turn had given fresh impetus to the French idea of the European Union as a countervailing power to the United States.

In March German chancellor Gerhard Schroeder declared that Germany would participate in war against Baghdad only if it was backed by a UN mandate. With only a third of Germans favoring an invasion of Iraq, he was reflecting a majority view. Three months later France, administered by the freshly reelected President Jacques Chirac, expressed its opposition to military action without "conclusive proof of Baghdad's role in exporting terrorism." After a meeting between the two leaders on July 30, Chirac said, "Any attack on Iraq will only be justified if a mandate was approved by the UN Security Council. That is the position of Germany and France."

Following Cheney's combative speech in late August, Chirac criticized "attempts to legitimize the deployment of unilateral and pre-emptive use of force"—not least because other nations would use this as a pretext to settle their own disputes. "This runs contrary to the vision of the collective security of France, a vision that is based on cooperation among states, respect of the law and the authority of the Security Council," he said. "We shall repeat these rules as often as needed, and notably over Iraq."[33]

Even Blair, the hitherto unquestioning ally of the United States, began to have second thoughts. While claiming in public that he was 100 percent with the United States, he privately urged Bush to reengage with the United Nations. A BBC poll in March showed that seven-eighths of the ruling Labor MPs opposed military action against Baghdad. What undermined the British hawks were statements by former Conservative foreign secretary Lord Hurd—"The Americans narrow their options if they insist on regime change without any international authority"—and former Chief of Defense Staff (equivalent of the US chair to the Joint Chiefs of Staff) Lord Field Marshal Bramall: "Overthrowing Saddam may not be morally or legally justified. And any evidence of the WMD was remarkably sparse." Bramall added that Britain risked "being dragged into a very very messy and long lasting Middle East war if it goes along with US plans for a military assault on Iraq." These sentiments were in tune with the popular opinion.[34]

It came as no surprise when, in early August, after meeting Blair in London, King Abdullah II of Jordan said that his interlocutor had confided to him "tremendous concerns" about an attack on Iraq. He told CNN that invading Iraq would open "a Pandora's box" while the Israeli-Palestinian conflict remained unresolved. Later the normally phlegmatic Egyptian president Mubarak said, "I told the American government: if you strike at the Iraqi people because of one or two individuals and leave the Palestinian issue [unresolved], not a single [Arab] ruler will be able to curb the popular sentiment. There might be repercussions, and we fear a state of disorder and chaos may prevail in the region."[35] Saudi foreign minister Saud al Faisal added his voice: "For the government of Iraq, the leadership of Iraq, any change that happens there has to come from the Iraqi people."

A broader perspective was provided by Pakistani president Gen. Pervez Musharraf. "It is already dangerous that all political disputes at the moment all around the world are unfortunately involving Muslims, and Muslims are feeling that they are on the receiving end everywhere," he said. "There is a feeling of alienation in the Muslim world and I think this [attack on Iraq] will lead to further alienation."

If, by rejecting the advice of such long-standing friends of the United States, President Bush invades Iraq, he will push the world inexorably toward the much-dreaded clash of civilizations between the West and the Muslim world with grave consequences for us all, thus unwittingly fulfilling the agenda of Osama bin Laden and extremists of his ilk.

POSTSCRIPT

We cannot have another Gulf War. We cannot have the people of Iraq suffering again. That would be wrong. . . . We should be ready to impose the will of the United Nations on them [Saddam and the elite around him] if they don't cooperate, but not by hurting the people of Iraq.
> —Clare Short, British secretary for international development,
> September 23, 2002

A ugust is a month of rest and relaxation in the Western world, a vacationing time. In the Middle East though, it is a period of unbearable heat, of long siestas in homes cooled by electric fans or air conditioning.

In recent decades August has figured ominously both globally and regionally. It was during this month that war clouds gathered in Europe in 1939 before bursting on September 1, with Germany invading Poland on that date. And it was on the second day of August in 1990 that Iraqi tanks charged into Kuwait at a time when President George Bush Sr. governed the United States—setting in train an international process that remained unfinished 12 years later when the White House in Washington was occupied by Bush Sr.'s son, George Walker.

During August 2002, though, the seat of the US government moved temporarily to the sprawling ranch of George W. Bush Jr. in Crawford, Texas. Between playing golf, holding informal barbecue parties, and making periodic forays into the American hinterland to raise funds for the Republican Party's mid-term election campaign, the US president gave brief press conferences. Here he would mention the danger that Iraqi dictator Saddam Hussein posed to the United

States against the background of a debate in the country about the pros and cons of a military action against Iraq, with Lawrence Eagleburger, former US secretary of state under his father, saying, "I am scared to death that the Richard Perles and [Paul] Wolfowitzes of this world are arguing that we can [topple Saddam] in a cakewalk. I am scared to death they are going to convince the President . . . and we'll find ourselves in the middle of a swamp because we didn't plan to do it the right way."[1] Responding to such utterances, presidential aides would tell the White House press corps that the national debate had moved far ahead of any plans by the Pentagon, with Bush himself trying to cool it by saying, "I'm a patient man."

While Bush professed patience, his Vice President, Dick Cheney, delivered a speech to the Veterans for Foreign Wars national convention in Nashville, Tennessee, on August 26, which combined belligerency with impatience. "The Iraqi regime has in fact been very busy enhancing its capabilities in the field of chemical and biological agents," he told his audience. "And they continue to pursue the nuclear program they began so many years ago." How did he know? "We've gotten this from the firsthand testimony of defectors,' he grimly revealed, "including Saddam's own son-in-law." (This was old hat, as the reader, having perused Chapter 6, would know.) From this Cheney went on to deduct that United Nations inspections and inspectors were inept and irrelevant, ignoring the vital fact that Unscom had relied heavily on information supplied by Iraqi defectors and the intelligence agencies of UN members, principally the United States, Britain, and Israel. Then, having scared his audience with an apocalyptic scenario of Saddam running amok with his weapons of mass destruction, he concluded that war with Iraq was "inevitable." Thus, as a counterpoint to "a patient Bush" emerged "an impatient Cheney."

Once the Labor Day holiday was past, Bush, working closely with his hawkish aides, unleashed a campaign which was designed primarily to improve the electoral chances of the Republicans at the mid-term election on November 5. Because Bush had lost the popular vote in the presidential contest in November 2000, he was keen to see the Republicans regain control of the Senate and retain their majority in the House.

The omens were unpromising. His popularity rating had dropped to 63 percent, the lowest since the 9/11 attacks, and the approval for his foreign policy handling was down to 54 percent, a loss of 14 points in a month. Equally alarming to his party strategists was the *Los Angeles Times* poll which showed that while 28 percent thought that the economy and jobs were the most important issue, only 11 percent considered homeland security and terrorism as their top priority.[2]

These statistics became available at a time when negative reactions to the Cheney speech began pouring in at the State Department in the form of reports from American embassies worldwide. These dispatches came in handy to Colin Powell in illustrating the diplomatic dangers of ignoring the UN on the Iraq issue. Going by the remarks attributed to his close aides in *Time*, Powell felt unbearably frustrated, having to battle the hawks perennially, preferring therefore to say little in public about Iraq. Quite independently, his case got a boost when in a long telephone conversation British prime minister Tony Blair, while agreeing with Bush on the ominous threat posed by Saddam, advised him not to bypass the UN Security Council.

So, a year after the tragedy of 9/11, Bush faced an almost universal international isolation, which was highlighted by the statement of Jean Chretien, the prime minister of neighboring Canada, a traditional ally of America: "As for going in and changing the [Iraqi] regime, as opposed to going in and ensuring that there are no weapons of mass destruction, we haven't signed on to that"[3] All this was in stark contrast to the time when, in the immediate aftermath of the September 11 attacks, world leaders rushed to express their backing for Bush's war on Al Qaeda.

Now, while Bush continued his refrain about Saddam's evil designs, his counterpart in Germany—the most populous nation in the European Union, and ranking third in the world's economies—Chancellor Gerhard Schroeder, who was in the midst of an election campaign, wondered aloud why there was suddenly this urgency about Iraq when there was no new evidence of its acquiring WMD. He pointed out that Washington had no idea how war on Iraq would impact the cohesion of the antiterror coalition it had assembled and the stability of the moderate pro-Western regimes in the region. He ruled out Germany's participation in any US-led invasion of Iraq even with UN and EU mandates.[4]

After Schroeder's talks with French president Jacques Chirac in early September, both leaders objected to Washington's unilateral change in the aims of the policy on Iraq to overthrowing Saddam— a departure from the consensus among US allies to contain and deter Baghdad through UN inspections as well as economic, political, and diplomatic pressure. They reiterated their demand for the unconditional return of UN inspectors to Iraq. Schroeder's unambiguous stance that Germany would not participate in an anti-Iraq war even if sanctioned by the Security Council, and would bar the Pentagon from using German air bases for attacking Iraq, would help him win the closely fought election. The opposition to America's go-it-alone policy was strong elsewhere in Europe as well. "Unilateral US military action could destroy the keystone of US diplomacy, the global antiterrorist alliance," warned Romano Prodi, the European Commission president.[5]

No wonder that when Bush tried to secure the backing of Chirac for a military attack on Iraq, he heard the latter express "serious doubts" about the validity, political and legal, of such action. He got a similar response from the presidents of Russia and China when he telephoned them.[6]

What further undermined Bush's hawkish position was the one-man campaign by Scott Ritter. It got a boost when he was invited to address the Iraqi parliament in Baghdad—a unique honor for a Westerner. "My country seems to be on the verge of making a historical mistake," Ritter told the Iraqi lawmakers on September 8.

'The rhetoric of fear that is disseminated by my government has not, to date, been backed by hard facts that substantiate any allegations that Iraq is today in possession of weapons of mass destruction or has links to terror groups responsible for September 11 attacks on the United States." So, what were the facts? "Iraq, during nearly seven years of continuous inspection activity by the United Nations, had been certified as being disarmed to a 90–95 percent level," he said.

Having engaged in espionage for the US, knowingly or unknowingly, Ritter conceded that "Iraq has legitimate grievances regarding the past work of the weapons inspectors, and for that reason has sought to keep inspectors from returning to Iraq." But, assessing the overall situation, he concluded that "The only path toward peace that will be embraced by the international community is one which begins by Iraq agreeing to the immediate, unconditional return of UN weapons inspectors operating in full keeping with the mandate as set forth by existing UN Security Council resolutions."

Paralleling the situation in the united States, there were two schools of thought in Iraq: the hawkish one was for keeping the inspectors out, whereas the dovish school was for reengaging with the UN on inspections but only as part of a comprehensive deal that eliminated the threat of US invasion and addressed such critical issues as the eventual lifting of sanctions. Explaining the Iraqi dilemma, Hans von Sponeck , a former UN humanitarian coordinator in Iraq, said: "The Iraqis have deep fears that inspectors would come back, carry out their work and create an artificial problem so Iraq gets bombed. But if they don't show signs that they are willing to resume discussions [with the UN], it will play into the hands of hard-liners in the US.'[7] The Iraqi hawks argued that since the US would use the returned UN inspectors to spy and help the Pentagon update its Iraqi target list, and then manufacture a crisis that would give the United States a pretext to invade Iraq, it was better to keep out the inspectors. But they lost to the other side.

Iraqi foreign minister Naji Sabri tried to implement the dovish mandate by pursuing a two-track strategy—one aimed at the Arab world and the other at China, France, and Russia, with the main focus on Russia. His visit to Moscow was successful. After talking with him, Russian foreign minister Igor Ivanov said, "I hope the UN Security Council will not face the issue of authorizing a strike on Iraq when [exercising] the right of veto will be necessary. I don't see a single well-founded argument that Iraq represents a threat to US national security."

When the Arab League foreign ministers, meeting in Cairo on September 4–5, declared their "total rejection of the threat of aggression on Arab nations, in particular Iraq, reaffirming that these threats to the security and safety of any Arab country are considered a threat to Arab national security," Sabri was visibly satisfied.[8]

This statement reflected the public opinion in the Arab world, incensed by Washington's overlooking of Israel's continued reoccupation of West Bank towns and cities, topped with Israeli prime minister Ariel Sharon's declaration that since the Oslo Accords were dead, he had no intention of handing over the administration of the West Bank's urban areas to the Palestinian Authority. Expressing a prevalent sentiment in the Arab world, Prince Khalid al Faisal, governor of the Saudi province of Asir, told Neil MacFarquhar of the *New York Times*, "It is very frustrating to see our people [Arabs] killed every day [in the Palestinian Territories]; you see them on television, you see women and children being bombed by American airplanes, American helicopters, American tanks and American money. This is disturbing. We think the Zionist movement is using this opportunity to make Islam and the Arabs the enemy of the West."[9]

In the Arab world the American-Israeli nexus was seen to be so strong that the issue of Iraq could not be delinked from Israel. "Many ordinary people and politicians [in the Arab world] feel that the moves against Iraq are an effort to redraw the map of the Middle East for the strategic interest of the United States and Israel," said Rami Khouri, an Amman-based American-educated Jordanian analyst with the International Crisis Group of Washington. "Everyone I know wants Saddam removed. Nobody I know wants the Americans to do it—because we believe they are the last people in the world who will work on behalf of Arab interests."[10]

A US attack on Iraq while the Israeli-Palestinian conflict continues to rage will lead to a violent eruption of anger in the Arab and Muslim world and make anti-American terrorism the only outlet of expression for many other nonfundamentalist groups of Muslims, most Arab and Muslim analysts warned. Disputing the US hawks' scenario that the military overthrow of Saddam would trigger "march of democracy" in the Middle East, they foresaw destabilization and chaos in the region.

Careful though Sharon was by saying little in public about Iraq and Saddam, there was no doubt in the minds of astute Arab and other analysts that Sharon and the pro-Israeli lobby in Washington were the driving force behind the campaign for "regime change in Baghdad." Equally disturbing to them was Bush's misguided strategy on countering terrorism—conceived and implemented by a small circle of intelligence and defense officials—with the sole stress on vengeance in the style of the American Wild West, and no interest in determining and rectifying the political causes of terrorism. Illustrative of this policy was the statement by Richard Armitage, US deputy secretary of state, during his visit to Lebanon regarding "the blood debt" that the Hizbollah—an Islamic fundamentalist group represented in the Lebanese parliament—owed to Washington for the October 1983 truck-bombing in Beirut that killed 241 American troops.

THE FIRST ANNIVERSARY OF 9/11 AND AFTER

As the United States prepared to remember the 3,052 people who perished in the tragedy of 9/11 with prayers and poignant ceremonies throughout the country, the Bush administration mounted a well-crafted media campaign to sublimate the atrocities committed by Al Qaeda, led by Osama bin Laden, with Iraq, governed by Saddam Hussein, the evil incarnate. Bush and his close aides made a deliberate and sustained attempt to channel the nation's grief and defiance expressed at highly charged 9/11 anniversary ceremonies into national and international resolve to take the antiterror war to Iraq. By deciding to have Donald Rumsfeld stand beside him as the band played "The Star Spangled Banner," Bush emphasized the military nature of the counterterrorism campaign as he visited the three sites where the hijackers had crashed their planes a year earlier.

By so doing, the Bush administration made no distinction between a private terrorist group, such as Al Qaeda, and Iraq, a member-state of the UN, which, for totally different reasons, had since 1990 been on the agenda of the UN Security Council, the only internationally recognized body authorized to deal with it.

The Bush White House felt impelled to implement this strategy when it realized that, according to three-fifths of Americans, their government could not claim victory in its antiterrorism war until and unless it had captured or killed bin Laden.

While Bush probably perceived a military confrontation with Saddam as an extension of his war on terrorism—unveiled with the bombing of the Taliban-administered Afghanistan harboring Al Qaeda—he had failed to build a case for an anti-Baghdad campaign on the back of the anti-Taliban one. Those congressional leaders entitled to classified intelligence briefings had so far failed to see or hear any fresh evidence that Baghdad posed an immediate threat to US security. A similar situation prevailed in Britain, the only European nation officially and vocally toeing Bush's line. An intelligence source who had read the Blair government's Iraq dossier long before its release on September 24 said, "It does not establish an overwhelming case for war based on new weapons Saddam may have acquired. The significant change is September 11 [2001], which has convinced military advisers that we cannot ignore Iraq the same way we ignored Afghanistan when it harbored Al Qaeda."[11]

Then there was the question of interpretation and analysis of the intelligence on Iraq. Differences arose in the interpretations given by the Washington-London axis and such professional disarmament experts as Hans Blix, head of the UN Monitoring, Verification, and Inspection Commission. At a joint press conference at Camp David on September 7, Bush and Blair showed some satellite pictures, indicating new construction activity (seemingly at Tuweitha, the original site of the French-built nuclear reactors destroyed by Israel in 1980), once identified as nuclear-related, as evidence that Iraq was working on a nuclear weapons program. On September 10, Blix said that Unmovic did not draw the same conclusion from the satellite images presented by Bush and Blair.[12]

That day Iraqi officials took a group of Baghdad-based international journalists to Tuweitha, and went through the three buildings in the satellite images published in the British press, alleging that Iraq had resumed nuclear weapons research. One building turned out to be a mere shed. The second site was a hulking carcass of a building which, according to Iraqi officials, was used during 1981–91 to deal with radioactive materials produced for diagnosing and treating cancer, and was bombed during the Gulf War. The third building, used for producing chemical agents to treat cancer, was "far from new," according to Amberin Zaman of the (London) *Daily Telegraph.* 'Its floors are well worn, its walls grotty and cracked." Zaman was taken to a small room by Dr. Hisham Atmed, head of the research team, where, pointing to a pair of Unscom labels pasted on the face of a stove-like steel contraption used to dry chemicals, he said: "The [UN] inspectors have seen everything." The complex was repeatedly scrutinized by Unscom, the escorting Iraqi official told the foreign journalists, adding that the inspectors of the International Atomic Energy Agency had visited it in January 2002. Finally came the barn-like structures that had featured on the Blair-supplied aerial photograph. "Inside a dark room, white fungi spring from manure-filled plastic bags," Zaman reported. Ali Nadeer, the head of the mushroom unit, picked a few mushrooms and munched them, the (secret) source of his enhanced sexual prowess. "I used to have one American wife; now I have two Iraqi wives," he told the bemused reporters.[13]

In New York, in his introductory remarks to the 57th UN General Assembly session on September 12, Kofi Annan said: "I stand before you as a multilateralist—by precedent, by principle, by charter, by duty." This was warmly received by the delegates. "Every government that is committed to the rule of law at home must also be committed to the rule of law abroad." He stressed that beyond the issue of self-defense, "When states decide to use force to deal with broader threats to international peace and security, there is no substitute for the unique legitimacy provided by the United Nations." In a thinly disguised reference to the United States, he said, 'For any one state, large or small, choosing to accept or reject the multilateral path must not be a simple path of political convenience. Even the most powerful countries know that they need to work with others."

At the top of Annan's list of the significant threats to international peace and security requiring the UN's attention was the Israeli-Palestinian issue. He called for an international peace conference, a proposal that would later be taken up by Tony Blair.

Speaking after Annan, President Bush emphasized the primacy of the United States—"We will use our position of unparalleled strength and influence to build an atmosphere of international order and openness in which progress and liberty can flourish in many nations"—and then focused almost exclusively on Iraq. "Saddam Hussein's regime is a grave and gathering danger," he said. "To suggest otherwise is to hope against the evidence. To assume this regime's good faith is to bet the lives of millions." He pointed out that Iraq retained "capable nuclear scientists and technicians and physical infrastructure," and had attempted to buy, unsuccessfully, "thousands of high-strength aluminum tubes for centrifuges to enrich uranium for a nuclear weapon." Once Iraq had fissile material, he warned , it could build a weapon in one year.[14]

Bush demanded Baghdad's compliance with the following demands: disclosure and removal of all WMD; active suppression of terrorism; a halt to the persecution of civilians of all ethnicities; return of the remaining prisoners of war from the Gulf conflict and the Iran-Iraq War; and cessation of any illicit trade outside the UN's oil-for-food program.

While promising that "We will work with the UN Security Council for the necessary resolutions," he emphasized that "the purpose of the United States should not be doubted." Setting out a guideline for the international community, he said, "If Iraq's regime defies us again, the world must move decisively to hold Iraq to account."'Summarizing his speech, Bush's aides stated that while the president acknowledged the UN's authority, he warned that its legitimacy would be at stake if it did not act on Iraq the way he wanted it to.

That day, in Washington, the White House released a twenty-page document on Iraq, entitled *A Decade of Deception and Defiance*. Disarmament experts were unimpressed. The report recycled a compendium of dated and circumstantial evidence that Saddam Hussein may be concealing the ingredients for WMD, and trying to develop a nuclear capability and weaponize biological and chemical agents. In the one page given to Iraq's support for international terrorism, there was a reference to an attempt to assassinate Bush Sr. in April 1993. Missing from the report was any allusion to Al Qaeda or a purported meeting between Muhammad Atta and Ahmad Ani in Prague.[15]

Yet the sixteen-paragraph preamble in the draft resolution, entitled "Further Resolution on Iraq" and designed to authorize Bush to assume war powers—that the White House forwarded to Congress on September 19—read: "Whereas members of Al Qaeda . . . are known to be in Iraq;" (paragraph 6).

Amazingly, this draft resolution made no mention of the dramatic development on September 16 when Iraq announced its acceptance of the return of UN inspectors "without conditions," and proposed discussing arrangements for resuming inspections. That evening Annan received a letter from Sabri to that effect. In it the Iraqi foreign minister referred to his meetings with Annan in New York on March 4 and May 2, and in Vienna on July 4—as well as to the talks held in Annan's office on September 14–15 with the participation of Amir Mousa, the Arab League secretary-general. It explained that the Iraqi government had made the latest decision in response to the appeals by Mousa; "other Arab, Islamic and friendly countries;" and Annan, who in his September 12 speech to the UN General Assembly had described inspections as the first essential step "towards a comprehensive solution that includes the lifting of sanctions and the timely implementation of other relevant Security Council resolutions, including 687."

Finally, the letter stressed that "all UN member-states" should respect the sovereignty, territorial integrity, and political independence of Iraq as stipulated in Article II of the UN Charter.[16]

There was a collective sigh of relief at the official and popular levels in the Arab world, with the leaders pleased that, unlike during the 1990 Kuwait crisis, this time Saddam had accepted their advice. He did so for a variety of reasons. He noticed Saudi Arabia breaking Arab ranks when its foreign minister Saud al Faisal told CNN on September 15: "If the UN Security Council takes a decision to implement a [particular] policy of the UN, then every country that has signed the UN Charter has to fulfill it." This implied that reversing its current policy of barring the Pentagon from using its bases in an anti-Iraq war, Riyadh would allow it to do so if the Security Council adopted a resolution authorizing "use of all necessary means" to disarm Iraq. On the positive side, Annan's September 12 statement regarding "a comprehensive solution" provided Saddam with a graceful way out.

Most importantly, convinced that Washington was set on over-throwing his regime irrespective of what he did or failed to do, and was using the WMD issue as a pretext, Saddam wanted to prove this crucial point to his Arab peers. The only way he could do so was to call Washington's bluff by opening up Iraq to unconditional inspec-tions. (Earlier his foreign minister Sabri had argued that if the WMD in the region were the real worry of Washington, Israel would require "regime change.") As days and weeks passed, Saddam would be helped in his argument by the shrill rhetoric of Bush and other Republican leaders in Washington and on the hustings about over-throwing his regime.

This would be topped by the incendiary remarks by Ari Fleischer, the White House spokesman, on October 1, the day the Iraqi foreign ministry published a twenty-nine-page dossier rebutting the charges made in the American and British documents on Iraq's WMD. When asked about the crippling costs of war—at $12.5 billion a month—he said, "The cost of a one-way ticket is substantially less than that. The cost of one bullet the Iraqi people take on themselves is substantially less than that." Asked if he was supporting assassina-tion, Fleischer replied, "Regime change is welcome whatever form it takes."[17] So much for America's ongoing war on terrorism, meaning political violence.

Earlier, on hearing of Iraq's unconditional acceptance of UN inspections, Fleischer's boss, President Bush, had behaved like a boy who found his ball taken away. When he regained his composure, he abandoned his expedient multilaterialism, expressed at the UN Gen-eral Assembly on September 12, and set out to move the goalposts. Working with Blair, his doggedly loyal British counterpart, Bush pro-duced a draft resolution that proposed UN security forces for the inspectors with powers to declare instant "no-fly/no-drive zones, exclusion zones, and/or ground- and air-transit corridors." By so doing Bush repeated the pattern of past US behavior, outlined at length in Chapter 6.

Bush combined his combative stance in the international arena with a similar posture at home. When Tom Daschle, the Senate majority leader, demanded the White House's answers to such vital questions as 'Will a major diversion of military resources undermine war on terrorism?' And 'Who will replace Saddam?' before the Senate could discuss the White House's draft 'Further Resolution on Iraq," Bush alleged that the (Democratic-controlled) Senate was "not interested in the security of the American people." By so doing Bush provided ammunition to those critics who had argued all along that the timing of prioritizing Iraq had to do with enhancing the Republicans' electoral chances rather than any serious and sudden threat by Saddam.

Describing Bush's remark as "outrageous," Daschle demanded that he apologize to Democratic war veterans and all Americans. Bush responded by calling a hurried press conference, and saying that "The security of the country is the commitment of both political parties and the responsibility of both elected branches of government."

To the chagrin of Democrats, Bush's electoral strategy had worked. The percentage of those who considered terrorism as more pressing than any other issue jumped from 11 to 47, almost equal to those who thought the economy the biggest problem. On the other hand, 52 percent felt that Bush had moved too fast to confront Saddam whereas 40 percent reckoned he would not move fast enough in the near future.[18] Also on the crucial question of war with Iraq, there was an equal division between unilateralists and multilateralists, 47 percent each. At the national political level, the ranks of the multilaterallists included former Democratic presidents Jimmy Carter and Bill Clinton. In his *Washington Post* article, Carter criticized the Bush administration for rejecting nuclear arms agreements, the biological weapons convention, the Kyoto protocol on global warming, anti-torture proposals, and punishment for war criminals. And in his article in the (London) *Observer* on September 8, Clinton argued that though the threat of Saddam's laboratories was real, it was not as immediate as the need to restart the Middle East peace process and stop the violence there, and that he was not sure the Iraqi problem would require an invasion.[19]

It was, however, left to Al Gore, who beat Bush in the popular vote for the presidency, to articulate comprehensively the dangers to which Bush's policy on Iraq was exposing the US and the world while addressing the Commonwealth Club in San Francisco. "President Bush is telling us that the most urgent requirement of the moment—right now—is not to redouble our efforts against Al Qaeda and bin Laden, not to stabilize the nation of [post-Taliban] Afghanistan . . . but instead to shift our focus and concentrate on immediately launching a new war against Saddam Hussein. And he is proclaiming a new, uniquely American right to preemptively attack whomsoever he may deem represents a potential future threat." Gore warned that "The course of action we are presently embarking on regarding Iraq has the potential to seriously damage our ability to win the war against terrorism and weaken our ability to lead the world in this new century."

Gore then expressed concern that Bush was seeking from Congress "the necessary authority to proceed immediately against Iraq and for that matter any other nation in the region, regardless of subsequent developments or circumstances." In short, Gore maintained, Bush and some in his administration were exchanging the tried-and-true practices of "deterrence" and "containment" for a policy of "dominance." He stressed that the action on Iraq needed international support. "If you are going after Jesse James, you ought to organize the posse first." If other nations asserted the same preemptive rights the United States does, "the rule of law will quickly be replaced by the reign of fear . . . by the notion that there is no law but the discretion of the American president." Gore wondered what precedent that would set, for example, for India facing Pakistan, or China against Taiwan, or Israel confronted by Iran. He added, "If what America represents to the world is leadership in a common-wealth of equals, then our friends are legion; [but] if what we represent is empire, then it is our enemies who will be legion."[20] Already the opinion among the British, historically and culturally close to Americans, had turned against the current US policy to the extent that an opinion poll revealed that 37 percent considered Bush "the greatest danger to world peace"—only six points behind Saddam.[21]

Yet Bush's White House summarily dismissed Gore's speech as 'irrelevant'.

The Bush administration's arrogance was by matched by its inarticulateness and lack of erudition. Straining to link Saddam and Al Qaeda, Bush mentioned (in his folksy way) "the danger of Al Qaeda becoming an extension of Saddam's madness," and added, "You can't distinguish between Al Qaeda and Saddam when you talk about the war on terror."[22] This from the president merely a fortnight after the White House document on Iraq had made no mention of Al Qaeda!

When well-read multilateralists argued against unilateralism in matters of war and peace by pointing out that the ban on unprovoked—or preventive—offensives against sovereign states had been the foundation of international law since the Treaty of Westphalia in 1648, and that a preemptive attack violated not only the UN Charter but also the NATO Charter, a member of Bush's policy-making team responded: "You can call it preemption, or preventative defense. But it is old fashioned self-protection, and it comes from the president's gut."[23]

This level of debating—indistinguishable from bar talk in a Texan town with an early history of vigilante justice—by a top policy maker of the US administration was reflective of the chief executive's intellectual and linguistic deficiencies. "Washington apes the style of a president who has no capacity for the use of language as a mode of leadership," noted James Carroll in the *Boston Globe*. "The problem comes when, having sought to lead through the imperative voice instead of the exhortatory or the explanatory, nothing changes. The world is beginning to act like America's sullen teenager, refusing to obey orders. As a candidate Bush was at a loss for words, and proud of it. Many voters were charmed. Others were appalled. Few understood, however, that this abdication of leadership by the intelligent use of language would be dangerous"[24]

The national and international concern grew after the White House released a thirty-three-page document, *The National Security Strategy of the United States*, on September 20. Parts of it reflected the enlightened approach of Thomas Jefferson, Abraham Lincoln, and George Marshall. By and large, though, dominated by reiterations of American power—military, economic and cultural—it sounded like a declaration of a Roman emperor or a Napoleon or John Bull—the portly, self-satisfied, and arrogant symbol of the sprawling British Empire. This version of Pax Americana was in the long line of past empires where the imperialist power, believing in its inherently superior values, preached the doctrine of "civilizing" the "natives"while dominating them, a theme aptly captured in Rudyard Kipling's poem, "The White Man's Burden."

Now President Bush's document visualized an overweening United States with such strong military muscle as to dissuade any potential adversary from challenging it. Under that overarching protective umbrella Washington will exercise its self-proclaimed right to strike preemptively any hostile country it believes is developing WMD. The paper went on to declare that international treaties were less effective in preventing the proliferation of nuclear arms than the use of military means. "[W]hen these pugnacious strategies become the dominant theme in American conduct, the nation risks alienating its friends and undermining the very interests that Bush seeks to protect," said the *New York Times*. "Arrogance subverts effective leadership. . . . Bush must be careful not to create a fortress America that inspires the enmity rather then envy of the world."

Ironically, the first draft of the document, written by Condoleezza Rice, an African-American who believes unabashedly in America's "imperial" destiny, was judged by Bush to be so overbearing or arrogant in parts that, according to White House sources, he edited it heavily.

Not that, in practice, it made much difference. Given Bush's earlier go-it-alone policies in international affairs, it came as no surprise to find him vetoing the call for an international peace conference by Tony Blair, fond of claiming "special relationship" with Bush. Having underlined the importance of the UN by announcing on September 12 the return of the United States to UNESCO after a gap of twenty years, Bush declared three weeks later that the UN would became irrelevant if the Security Council did not adopt the resolution on inspections in Iraq the US had submitted in association with Britain—in the face of opposition by China, France, and Russia, representing a majority among the permanent five and four times more people collectively than the Anglo-American alliance.

Their stance hardened when, following a two-day meeting with the Iraqi delegation, led by Amir Saadi, in Vienna, Blix announced an agreement on October 1. "The Iraqi representatives declared that Iraq accepts all rights of inspection provided for in all the relevant Security Council resolutions [including 1284]." That included all sensitive sites, including defense and intelligence ministries and mosques. "All sites are subject to immediate, unconditional and unrestricted access," Blix said. "However, the Memorandum of Understanding of 1998 establishes special procedures for access to eight presidential sites." As a goodwill gesture, the Iraqis handed over four CD-Roms of information on nuclear facilities to the IAEA.

Instead of welcoming the practical arrangements that the Iraqis had worked out with the Unmovic and IAEA chiefs, Washington leaked the draft resolution it had shown to China, France, and Russia—well aware that Iraq had said earlier that it would not accept any new resolution that altered the established inspections procedures.

The American draft resolution, backed by the British, began with the assertion that "Iraq is still, and has been for a number of years, in material breach of its obligations under relevant resolutions;" required Baghdad to provide within thirty days of the adoption of this resolution "an accurate, complete and full declaration of its programs to develop weapons of mass destruction, ballistic missiles and unmanned aerial vehicles;" specified that "inspection teams . . . accompanied at the bases by sufficient security forces . . . shall have the right to declare for the purposes of this resolution no-fly/no-drive zones, exclusion zones, and/or ground- and air-transit corridors, which shall be enforced by UN security forces or by members of the Council;" and ended with the proviso that "false statements or omissions in the declaration submitted by Iraq to the Council and failure by Iraq at any time to comply and cooperate fully with the provisions laid down in this resolution shall constitute a further material breach of Iraq's obligations, and that such breach authorizes member states to use all necessary means to restore international peace and security in the area."

Since Baghdad had stated up front that it would reject any new resolution changing the already established procedures, two outcomes are possible. Either, in the process of back-room bargaining with China, France, and Russia, Bush drops the "all necessary means" proviso and softens others in the draft resolution to the extent that it becomes acceptable to Baghdad. Or, using carrot and stick, Bush succeeds in getting his tough resolution passed with the required nine Security Council votes—and the three dissenting permanent members abstaining (as they had done on Resolution 1284 in December 1999)—will be set for the US-led invasion of Iraq with at least a token participation by such Arab countries as Kuwait and Qatar.

As in the 1991 Gulf War, the Pentagon will unleash nonstop bombing and cause untold carnage—in lives and property, public and private. How long the air campaign will last, and whether it will lead to the Iraqi army turning against Saddam—as the Iraqi opposition is predicting—thus sparing Bush the difficult decision about committing US ground troops, no one can tell with certainty.

What is certain though is that at the end of it all, it will be ordinary Iraqis who will suffer most, as they did in the 1991 conflict. To expect them to come out in the streets and welcome the Americans, arriving by tanks and helicopters, as liberators seems far-fetched. A people who have endured the rigors of the ,most comprehensive economic sanctions in history for twelve long years, primarily due to the merciless intransigence of successive US governments, are unlikely to forget either the harm done to them or forgive its principal perpetrator.

Referring to the 1991 Gulf War, Wamidh Nadhmi, professor of political science at Baghdad University, told Rajiv Chandrasekaran of the *Washington Post:* "That war was seen in certain circles not as an American aggression but as a reply to Iraq's invasion of Kuwait. With the continuation of sanctions, and when sanctions started hurting the civilian population more than the government, the people started to think that Iraqi society at large is the real target of the Americans."[25] That popular perception has not changed—nor has the concept of "an eye for an eye" that is an integral part of the tribal culture that runs deep among Iraqis.

NOTES

CHAPTER 1. LIFE IN IRAQ

1. 661 is the number of the UN Security Council resolution on the subject.

2. Nuha al Radi, *Baghdad Diaries* (London: Saqi Books, 1998), p. 59.

3. Cited in Sarah Graham-Brown, *Sanctioning Saddam: The Politics of Intervention in Iraq* (London and New York: I. B. Tauris, 1999), p. 184.

4. Interviews in Baghdad, July 2000.

5. Cited in *Middle East International*, April 10, 1998, p. 17.

6. Agence France-Presse, July 24, 2000.

7. Nuha al Radi, *Baghdad Diaries*, p. 76.

8. *Middle East International*, September 3, 1999, p. 20; Reuters, November 2, 1999.

9. The estimates given by the World Health Organization in March 1996 were "500,000 dead during 1990–94," and by Unicef in July 2000, "500,000 dead during 1991–98." *Guardian* (London), October 10, 2001.

10. *Sunday Times* (London), July 16, 2000.

11. Interview with a UN source in Baghdad, July 2000.

12. *The Middle East and North Africa 2001* (London: Europa Publications, 2001), p. 458.

13. Nuha al Radi, *Baghdad Diaries*, p. 63.

14. Ibid., p. 95.

15. Interview in London, October 2000.

16. Ibid., October 2000.

17. CBS TV transcript, May 12, 1996.

18. *Washington Post*, January 28, 1999.

CHAPTER 2. BABYLON TO BAATHIST ERA

1. Shias differ from Sunnis in doctrine, ritual, law, theology, and religious organization. While sharing monotheism, prophet-hood, and resurrection with Sunnis, they also believe in *aadl* justice, just nature of God, and *Imamat*, supreme leadership of Muslims— that is, being divinely inspired, Imams are infallible. Shias make up about 15 percent of the global Muslim population of 1.25 billion, with only four of the fifty-seven Muslim countries being Shia-majority: Azerbaijan, Bahrain, Iran, and Iraq.

2. See Chapter 4, p. 156.

3. Since then, July 17 has become Iraq's national day and is celebrated in a way that Americans do the Fourth of July. One of the bridges on the Tigris in Baghdad is called "July 17."

4. That this was a deliberate Kuwaiti policy became evident with the discovery of a memorandum by Brigadier Saad al Fahd al Sabah, director-general of Kuwait's State Security Department (SSD), to the interior minister Salim al Salim al Sabah on November 20, 1989. It summarized the agreements he had reached with William Webster, the CIA director, during their meeting at the agency headquarters in Langley, Virginia, a week earlier. "We agreed . . . that information would be exchanged [between the SSD and the CIA] about the armaments and political structures of Iran and Iraq," read paragraph 2 of the document. "We agreed with the American side that it was important to take advantage of the deteriorating economic situation in Iraq to put pressure on that country's government to delineate our common border," stated paragraph 5. The English translation of this memorandum, discovered at the headquarters of Kuwait's SSD by the occupying Iraqis, was placed before the UN secretary-general

by Iraq's ambassador to the United Nations on October 29, 1990. The CIA said that the document was a forgery.

5. Cited in Hiro, *Desert Shield to Desert Storm* (HarperCollins, New York: Routledge, 1992), p. 84.

6. Ibid., p. 93.

7. *Guardian* (London), August 24, 1990; *Independent* (London), August 24, 1990.

Chapter 3. Iraq and the Invasion of Kuwait

1. Dilip Hiro, *Desert Shield to Desert Storm*, pp. 387–88.

2. Dilip Hiro, *Dictionary of the Middle East* (Baskingstroke: Macmillan Press/New York: St. Martin's Press, 1996), p. 100.

3. General Sir Peter de La Billiere, *Storm Command: A Personal Account of the Gulf War* (London: HarperCollins, 1992), pp. 304–5.

4. *New York Times*, March 8, 1991; *Independent* (London), March 8, 1991.

5. Anthony H. Cordesman, and Ahmed S. Hashim, *Iraq: Sanctions and Beyond*, (Boulder, CO and Oxford: Westview Press, 1997), pp. 101–2.

6. ABC News, February 7, 1998, cited in David Wurmser, *Tyranny's Ally: America's Failure to Defeat Saddam Hussein* (Washington, D.C.: The AEI Press, 1999), p. 142.

7. Cited in Andrew Cockburn and Patrick Cockburn, *Out of the Ashes: The Resurrection of Saddam Hussein* (New York: Harper-Collins, 1999), p. 37.

8. *Gulf States Newsletter*, February 22, 1999, p. 3.

9. Interview with Dr. Haidar Muhammad Hussein al Kalidar, caretaker of the Imam Ali shrine, Najaf, July 2000.

10. *Guardian* (London), March 28, 1991. Earlier the White House had said that the United States would shoot down Iraqi helicopters used against the rebels *only* if they posed a threat to the coalition forces inside Iraq. *New York Times*, March 27, 1991.

11. David Wurmser, *Tyranny's Ally*, pp. 10–11.

12. Nuha al Radi, *Baghdad Diaries*, p. 56.

Chapter 4. The Baath and Saddam

1. Andrew Cockburn and Patrick Cockburn, *Out of the Ashes*, p. 245.

2. Dilip Hiro, *The Longest War* (London:Paladin Grafton Books, 1989/New York: Routledge, 1992), pp. 65–66 and 98.

3. Scott Ritter, *Endgame: Solving the Iraq Problem—Once and for All* (New York and London: Simon and Schuster, 1999), p. 75.

4. Anthony H. Cordesman and Ahmed S. Hashim, *Iraq* (Westport, CT and London: Praeger, 1999), p. 155.

5. Dilip Hiro, *The Longest War*, pp. 65–66.

6. Dilip Hiro, *Desert Shield to Desert Storm*, p. 443.

7. Interviews in Baghdad, July 2000.

8. Anthony H. Cordesman, *Iraq and the War of Sanctions: Conventional Threats and Weapons of Mass Destruction* (Westport, CT and London: Praeger, 1999), p. 156.

9. Said K. Aburish, *Saddam Hussein: The Politics of Revenge*, (London and New York: Bloomsbury, 1999), p. 233.

10. *The New Yorker*, November 1, 1993.

11. *BBC Summary of World Broadcasts*, August 14, 1995; *Wall Street Journal*, August 14, 1995.

12. Visit to the Saddam International Tower, July 2000.

13. Visits to Baghdad, Karbala, Najaf, and Babylon, August 2000.

14. Inter Press Service, January 20, 1998; *Guardian*, February 4, 1998.

Chapter 5. The Opposition and Its Foreign Links

1. *The Nation*, May 10, 1999, p. 20. The conference was held in Austria because none of Iraq's neighbors wanted it on their soil.

2. *Washington Post*, June 15, 1996, January 26, 1997; Andrew Cockburn and Patrick Cockburn, *Out of the Ashes*, pp. 188–89.

3. Andrew Cockburn and Patrick Cockburn, *ibid.*, p. 220.

4. According to one version, the CIA engaged an Egyptian intermediary to deliver the communications equipment to

the al Shahwani brothers, and that he divulged his mission to the Iraqis probably for money, handing over the equipment to them. In another version, the Iraqi GID infiltrated a group of Kurdish nationalists who were privy to the CIA's plans. And, according to the third version, the CIA used one of the Iraqi truck drivers plying between Amman and Baghdad to deliver the equipment, and he got caught by the Iraqi GID, which maintained a close watch on all such truck and taxi drivers, whether Iraqi or Jordanian.

5. Among the alledged CIA operators was Timothy McCarthy, who published an op-ed article on Iraqi disarmament in the *International Herald Tribune* on December 27, 1999, and was later identified by Iraq as a member of thirteen Unscom inspection teams.

6. Interview with an Iraqi exile in London, January 2000.

7. *Middle East International*, September 6, 1996, pp. 3–6; November 8, 1996, pp. 16–17.

8. Cited in Andrew Cockburn and Patrick Cockburn, *Out of the Ashes*, pp. 237–38.

9. Inter Press Service, September 3, 1996.

10. *Le Monde*, September 3, 1996.

11. Inter Press Service, September 3 and 6, 1996. A week later, when he appeared to be on the verge of signing an agreement with Baghdad on autonomy for Kurds within Iraq, Barzani declared that Saddam Hussein was not an enemy of the Kurdish people.

12. Inter Press Service, September 14, 1996.

13. *Middle East International*, September 20, 1996, pp. 5–6.

14. Anthony H. Cordesman and Ahmed S. Hashim, *Iraq*, p. 211.

15. *Washington Post*, September 20, 1996; Andrew Cockburn and Patrick Cockburn, *Out of the Ashes*, p. 244.

16. *Washington Post*, October 22, 1998; *Middle East International*, November 27, 1998; *The Nation*, May 10, 1999, p. 22.

17. *Washington Post*, October 22, 1998; *Observer* (London), November 15, 1998; *New York Times*, November 16, 1998.

18. *Washington Post*, November 23, 1998; *International Herald Tribune*, November 30, 1998; *Gulf States Newsletter*, February 22, 1999.

19. *Washington Post*, August 6, 1999.

20. The IMA's spokesman, Tawfiq al Yassiri, a Shia officer, defected in 1991.

21. *The Nation*, August 19, 2002, p. 6.

CHAPTER 6. IRAQ, THE UNITED NATIONS, AND THE UNITED STATES

1. See p. 174; Scott Ritter, *Endgame*, p. 107.

2. *Middle East International*, September 27, 1991, pp. 9–10; Tim Trevan, *Saddam's Secrets: The Hunt for Iraq's Hidden Weapons* (London: HarperCollins, 1999), pp. 103–9.

3. The names of the three key US intelligence agents, known to *Washington Post* reporter Barton Gellman, were withheld for security reasons when his story was published on March 2, 1999.

4. *Washington Post*, March 2, 1999.

5. *Middle East International*, September 8, 1995, p. 6.

6. Scott Ritter, *Endgame*, pp. 135–36; *Daily Telegraph*, March 8, 1999.

7. Scott Ritter, *Endgame*, p. 140. Author's italics.

8. Ibid., p. 154.

9. *Jane's Intelligence Review*, July 1997, pp. 312–16, and August 1997, pp. 365–67; *New York Times*, November 25, 1997; *Jerusalem Post*, November 28, 1997. Interviews in Baghdad, July 2000.

10. Scott Ritter, *Endgame*, p. 190.

11. United Nations Special Commission, "Report to the Security Council S/1997/774, dated October 6, 1997."

12. Richard Butler, *Saddam Defiant: The Threat of Weapons of Mass Destruction, and the Crisis of Global Security* (Washington, D.C.: Public Affairs, 1999), p. 107.

13. "Of the approximately 1,000 people Unscom used during my administration, perhaps 250 were American; another 150 were British," wrote Richard Butler. *ibid.*, p. 94.

14. "Ritter's Private War," *The New Yorker*, November 9, 1998, pp. 56–73.

15. *Sunday Times* (London), November 16, 1997; *Independent* (London), December 18, 1997.

16. *Washington Post*, August 28, 1998. Author's italics.

17. *Washington Post*, August 28, 1998.

18. *Observer* (London), March 1, 1998; Richard Butler, *Saddam Defiant*, pp. 145, 147.

19. *New York Times*, November 8, 1998.

20. *Washington Post*, February 24 and 25, 1998.

21. Scott Ritter, *Endgame*, pp. 188–89; *Washington Post*, March 20, 1998.

22. Richard Butler, *Saddam Defiant*, pp. 166–67; Tariq Aziz's letter to the UN Security Council, S/1998/342, dated April 22, 1998.

23. *Washington Post*, August 28, 1998.

24. Anthony H. Cordesman, *Iraq and the War of Sanctions*, p. 315.

25. Richard Butler, *Saddam Defiant*, pp. 171-2.

26. Anthony H. Cordesman, *Iraq and the War of Sanctions*, p. 304.

27. Richard Butler, *Saddam Defiant*, p. 175. In his interview with the *New York Times*, he said that he demanded that Iraq submit documentation "involving areas of official decision-making, especially on Iraq's concealment policy." *New York Times*, June 17, 1998.

28. Regarding the biological file, after the July 17–23 meetings in Baghdad on the subject, Aziz reportedly told Butler in a letter that "the meeting[s] did not succeed in closing the gaps between the two sides." Richard Butler, *Saddam Defiant*, pp. 174, 179.

29. Richard Butler's allegation was said to be supported by satellite images collected by the United States showing delivery of the materials at the farm after Hussein Kamil Hassan's defection

on August 8, 1995. *Middle East International*, July 3, 1998, pp. 10–11.

30. Richard Butler, *Saddam Defiant*, pp. 177–78. According to Butler, over 100,000 special munitions allegedly consumed from 1981–88 had remained unaccounted for.

31. Richard Butler, *Saddam Defiant*, p. 184.

32. *International Herald Tribune*, August 6, 1998; Richard Butler, *Saddam Defiant*, pp. 187–88.

33. *Washington Post*, November 16, 1998.

34. Scott Ritter, *Endgame*, p. 182.

35. *New York Times*, August 27 and September 4, 1998.

36. *ibid.*, October 2, 1998; *International Herald Tribune*, November 12, 1998; *Sunday Times* (London), November 22, 1998. The FBI began investigating whether Ritter's dealings with Israel had compromised US security.

37. Iraqi foreign minister Muhammad al Sahhaf's letter to Kofi Annan, S/1998/204, dated March 8, 1998.

38. Scott Ritter, *Endgame*, pp. 195–96.

39. Anthony H. Cordesman, *Iraq and the War of Sanctions*, pp. 374–75.

40. *Washington Post*, November 22, 1998.

41. Richard Butler, *Saddam Defiant*, pp. 218–19.

42. *Washington Post*, December 16, 1998; Richard Butler, *Saddam Defiant*, p. 224.

43. Dilip Hiro, *Neighbors, Not Friends: Iraq and Iran after the Gulf Wars* (London and New York: Routledge, 2001), pp. 161–63.

44. *New York Times*, January 3, 1999.

45. Associated Press, November 26, 1999.

46. Associated Press, January 5, 2000.

47. Agence France-Presse, February 15 and 16, 2000.

48. *Daily Telegraph*, February 17, 2000.

49. *International Herald Tribune*, August 24, 2000.

50. *Washington Post*, August 31, 2000.

Chapter 7. Iraq and the Region

1. *Middle East International*, January 10, 1997, pp. 11–12; January 24, 1997, pp. 19–20.

2. *Observer* (London), November 16, 1997; *The Times* (London), November 17, 1997.

3. Cited in *Middle East International*, February 13, 1998, p. 4; Anthony H. Cordesman, *Iraq and the War of Sanctions*, p. 246.

4. Cited in Inter Press Service, February 10, 1998.

5. *Washington Post*, October 22, 1998.

6. Cited in Anthony H. Cordesman, *Iraq and the War of Sanctions*, p. 237.

7. *Washington Post*, November 23, 1998; *International Herald Tribune*, November 30, 1998.

8. *Washington Post*, January 29, 1999.

9. Reuters, February 3, 1999.

10. *Middle East International*, February 12, 1999, p. 10.

11. *Gulf States Newsletter*, February 22, 1999.

12. See http://leb.net/iac/nofly.html.

13. Sarah Graham-Brown, *Sanctioning Saddam: The Politics of Intervention in Iraq* (London and New York: I. B. Tauris, 1999), p. 106.

14. The annual cost of maintaining the two no fly zones was $1 billion.

15. Associated Press, November 26, 1999.

16. Reuters, February 15, 2000; Agence France-Presse, February 15 and 16, 2000.

17. Cited in *Middle East International*, August 18, 2000, p. 14.

18. Agence France-Presse, October 8, 2000.

19. *International Herald Tribune*, September 27, 2000.

20. *New York Times*, November 5, 2000.

21. Associated Press, October 21, 2000.

22. Associated Press., October 21, 2000.

23. Since 1988, Iran had released some 57,000 prisoners of war and Iraq about 40,000. In dispute were 3,000 Iranian POWs that Tehran said Baghdad was holding. *Middle East International*,

April 21, 2000, p. 13. By contrast, some 10,000 Iraqi POWs had sought asylum in Iran. *Kayhan International*, August 24, 1999.

24. *International Herald Tribune*, October 16, 2000.

Chapter 8. Oil, the Defining Element of Iraq

1. Said K. Aburish, *Saddam Hussein: The Politics of Revenge*, pp. 134–35.

2. *Middle East International*, July 23, 1993, p. 10, and April 15, 1994, p. 13.

3. *BP Statistical Review of World Energy 1997* (London: British Petroleum Corporation, 1998), pp. 7, 10.

4. *New York Times*, June 19, 1998.

5. Inter Press Service, October 17, 1997.

6. *Financial Times*, June 17, 1998.

7. *Observer* (London), September 24, 2000.

8. *Washington Post*, February 20, 2000.

9. *International Herald Tribune*, March 28, 2000.

10. *Observer* (London), September 24, 2000; *BP Amoco Statistical Review of World Energy 2000*, (London: British Petroleum Corporation, 2000), pp. 7, 10.

11. *Observer* (London), September 24, 2000.

Chapter 9. Iraq after 9/11

1. *International Herald Tribune*, September 17, 2001; *Daily Telegraph*, September 23, 2001.

2. *New York Times*, October 10, 2001.

3. Cited in *Financial Times* (London), September 17, 2001.

4. Hypocrite *munafiq* is the one who claims to be Muslim but is not due to his failure to follow Islamic requirements in his life. According to the Quran 4:144, "Surely the hypocrites will be in the lowest reaches of the Fire [of Hell]; you will not find for them any helper."

5. The estimates given by the World Health Organization in

March 1996 were "500,000 dead during 1990–94," and by Unicef in July 2000, "500,000 dead during 1991–98." *Guardian* (London), October 10, 2001.

6. Reuters, October 8, 2001; *The Times*, October 8, 2001.

7. *Washington Post*, May 2, 2002.

8. The Defense Policy Board's members included Dan Quayle, former vice president; Henry Kissinger, former secretary of state; James Schlesinger and Harold Brown, both former defense secretaries; Newt Gingrich, former speaker of the US House of Representatives; and James Woolsey, former CIA director.

9. Cited in *Daily Telegraph*, December 22, 2001.

10. See http://www.whitehouse.gov/news/2002/01/20020129-11.html.

11. *New York Times*, February 4, 2002.

12. Reuters, February 1, 2002.

13. *New York Times*, January 23, 2002.

14. *Guardian* (London), February 10, 2002.

15. *Financial Times* (London), February 15, 2002.

16. *New York Times*, March 12, 2002.

17. *Sunday Times* (London), March 10, 2002.

18. *Washington Post*, May 2, 2002.

19. *International Herald Tribune*, November 22, 2001.

20. *Washington Post*, September 30, 2001.

21. *ibid.*, February 21, 2001.

22. *International Herald Tribune*, February 2, 3, 5, and 6, 2002.

23. Reuters, May 22, 2002.

24. *International Herald Tribune*, March 18, 2002.

25. Rehabilitating Iraq's military infrastructure with conventional arms would cost Baghdad an estimated $22 billion.

26. Dilip Hiro, *Neighbors, Not Friends*, p. 302.

27. *Sunday Times* (London), March 24, 2002.

28. *Washington Post*, August 10, 2002.

29. *Sunday Times* (London), August 4, 2002.

30. *Washington Post*, July 6, 2002.

31. *International Herald Tribune*, August 15 and 26, 2002.

32. *New York Times*, February 23, 2002.

33. *ibid.*, August 30, 2002.

34. While opposition to war grew by nine points in a month to 61 percent, support for it fell by nine points to 28 percent. *The Times* (London), September 4, 2002.

35. Cited in *Observer* (London), September 1, 2002.

POSTSCRIPT

1. Cited in *Sunday Times* (London), September 1, 2002.

2. *The Times* (London), September 2, 2002.

3. *International Herald Tribune*, September 10, 2002.

4. *New York Times*, September 5, 2002.

5. *Washington Post*, September 11, 2002.

6. *ibid.*, September 7, 2002. In an interview with the *New York Times*, Jacques Chirac said, "I condemn the regime in Iraq for all the reasons we know, for all the dangers it puts on the region and the tragedy it constitutes for the Iraqi people who are held hostage by it. . . . I do wish for it [deposition of Saddam]."

7. *Financial Times* (London), September 7–8, 2002.

8. *Washington Post*, September 6, 2002.

9. *New York Times*, September 14, 2002.

10. *New York Times*, September 12, 2002.

11. *Sunday Times* (London), September 8, 2002.

12. *Washington Post*, September 11, 2002.

13. *Daily Telegraph* (London), September 11, 2002.

14. The White House dossier on Iraq, released the same day in Washington, said "a few months," whereas the document released by Tony Blair a fortnight later would mention "two years."

15. *Washington Post*, September 13, 2002.

16. *International Herald Tribune*, September 18, 2002. Consisting of seven clauses, Article II of the UN Charter reads *inter alia*, "All Members shall refrain in their international relations from the threat or use of force against the territorial integrity or political independence of any state."

17. *Daily Mirror* (London), October 2, 2002; *International Herald Tribune*, October 2, 2002.

18. *Washington Post*, September 29, 2002.

19. Addressing the Labour Party conference in the British city of Blackpool in early October, Clinton described an American preemptive attack on Iraq as "wrong," and warned that "'preemptive action today may come back with unwelcome consequences in the future because I don't care how precise your weapons and bombs are, when you set them off, innocent people die." *New York Times*, October 3, 2002.

20. *Guardian* (London), September 24, 2002; *Sunday Times* (London), September 29, 2002.

21. *Observer* (London), September 29, 2002.

22. *Washington Post*, September 27, 2002.

23. *New York Times*, September 11, 2002.

24. Cited in *International Herald Tribune*, September 6, 2002.

25. *Washington Post*, September 15, 2002.

FREQUENT COMMENTS
AND QUESTIONS

1/ Saddam is an aggressor. He has invaded two neighboring countries, Iran and Kuwait.
A: Yes. When Saddam attacked and occupied Kuwait in 1990, the US declared him an aggressor, rallied the UN Security Council, led a military coalition against Iraq, and expelled the Iraqis from the emirate. In contrast, when he invaded Iran in September 1980, Washington declared itself neutral in the war. At the UN Security Council, putting the aggressor and its victim on a par, it supported a resolution which called for a cease-fire. Actually, using back channels, the administration of US president Jimmy Carter had encouraged Saddam to attack Iran, whose military plans were known to the pro-American rulers of Saudi Arabia and Kuwait weeks before the invasion. See chapter 3, p. 29. For further details, see Dilip Hiro, *The Longest War: The Iran-Iraq Military Conflict* (1991), pp. 71–72.

2/ Saddam is once again threatening his neighboring countries.
A: Which ones? As it is, in early September 2002 the Arab League's foreign ministers rejected "the threat of aggression on Arab nations, in particular Iraq," and reaffirmed 'that these threats to the security and safety of any Arab country are considered a threat to Arab national security." Later when the George W. Bush administration turned to the UN in its conflict with Baghdad, Iraq listened to the advice of Arab capitals and accepted the unconditional return of UN inspectors, thereby keeping intact the Arab League support. Unlike in 1990, this time Iraq has not occupied a

fellow Arab state. See further, Dilip Hiro, "Iraq woos its neighbors" at www.thenation.com/doc.mhtml?i=20020819&s=hiro

3/ Saddam gassed his own people.

A: US officials are evidently referring to the Iraqi military's use of chemical weapons in the Iraqi Kurdistan town of Halabja in March 1988 during the Iran-Iraq War, and then in the area controlled by the Tehran-backed Kurdish insurgents after the cease-fire in August. Since Baghdad's deployment of chemical arms in war as well as peace was known at the time, the question is: What did the US government do about it then? Nothing. Worse, so strong was the hold of the pro-Iraq lobby on the Republican administration of President Ronald Reagan, it succeeded in getting the White House to frustrate the Senate's attempt to penalize Baghdad for violating the Geneva Protocol on Chemical Weapons, which it had signed. This led Saddam to believe that Washington was firmly on his side — a conclusion that paved the way for his invasion of Kuwait and the 1991 Gulf War.

During the five years following October 1983, Iraq used 100,000 chemical munitions. From the initial use of such agents in extremis to repel Iranian offensives, the Iraqis went on to deploy them extensively as a vital element of their assaults in the spring and summer of 1988 to retake lost territories. At the time, even as the US government had knowledge of these attacks, it provided intelligence and planning assistance to the Iraqi army, according to an August 18 report by Patrick Tyler in the *New York Times*.

Contrary to its proclamations of neutrality in the war, Washington had all along been pro-Iraq. This tilt became an embrace after the reelection of Reagan as president in November 1984, when Iraq and the United States reestablished diplomatic ties. From mid-1986, assisted by the Pentagon, which secretly seconded its air force officers to work with their Iraqi counterparts, Iraq improved its accuracy in targeting, hitting Iran's bridges, factories, and power plants relentlessly, and extending its air strikes to the Iranian oil terminals in the Lower Gulf.

It was against this backdrop that Iraq began striking Tehran with its upgraded Scud ground-to-ground missiles in late February 1988. To recapture Halabja, a town of 70,000 about fifteen miles from the border, from Iran and its Kurdish allies, who had seized it in March, the Iraqi air force attacked it with poison-gas bombs, killing 3,200 to 5,000 civilians. The images of men, women, and children frozen in instant death, relayed by the Iranian media, shocked the world. Yet no condemnation came from Washington.

It was only when, following the truce with Tehran on August 20, Saddam made extensive use of chemical agents to retake 4,000 square miles controlled by the Kurdish rebels, that the Security Council decided to send a team to determine if Iraq had deployed chemical arms. Baghdad refused to cooperate.

But instead of pressing Baghdad to reverse its stance or face an immediate ban on the sale of US military equipment and advanced technology to Iraq by the revival of the Senate's bill, US secretary of state George Shultz chose merely to say that interviews with the Kurdish refugees in Turkey, and "other sources" (which remained obscure), pointed toward Baghdad's using chemical weapons. These two elements did not add up to "conclusive" proof. Such was the verdict of Shultz's British counterpart, Sir Geoffrey Howe. "If conclusive evidence is obtained, then punitive measures against Iraq have not been ruled out," he said. But as neither he nor Shultz is known to have made a further attempt to get at the truth, Baghdad went unpunished. See further, Dilip Hiro, "Iraq and Poison Gas" at www.thenation.com/Special Report/August 28 2002/.

4/ Saddam is a terrorist.
A: According to the single page, headlined "Support for International Terrorism," in the White House's twenty-page document, *A Decade of Deception and Defiance*, released on September 12, 2002,

the last terrorist act sponsored by Iraq was a failed attempt to assassinate former US president George Bush in April 1993 during his visit to Kuwait. See further, chapter 4, pp. 63–64.

5/ Saddam is harboring Al Qaeda.
A: The White House's document, A *Decade of Deception and Defiance,* published on September 12, 2002, makes no reference either to Al Qaeda or to an alleged meeting between Muhammad Atta, the hijacker involved in 9/11, and Ahmad Ani, an Iraqi intelligence official posted in Prague. See further, chapter 9, pp 214.

6/ Saddam is funding Palestinian suicide bombers.
A: Iraq is giving $25,000 each to the families of the Palestinian suicide bombers. After the outbreak of the Palestinian intifada against the Israeli occupation in September 2000, the Palestinian Authority handed over a $2,000 check to the family of the Palestinian killed in the uprising to compensate it for the loss. Following this, the Arab Liberation Front, a pro-Iraq Palestinian faction, started giving a $10,000 check to the family of the latest Palestinian "martyr." Later, when Palestinian militants resorted to suicide bombings, the Front raised the compensation by $15,000. Of some 1,500 Palestinians killed during the first two years of the intifada, only 70 were suicide bombers. In other words, Saddam had not singled out Palestinian suicide bombers. See further, chapter 9, pp. 190–191.

7/ Saddam has violated human rights grossly.
A: Saddam has been violating human rights ever since he became vice president of Iraq in 1975. But that did not deter the US from assisting his regime financially, militarily, and intelligence-wise during the 1980–88 Iran-Iraq War and later. China has been violating human rights in Tibet since 1959. More recently it has been persecuting the followers of Falon Gong, a religious movement, on

a massive scale. Yet Washington eased China's entry into the World Trade Organization in 2001. See further, chapter 9, p. 191.

8/ Saddam is in breach of several UN Security Council resolutions.
A: Every time Iraq breached a UN Security Council resolution, the council took action against it. To say that the council was not tough enough in its responses, as British prime minister Tony Blair now does, is churlish. He and his US counterpart never mention the numerous times they succeeded in getting their way at the council. For details of Security Council responses, see chapter 6, pp. 100, 112, 116–117. For greater detail, check the United Nations Security Council (Numbered) Resolutions in the index of Dilip Hiro's *Neighbors, Not Friends: Iraq and Iran after the Gulf Wars* (2001).

9/ As Iraq has broken the UN Security Council cease-fire Resolution 687 (April 1991), the US is entitled to resume hostilities against it, and does not require a separate Security Council resolution.
A: The UN Security Council, composed of five permanent members and tenelected is a collective body. It is up to the council to decide, by the prescribed procedures, whether or not Baghdad breached its Resolution 687, how serious a breach it is, and how to penalize Iraq for it. No single member has the unilateral right to draw its own conclusion—and simultaneously claim that it is acting under the Security Council aegis. What a permanent member is entitled to is the right to veto a resolution, passed by the required majority of nine, it does not like. The United States can attack Iraq unilaterally by claiming that it acted in self-defense, which is allowed according to the UN Charter Article 51. But then it must prove that Iraq threatened it specifically. So far Baghdad has done no such thing. For the US to invade a sovereign country on the assumption that it *will* threaten it sometime in the future is illegal under international law.

10/ Once the US has adopted the doctrine of preemption, its preemptive strike on Iraq will be amply justified.

A: The White House document *The National Security Strategy of the United States*, issued on September 18, shifts US military strategy away from containment and deterrence to preemptive action against hostile states and terrorist groups developing weapons of mass destruction. As a sovereign nation, the US is entitled to devise its military strategy as it sees fit. But so long as it is a member of the United Nations, it must abide by the UN Charter. There is no place for a preemptive war in the charter. It is up to the George W. Bush administration to convince two-thirds of the 190 members of the UN on this issue and modify the charter accordingly. Until then it must abide by the charter.

11/ Those European states that refuse to back the US on the Iraqi issue are not facing up to the danger posed by the alliance of the terrorist groups with one or more of the tripartite "axis of evil"— Iraq, Iran, and North Korea—and are appeasers.

A: Following the bombings of the US embassies in East Africa, the Bill Clinton administration appointed an advisory panel, called the Gilmore Commission, to examine the possibility of a terrorist group acquiring WMD from a rogue state. In its December 1999 report, the commission concluded that the rogue states would be averse to entrusting such weapons to a terrorist group because of the unpredictability of the group's behavior to the extent of turning the weapon against its sponsor, and that a rogue state itself would be unlikely to use WMD due to the prospect of shattering reprisals.

To dub the Europeans differing with Washington as "appeasers"—the term applied to British premier Neville Chamberlain in his dealings with Adolf Hitler in the late 1930s—is wrong. Unlike Hitler, Saddam is not threatening territorial expansion, having come to grief in the case of Kuwait. Impoverished, de-industrialized Iraq in 2002 has little in common with the militarist, industrialized Germany on the eve of World War II. Finally, no politician in the international community is suggesting buying off Saddam with concessions.

12/ Saddam kicked out UN inspectors.

A: Wrong. Advised by Peter Burleigh, the US ambassador to the UN, Richard Butler, the executive chairman of Unscom, withdrew UN inspectors so that the Pentagon could start its hundred-hour blitzkrieg on Iraq, without even informing other Security Council members. By so doing, Butler did an inadvertent favor to Saddam. Earlier, in its tussles with Unscom, Iraq barred UN inspectors of US nationality, and later expelled them. But it never expelled UN inspectors per se. See further, chapter 6, pp. 129–130.

13/ Saddam behaved in a way that led to the withdrawal of UN inspectors.

A: This statement made by Colin Powell is an interpretation of what happened. A contrasting interpretation is that by late 1998, the Clinton administration had concluded that the UN inspections had yielded as much as they could, and that it was also time to make military use of all the intelligence it had collected legitimately through satellite imaging and briefings by Iraqi defectors, and illegitimately by planting its intelligence operatives on the Unscom staff. See further, chapter 6, pp. 97, 101–102, 127, 129.

14/ Saddam's deep hostility to Israel is a barrier to peace in the Middle East.

A: At the Arab summit in Beirut in March 2002, Iraq endorsed the peace plan advanced by Saudi crown Prince Abdullah, which offered Israel total peace for its total withdrawal from the Occupied Arab Territories, including the Arab East Jerusalem and the Syrian Golan Heights.

15/ Saddam possesses chemical and biological warfare agents, and will soon acquire nuclear weapons.

A: A day before vice President Dick Cheney stated the above, Hans Blix, head of the UN Monitoring, Verification, and Inspection Commission, and an expert on disarmament since 1971, said in a television interview that there was no "clear-cut" evidence that Iraq possessed weapons of mass destruction. What the White House provided in its twenty-page document, A *Decade of Deception and Defiance*, published on September 12, 2002, was described by experts as a recycled mixture of dated and circumstantial evidence that Saddam may be hiding the ingredients for WMD, and seeking to develop a nuclear capability and to weaponize biological and chemical agents. On nuclear arms the White House dossier repeated the earlier assessment made by the London-based International Institute for Strategic Studies that Iraq could build nuclear weapons but *only* if it managed to acquire enriched uranium from an outside source. See further, Dana Priest and Joby Warrick, "Document against Iraq gives little new data about weapons," in the *Washington Post*, September 13, 2002.

After months of hype, Tony Blair released a fifty-page document, *Iraq's Weapons of Mass Destruction: The Assessment of the British Government*, on September 24. In essence what this document produced were pictures of two sites with high walls and watchtowers which, its authors claimed, were for "military purposes." It stated, without providing evidence, that Iraq had developed mobile laboratories that could be used in war. The agents were sarin, mustard gas, anthrax, and botulinum toxin. It was "likely" that Saddam Hussein had passed on the authority for their use to his younger son, Qusay. In the nuclear field, the Iraqi president had recalled local specialists and sent a delegation to "Africa"—a continent of 52 countries, the unnamed African state being Congo—to acquire uranium, unsuccessfully. It would take him five years to produce a nuclear weapon on his own, and two years if he acquired weapons-grade material from outside. The document claimed that Iraq had twenty Al Hussein ground-to-ground missiles, with a range of 400 miles. Earlier the London-based International Institute for Strategic Studies had put the figure at twelve.

By deliberately releasing the dossier at 8 A.M.—only a few hours before the start of the debate in Parliament—Blair deprived the parliamentarians of sufficient time to study it properly. So they ended up discussing the document without digesting it and without the advantage of access to its summaries and analysis by expert journalists and specialists. In the words of Menzies Campbell, foreign affairs spokesman of the left-of-center Liberal-Democrats, "Where is the evidence that containment and deterrence have now failed to the point at which military action is deemed necessary?"

In any case, once Iraq had agreed to allow UN inspections unconditionally, Blair's exercise became superfluous. What his government should have done was to forward the information it had to the UN Monitoring, Verification, and Inspection Commission in New York and the International Atomic Energy Agency in Vienna—as indeed it had on many occasions between 1991 and 1998.

For Iraq's response to the American and British dossiers, see: www.uruklink.net/iraqnews/enews20.htm.

16/ The reason why the White House does not spell out the details of the information it has on Saddam's progress in producing nuclear arms is that it does not want to compromise its highly classified intelligence source.

A: In that case, the least Washington can do is to share this highly confidential information with its NATO allies. This is what it did in the case of Al Qaeda and Osama bin Laden after 9/11. And its NATO partners were sufficiently convinced to declare that the attack on the US had originated from abroad. This in turn led to the activation of Article 5 of the NATO Treaty and allowed the Pentagon unlimited use of NATO airspace, etc.

Let us consider Pakistan, which possesses an arsenal of nuclear arms, and which is susceptible to military coups. It is widely known that the United States has made contingency plans, in conjunction with Israel and India, for seizing Pakistani nuclear arsenals if fundamentalist generals succeed in overthrowing pro-American President Gen. Pervez Musharraf.

If Washington is fully primed to tackle a situation where a country already possesses nuclear arms, it can easily take care of Saddam Hussein's putative atomic bomb. Let us suppose that Iraq has progressed far enough to assemble a nuclear bomb. To ensure its effectiveness, Baghdad would have to test one. And a nuclear test, even if conducted underground, would be picked up by the US and other countries. It would not take the Pentagon too long to neutralize this threat.

17/ The suffering of the Iraqi people stems from the policies followed by Saddam. So he should stop blaming the United States for their misery.

A: Most outsiders, including US policy makers, thought that the Iraqi people would blame Saddam for the misery that has visited them since his invasion of Kuwait, and that they would see the connection between the cause (Iraq's aggression) and the effect (UN sanctions, international isolation). This has not happened. Why? "Iraqis don't take individual responsibility for the invasion of Kuwait," explains "Dhia," a London-based Iraqi professional who does not belong to any opposition group and visits Baghdad periodically. "The sanctions that flowed from that event have created a popular feeling of 'us' and 'them,' the West. When it comes to apportioning blame, most Iraqis think at the first level, and don't get into secondary and tertiary reasons. They say that Saddam put them in harm's way but did not cause harm. That was caused by the West, led by America. 'Saddam did not drop bombs on us, did not cut off our electricity and phones and water supplies; others did that,' they say." And sanctions had provided Saddam with a perfect alibi for all the ills in the country. "If roads are pot-holed, if phones don't work, if there aren't enough medicines in hospitals, Saddam blames the sanctions. On the other hand, he takes full credit for any improvement, however slight—like, say, flower beds appearing in Saadoun Street in Baghdad [a thoroughfare]." Sanctions have helped Saddam to further tighten his hold over society in which rationing is at the core of his control mechanism. See further, Dilip Hiro, *Neighbors, Not Friends,* pp. 290–91.

18/ By lifting sanctions we will let Saddam resume armament.

A: Paragraph 20 in Section C of UN Security Council Resolution 687 states that once the conditions regarding disarming Iraq and paying compensation to those who suffered due to Baghdad's aggression against Kuwait had been satisfied, then "the prohibitions against the import of commodities and products originating in Iraq and the prohibitions against financial transactions related thereto contained in Resolution 661 (1990) shall have no further force or effect." But Security Council Resolution 1284 (December 1999) altered the lifting of sanctions to suspension for 120 days at a time. Not surprisingly, Baghdad refused to accept 1284—until September 16, 2002.

The last in the list of questions that Iraqi foreign minister Naji Sabri submitted to Kofi Annan in March 2002 reads: "Does the Security Council agree with Iraq's legitimate right to self-defense in accordance with Article 51 of the [UN] Charter, and whether this allows Iraq to acquire conventional defensive weapons?" To the best of our knowledge, Iraq has not yet received an answer to this question from the Security Council.

19/ Saddam understands only relentless pressure.

A: This runs counter to the age-old wisdom of using carrot and stick to achieve one's aim. Saddam did follow the pattern of cheat-and-retreat. He also saw how the US began moving the goalposts, starting with US secretary of state Warren Christopher's *New York Times* article in April 1994. It became obvious to him as well as to most dispassionate outsiders that no matter what he did, the US would not allow the clean bill of health to be issued or made effective, by vetoing such a resolution at the Security Council.

20/ The US military action, followed by its occupation of the country, will bring democracy to Iraqis as it did to Japanese after World War II.

A: The length and pervasiveness of the US occupation of Iraq will be determined by the stability of the post-Saddam regime. If the fledgling government proves too fragile, Washington may well decide to put Iraq through the democratization process that Gen. Douglas McArthur did in Japan after its defeat in 1945. Will the US achieve the same result? No. Because, unlike the decimation that Washington is itching to inflict upon Saddam's regime, McArthur kept intact the regime of Emperor Hirohito, and used it as his main instrument to democratize the country, which experienced no break in its monarchical order.

21/ At the UN Security Council, France and Russia are siding with Iraq because French and Russian oil companies have signed lucrative contracts with Iraq that will become operational as soon as the UN economic sanctions against Iraq are lifted. This is sheer greed on the part of the Russians and the French.

A: It is the prime duty of a government to look after its national interests. The US does it all the time—even at the expense of breaking its international obligations. Remember the Bush Jr. administration imposing tariffs on imported steel in violation of the World Trade Organization rules? In the oil-rich Arabian Peninsula, the US arms manufacturers and other corporations reaped a rich harvest of lucrative contracts in Kuwait, Saudi Arabia, and other Gulf monarchies after the 1991 Gulf War. And US oil companies, in collusion with their European subsidiaries, rushed to secure contracts for repairing Iraq's petroleum industry from the mid-1990s. See further, chapter 7, pp. 166

APPENDIX II

INFREQUENT COMMENTS AND QUESTIONS

1/ Iraqi officials keep saying that American inspectors and other staff working for Unscom spied for their government. Is there any truth in this?

A: There is ample evidence of this. The details are to be found in the stories published in the *Washington Post, New York Times, Wall Street Journal,* and *Boston Globe* from mid-1998 to early 1999—and in Scott Ritter's book *Endgame* (1999). After years of silence, the extremely discreet Rolf Ekeus, head of Unscom during 1991–97, told Swedish Radio in August 2002 that the US had planted its nationals, who were engaged more in trying to locate Saddam Hussein than carry out inspections or monitoring, into Unscom. The details of the complex "Shake the Tree" operation, implemented by a team of US inspectors and technicians, to eavesdrop on the highly confidential Iraqi military communications are described in chapter 6, pp. 102, 105–109, and 112–113. The US director of this operation shared this classified information with a fellow American and a former government official, Charles Duelfer, to ensure that Unscom's eavesdropping procedures remained intact—but not with Duelfer's boss, Ekeus, or even his openly pro-American successor, Richard Butler. Furthermore, US undercover agents were assigned to contact the commanders of the elite Special Republican Guard on the eve of a planned anti-Saddam coup on June 26, 1996. The details are in chapter 6, pp. 82–84. Ritter refers to the close links between Butler and the US national security adviser, Samuel Berger, to the extent of daily briefings on ongoing inspections that were agreed to beforehand with Berger. Barton Gellman in the *Washington Post* of August 28, 1998 refers to "a standard procedure" whereby "Mr Butler's senior staff briefed a liaison officer from the CIA on the target [for inspection]." For further details, check the Index for "Barton Gellman," "MoeDobbs," "Charles Duelfer," "Operation 'Shake the Tree,'" and "Scott Ritter," and follow up.

2/ OK, but there is the argument that by trying to deceive Unscom repeatedly, Saddam drove the US to resort to underhand methods and misuse the UN.

A: This argument assumes that what the US did was to react to the acts of deception by Saddam. But there is at least one known example of Washington abusing the UN for its intelligence ends when it did *not* have the kind of rationale provided by Saddam. That was in 1975. Following the March 1975 Algiers Accord between Iran and Iraq, the Shah of Iran withdrew his support to the Iraqi Kurds fighting the Baghdad government from Iranian soil. Due to the resulting humanitarian crisis, the UN sent its aid personnel, drawn from a few contributing member-states, including the US, to Iran. The US contingent included American intelligence agents with a mandate to salvage as much of the Kurdish military campaign against Baghdad as they could. See further, Dilip Hiro, *Neighbors, Nor Friends: Iraq and Iran after the Gulf Wars* (2001), p. 118.

3/ After the Gulf War, the United States, assisted by Britain, imposed air exclusion zones on the Baghdad government in the North and the South, covering more than 60 percent of Iraq. Are these authorized by the UN Security Council?

A: The US and the UK cite Security Council Resolution 688 (April 1991) to rationalize their imposition of these zones. But there is no mention of such zones in that document. Indeed, as the resolution was not passed under Chapter VII of the UN Charter, it did not authorize use of force by a UN member-state to implement it. When challenged, the US argues that its action is "derivative" of Paragraph 6 of Resolution 688, which appealed "to all Member States and to all humanitarian organizations to contribute to these humanitarian relief efforts" for the Kurdish refugees created by the failure of the Kurdish uprising after the Gulf War. The linkage between humanitarian relief and stretching an air umbrella over this region remains unclear. For example, the UN's World Food Program has continued to provide free food to tens of thousands of indigent Iraqi families living under the direct control of the Baghdad government. In any case, even that sort of reasoning cannot rationalize "Operation Southern Watch," which was imposed in August 1992—16 months after Resolution 688 was adopted. After consulting the British and French leaders, US president George Bush Sr. decided to impose an air exclusion zone in the South to safeguard the Shias there. This had more to do with Bush Sr. punishing Saddam for his long standoff with Unscom and the IAEA on disarmament in the previous month than protecting the Shias in the South. The Pentagon's standard statement that "The purpose of the no fly zone [in southern Iraq] is to ensure the safety of Coalition aircraft monitoring compliance with United Nations Security Council Resolution 688" is a typical example of a circular argument. The fact that enforcing an air exclusion zone in the South did not stop Baghdad's ground-based attacks on the southern marshes providing refuge to Iraqi fugitives, often dodging conscription, underlined Washington's purported concern for civilians. That the real reason for maintaining the air exclusion zones in the North and the South was political, rather than humanitarian, became public when US secretary of state Madeleine Albright said in November 1999, "I believe that through our . . . continued patrolling of northern and southern no fly zones, we are able to keep Saddam Hussein in his box."

Of the two air exclusion zones, the southern one has proved strategically valuable to Washington. The Pentagon perceives it as a means of denying Baghdad the opportunity to train its pilots in the southern Iraqi airspace and as a source of intelligence input in its early warning system. See further, chapter 7, pp. 147–149.

4/ Some experts argue that every time the US bombed Iraq, it lost ground diplomatically and generated hatred among Iraqis. Is that true?

A: There is much evidence to support this view. Besides the forty-three days of nonstop bombardment of Iraq during the Gulf War, the Pentagon bombed Iraq in January and June 1993, September 1996, December 1998, and February 2001. This series of military strikes convinced most Iraqis that Washington was against them as a people rather than against Saddam and his coterie. The negative diplomatic impact of the hundred-hour blitzkrieg of "Operation Desert Fox" in December 1998—condemned by China, France, and Russia—was so severe that it took the Security Council a whole year to come up with a new inspection and monitoring regime under Resolution 1284. China, France, and Russia refused to back the resolution, and abstained—primarily because it altered the provision of complete lifting of sanctions, as specified in Resolution 687 (1991), to a suspension of 120 days at a time.

Secondly, because the Pentagon's massive Operation Desert Fox could not be implemented while the UN inspectors were inside Iraq, they were withdrawn by Unscom chief Richard Butler. By so doing, he provided Saddam a chance to negotiate their return. Finally, as Americans must know from their own experience, when a country is attacked, its citizens rally around their leader, no matter how inept and/or brutal. This is what Americans did after September 11, 2001. And this is what Iraqis do every time their homeland is hit by US bombs and missiles.

5/ There is a big gap between how the people in the West and the Arab and Muslim world view events of international importance. This became starkly obvious during the Pentagon's attack on

Afghanistan in 2001. The presentation of the US military strikes on the Arabic-language television channels, especially the popular Qatar-based Al Jazeera satellite television, had little in common with what appeared on the screens showing material supplied by the BBC or CNN and other American channels. What lies at the root of this disjunction? And between these two broad systems, which one is more objective and trustworthy?

A: To say that the media, especially the broadcasting ones, play a vital role in shaping popular perceptions would be to state the obvious. What even the most enlightened Western journalists fail to realize is that (a) most people in the world get their information primarily from their national radio and television, and (b) most people trust their own media, however censored or distorted. In the English-speaking world, given equal access to CNN and the BBC, Americans turn to CNN and Britons to the BBC, with each group trusting more its own television channel than the rival. By the same token, most Egyptians stick with their own radio and television channels, as do most Syrians. The situation is particularly acute in Iraq. Due to the communications and educational embargo since 1990, most Iraqis don't know what a fax is, or a mobile phone. Even middle- and upper-middle-class Iraqis have no access to foreign publications or television. The people living in Iraq are exposed to nothing but the state-run Iraqi radio and television.

The subject of the disjunction between the West and the Arab and Muslim world is very broad, and beyond the scope of this book. Suffice it to say that this gap, already very wide, will grow dangerously wider if there is an invasion of Iraq by the US or US-led coalition.

The question of objectivity was addressed succinctly by Max Rodenbeck, the Cairo-based correspondent of the *Economist*, in a *New York Times* article in April 2002. "As network coverage of Vietnam shocked Americans with the immediacy of a far-off war, satellite television's insistent, graphic imagery of the [Palestinian] intifada has taken this bloody drama into millions of Arab households," he wrote. "The drama generates not weariness with war but a thirst for justice, for sacrifice and revenge. . . . Some Palestinian casualties have become household names from Morocco to Muscat—Muhammad Dura, the twelve-year-old boy from Gaza whose father could not shield him from a hail of Israeli gunfire, or Wafa Idris and Ayat Akhras, the first female suicide bombers." Yet, argued Rodenbeck, "Arab coverage of the conflict is not really much more one-sided than, say, America's gung-ho coverage of the Gulf War. Or, for that matter, Israeli reporting on the intifada. It does not require subtle manipulation to frame the ongoing tragedy as an epic struggle of the weak against the strong. The imagery saturating Arab screens of tanks crushing ambulances and helicopters rockets refugee camps is, alas, all too real."

6/ Paragraph 14 of Security Council Resolution 687 (1991) specifies "the goal of establishing in the Middle East a zone free from weapons of mass destruction and all missiles for their delivery." Eleven years on, the Security Council has taken no steps in this direction. Why has not the US, the sole superpower, goaded the council to act?

A: For the simple reasons that the Middle East includes Israel, a country that is widely known to have been in possession of atomic bombs since 1968, and whose present arsenal according to the estimate of *Jane's intelligence Review* in 1997, includes "over 400 thermonuclear and nuclear warhead." In addition, biological and chemical weapons research and production have been in progress at the Israeli Institute for Biological Research (IIBR) Nes Tziona, south of Tel Aviv (which is unmarked in maps), since 1952. the government expanded the facility in 1998. It officially acknowledged in 1983 that Marcus Klinberg, deputy head of the IIBRwas given life sentence for leaking "sensitive" information to the Soviet Union. See further, Dilip Hiro, *Dictionary of thte Middle East,* pp. 197–98, and *Middle East International,* October 11, 2002, pp. 26–27.

7/ Everybody is aware that Saddam tried to cheat the UN repeatedly on its disarmament program. That is a given. But is it true

that as Iraq's disarmament progressed, the US kept shifting the goalpost, forcing Saddam to conclude that no matter what he did, Washington would never allow the sanctions to be lifted?

A: Yes. The evidence is in chapter 6. The key moment came in June 1998 when Richard Butler, Unscom chief, told Tariq Aziz that even if the disarmament of the weapons of mass destruction had been judged to be completed, he would want to know the details of the conceal- ment mechanism that the Iraqi government had set up for the WMD. The question that arises is: Was this investigation—akin to investi- gating a crime rather then disarming a country—part of the original UN mandate on disarmament, leaving aside the issue of some Amer- ican inspectors in Unscom focusing on the whereabouts of Saddam?

8/ We are familiar with Iraq hindering UN inspectors from car- rying out their mandate, and the US punishing the Iraqi govern- ment for doing so. But what are the overall figures: How many inspections were carried out, and how many times did Iraq refuse access to a requested site?

A: Compared to inspections carried out by nearly six thousand inspec- tors during 91 months (May 1991–December 1998), there were a little over one hundred Iraqi refusals, about one a month.

9/ Is it possible to have 100 percent disarmament?

A: No, according to Hans Blix, executive chairman of the UN Mon- itoring, Verification, and Inspection Commission (Unmovic), the latest in a series of disarmament experts who have said so. See fur- ther, chapter 6, p. 128.

10/ The United States and Britain have kept track of the number of Security Council resolutions that Iraq has breached, and put this information on websites. Do they have a similar figure for Israel, and have they put it out on their websites?

A: Maybe the US and the UK have worked out the figure for Israel.

But they have not publicized it. According to Professor Steven Zunes of San Francisco University, since 1968 alone Israel has violated 32 resolutions that included condemnation or criticism of its government's policies and actions. The details were published respectively in the Israeli *Ha'aretz* and *Newsday* newspapers on October 8 and 9, 2002. their respective websites are www.haaretzdaily.com and www.newsday.com.

11/ Going by the reports of Western journalists visiting Iraqi Kurdistan, the region seems to be ably and peacefully administered by Masud Barzani of the Kurdistan Democratic Party (KDP) and Jalal Talabani of the Patriotic Union of Kurdistan (PUK). Is that so?

A: Most Western reporters' dispatches are deficient on the state of KDP-PUK relations, which are far from normal. Following a parliamentary election in May 1992, the KDP and the PUK shared power equally. That lasted two years. Then they fought each other bitterly—to the point that Barzani called on Saddam to help him defeat Talabani in late August 1996. Saddam obliged. It took American and British mediators two years to get the rival parties to agree to a peaceful coexistence based on each side compromising its rigid position on such issues as sharing revenues. But it was not until September 2002 that they finally agreed to implement their four-year-old accord. All along Barzani has maintained his economic link with Saddam—his supplier of Iraqi oil and oil products at heavily discounted prices for resale to Turkish traders with a large markup—to underwrite the expense of administering his part of Kurdistan. Fresh elections to the parliament were due in 1996. Yet there are no plans for a fresh election. Washington dares not press for it because Turkey will view it as a preamble to the emergence of an independent Kurdistan, its nightmare.

12/ We hear a lot about the Iraqi opposition coming together and the series of meetings their leaders are holding in Washington or London. But why don't we hear much about the

shady background of the leading opposition figure, Ahmed Chalabi, who was given two prison sentences in Jordan for embezzling the funds of his Petra Bank after he fled Amman in 1989, or that until recently the State Department had refused to deal with him or his Iraqi National Congress?

A: Draw your own conclusions. See further, www.observer.co.uk/international/0,6903,800986,00.html.

13/ Some analysts are arguing that "regime change" in Iraq isa euphemism for the invasion of a sovereign state. Is "imperial America," the term used by among others Condoleezza Rice, on the verge of entering an imperialist phase?

A: It seems that way. There is enough in 'The National Security Strategy of the United States," a document drafted by Condoleezza Rice and adopted by President George W. Bush on September 20, 2002, to support the thesis that the United States has formally entered a neo-imperialist phase, where it seeks worldwide dominance not only in diplomacy and military but also in culture.

14/ There is a growing school of analysts and commentators who argue that the Bush Jr. administration's Middle East policy is driven by the pro-Israeli lobby, which is close to the neo-conservative ideologues. Is that so?

A: The evidence so far points in that direction. Nothing illustrated the power of the pro-Israeli lobby more vividly than when President George W. Bush publicly and insistently demanded in early April that Israel withdraw its forces from the West Bank. "Now," he declared,. "and I mean now." Israeli prime minister Ariel Sharon paid no attention, took his time, and withdrew the troops four weeks later. For this open defiance of the world's most powerful person, he got invited to the White House for a cordial meeting with the leader whose advice he had blatantly ignored. The US hawks and pro-Israeli lobbyists are pursing the strategic aim of making Israel's eastern front secure. Beyond Jordan, a military cipher, lie

Iraq and Iran. Their overall objective is to ratchet up the policy of keeping Saddam in a box to his overthrow, under the rubric of a preemptive strike. If, as, and when that aim is achieved, they will turn their guns on Iran, a member of Bush's "axis of evil."

Regarding the third member of the "axis," North Korea, it represents no threat to Israel. So, while the world attention was turned on Iraq, the Bush administration sent James Kelly, a senior diplomat, to Pyongyang for talks in early October 2002, even though, according to the CIA, North Korea possesses chemical weapons and enough fissile material for two atomic bombs. It suppressed the news of the North Koreans admitting having a nuclear arms program (to Kelly on October 4) until Bush had signed into law the congressional was powers resolution on October 16.

15/ What are the implications of the US unilaterally adopting the doctrine of preemption in the international arena?
A: Pretty alarming. If Russia were to follow the example of the United States, it would preempt the Chechen threat by invading Georgia, where, it claims, the Chechen terrorists are now based. And if India follows Washington's lead, it will attack Pakistan to preempt the threat of cross-border terrorism being perpetrated by Kashmiri and non-Kashmiri Muslim fundamentalists. And so on. . . .

16/ With Christians like Tariq Aziz and holding important positions in the Iraqi regime, President Saddam Hussein cannot be an Islamic fundamentalist. Yet in a rare interview to a non-Arab politician or journalist in August 2002, he told George Galloway, a British member of Parliament: "If Crusaders attack us, we will fight on the streets, from the rooftops, from house to house." What should one make of his description of Americans as "crusaders"?
A: Saddam intensified his suppression of Islamic militants in Iraq on the eve of his attack on the Islamic Republic of Iran in September 1980. But he is opportunistic enough to invoke Islam to widen his base of support. On the eve of the 1991 Gulf War, for instance, he decreed

that the credo "Allah-u Akbar (God Is Great)" be inscribed on the Iraqi tricolor. He will most likely depict Washington's invasion of Iraq as aggression against a Muslim country and therefore against Islam. The subsequent rise in militant anti-Americanism in the Middle East will increase Israel's isolation, thus defeating one of the Bush Jr. administration's strategic aims and abetting Saddam's agenda.

Furthermore, the negative repercussions will also be felt in the surrounding non-Arab, but Muslim, region — in Turkey, Afghanistan and Pakistan. A dramatic upset in Pakistan might put the country's nuclear arsenal in the hands of fundamentalist generals. At the very least these developments will curtail foreign governments' cooperation with Washington's war on terrorism and swell the terrorist ranks by driving some radical, non-fundamentalist groups among Muslims to political violence.

17/ When George W. Bush first assumed office, there was talk of relaxation of sanctions leading to the entry of US oil corporations into the untapped Iraqi petroleum reserves. Whatever happened to that scenario?
A: There have always been ideological and pragmatic schools of thought in the foreign policy establishment of the US. In the case of the Middle East, the ideologues back Israel, right or wrong, and the pragmatists prioritize the interests of oil companies, crucial to the American economy. Given the deep roots that Vice President Dick Cheney as well as the Texan-based George W. Bush and his father have in the oil industry, it was expected early on that in the new administration oil interests would prevail at the expense of the Israeli lobby. The first sign that this was a vain hope came when the Bush Jr. White House endorsed the congressional plan to extend by five years the Iraq-Libya Sanctions Act, 1996, due to expire in August 2001.

18/ Recently, US hawks have taken to popularizing the idea of invading Iraq on the grounds that Saddam's overthrow will open

the rich Iraqi oil fields to US corporations. This is a vital consideration for American petroleum companies and their British counterparts who have been frozen out of the Iraqi market due to the policies of their respective governments. US corporations' access to Iraqi oil fields, say the hawks, will result in reducing the United States' growing dependence on petroleum from Saudi Arabia—a country which, as the homeland of 15 of the 19 hijackers responsible for the 9/11 attacks, has become deeply unpopular with Americans.

A: One of the unpublicized prices that Washington and London paid for their Operation Desert Fox in December 1998 was that Saddam banned direct sales of Iraqi oil to American or British companies or traders, forcing them to buy the commodity from the Russian, French, or Chinese intermediaries, thus forgoing their trading profit margins.

19/ So, in the final analysis, will the forthcoming war with Iraq be about oil—just as the 1991 Gulf conflict was?

A: Yes. This is one point on which both the US hawks, who are determining the Iraq policy, and Iraqi officials, from Saddam downward, are agreed. As Tariq Aziz put it, "The weapons of mass destruction is just an excuse. The Americans are after the Iraqi oil." Explaining the 1991 Gulf War, the worldly-wise Muhammad Bagga, an old resident of Saddam City, Baghdad, told me: "The big Western powers got angry because Saddam Hussein wanted to benefit all Arabs from Iraq's oil." See further, chapter 1, p. 19.

QUESTIONS SUBMITTED BY IRAQI FOREIGN MINISTER NAJI SABRI TO UN SECRETARY-GENERAL KOFI ANNAN, MARCH 7, 2002

ACCOMPANYING NOTE

from UN Secretary-General Kofi Annan
19 March, 2002

His Excellency
Mr. Ole Peter Kolby
President of the Security Council
New York

Dear Mr. President,

I have the honour to convey to the Security Council a number of questions handed to me by the Foreign Minister of Iraq, Mr. Naji Sabri, on March 7, 2002. As I indicated in my briefing to the Council on March 8, the questions have been rearranged and clustered for the sake of clarity and expediency. Many of the questions lie within the competence of the Executive Chairman of UNMOVIC, Dr. Hans Blix, in coordination with the IAEA, to answer. However, a number of the questions are addressed to the Security Council.

I should be grateful if you would bring the attached list of questions to the attention of the members of the Security Council. As it is anticipated that the next round of dialogue with the Iraqi delegation will be held during the second half of April, I would appreciate receiving any response the Security Council may wish to provide by 10 April at the latest.

Please accept, Mr. President, the assurance of my highest consideration.

Signed,
Kofi A. Annan

CLUSTERED QUESTIONS

I. Disarmament/Inspection Issues

Some members of the Security Council state that disarmament talks, as described in Section C of resolution 687, have not been completed. Iraq is not against certainty as a principle.

- What has been achieved in seven years and seven months of Iraq's cooperation with UNSCOM and the IAEA in the disarmament area?
- How can UNMOVIC start its activities based on what has been accomplished?
- What are the disarmament tasks and the remaining questions to be clarified through inspections, how much time is needed to accomplish these inspections?
- How long would it take UNMOVIC to reach a degree of certainty that Iraq has retained no WMD and to present a report to the Security Council appropriately?
- What kind of inspections is UNMOVIC planning to conduct?
- Would inspections be conducted with the necessary respect of the sovereignty, independence and territorial integrity of Iraq and in accordance with the relevant international conventions?

- What are the Terms of Reference for UNMOVIC, limits of powers of its Executive Chairman and the College of Commissioners?
- Would the Secretary-General supervise the work of UNMOVIC?
- Does UNMOVIC's composition include individuals who have been members of UNSCOM involved in spying activities?
- What are the guarantees that UNMOVIC would not use the same inspection formula which led to the bombing of Iraq in 1998?
- How could US and UK inspectors fulfill a neutral international mandate?

II. Issues relevant to relations between Iraq and the Security Council

Iraq insists on the principle of concurrence in the implementation of the corresponding obligations in order to build confidence between Iraq and the Security Council.

- Do threats to invade Iraq and to change the national government by force violate Security Council resolutions, rules of international law, Charter of the United Nations and Iraq's sovereignty, independence and territorial integrity?
- Could one permanent member of the Security Council have a right to its own interpretation of resolutions in order to take unilateral decisions regarding Iraq?
- Is it possible to normalize relations between the Security Council and Iraq under the circumstances when calls are made for invading Iraq and overthrowing its national government by force?
- Could the elimination of the no-fly zones be guaranteed?

·What are the views of the Security Council on decla-
rations that the economic sanctions imposed on Iraq
would not be lifted in accordance with relevant resolutions as long as the current national government
remains in place?

·Has the Security Council implemented its obligations
pursuant to resolution 687 (1991) regarding the lifting
of the sanctions, respect of Iraq's sovereignty, independence and territorial integrity and the establishment in the Middle East of a zone free from weapons
of mass destruction (paragraph 14)?

III. Iraq's requests for compensation and right of self-defense

·Would Iraq be compensated for the destruction of its
economic, educational and other infrastructure caused
by the embargo and violations of Iraq's sovereignty?

·Is there an intention to dispatch a team of experts to
Iraq to assess the cost of reconstruction in order to
submit a report, which would help the Security
Council to consider the issue of compensation?

·Does the Security Council agree with Iraq's legitimate
right to self-defense in accordance with Article 51 of
the Charter and whether this right allows Iraq to
acquire conventional defensive weapons?

INDEX

uprising and, 41-43; US
hostages taken by, xv
Iran-Iraq War: about, 28-33; Arab
support during, 138-39; economic casualties of, 159-61;
impact of, 21-22, 55; Kurds
during, 74; policy of UN
during, 96
Iraq: anti-American feeling in, 6,
17-19, 47, 196-97; under the
Baathists, 26-28; under British
control, 22-25; creation of, 22-
23; military strength of, 88-89,
177-78, 194; post-Saddam,
198-99; Republican, 25-26;
strategic importance of, 137-
38; sympathy for, 140, 142-47,
149-51; territory of, 137-38;
terrorists and, 180-82, 190;
between wars, 33-34
Iraq Liberation Act (ILA), 89-92
Iraq National Oil Company
(INOC), 157-58
Iraq Petroleum Company (IPC),
157-58
Iraqi exiles, 93
Iraqi Kurdistan Front (IKF), 75
Iraqi Military Alliance (IMA), 93-94
Iraqi National Accord (INA), 77-
78, 79-84
Iraqi National Congress (INC),
75, 76-81, 89-90, 92, 93, 187
Iraqis, working abroad, 13, 14-15
Islam, Saddam Hussein and, 71-
72, 195-96
Israeli-Palestinian conflict, 37,
139-40, 142, 144, 150, 151,
158, 170-71, 178, 183-84, 191,
195-96

Jordan, 82, 139, 140, 141, 150,
152, 202

Kay, David, 98-99
Kazar, Nazim, 57
Kerry, John, 187
Khomeini, Ayatollah Ruhollah,
xv, 28, 29, 31-32
Kurdistan Autonomous Region
(KAR), 73-75
Kurdistan Democratic Party
(KDP), 73-75, 77, 78-79, 84-
88
Kurds: coups planned by, 79-89;
creation of Iraq and, 23; oil
industry and, 163-64; rebel-
lions by, 27, 43-48; Saddam's
policies toward, 68-69, 73-75;
Turkey and, 140-41; violence
among, 78-79, 85, 140-41
Kuwait: backing of U.S. by, 114;
democracy in, 200; invasion
of, 35-36; oil industry and,
169; reasons behind invasion
of, 33-34, 138-39; relations
between Iraq and, 184; support for Iraq by, 138, 143

La Billiere, Peter de, 39-40
Lake, Tony, 81
landholders, 3
League of Nations, 22, 23, 96
Lewinsky scandal, 114
Libya, 173
livestock, 10

mail embargo, 8
al Majid, Ali Hassan, xiv, 57, 74
maps: Baghdad area, ix, x, xi; no-
fly zones, vii; surface oil
pipelines, viii
medicine, lack of, 9-11
military-industrial projects, 59-60
military expansion, 61
Military Intelligence, 59-60

DILIP HIRO

Born in the Indian subcontinent, Dilip Hiro was educated in India, Britain, and the United States, where he received a Master's degree at Virginia Polytechnic Institute & State University. He then settled in London in the mid-1960s, and became a full-time writer, journalist, and commentator. His articles have appeared in the *Washington Post, Los Angeles Times, Wall Street Journal, Boston Globe, Toronto Star, The Nation,* the *Sunday Times, Observer, Guardian,* the *Times, Independent, International Herald Tribune, Times Literary Supplement, Economist, New Statesman, Spectator,* and *Middle East International.* He is a frequent commentator on Middle Eastern, Central Asian, and Islamic affairs on National Public Radio, BBC Radio and Television, CBC (Canada), CBS Network (USA), Channel 4 (UK), Channel 5 (UK), CNN, Pacifica Radio Network (USA), Radio France Internationale (France), RTE (Ireland), Sky TV (satellite), and Vatican Radio.